GOING TO THE WARS

GOING
TO THE WARS

A Journey in Various Directions

John Verney

PAUL DRY BOOKS
Philadelphia   2019

First Paul Dry Books edition, 2019

Paul Dry Books, Inc.
Philadelphia, Pennsylvania
www.pauldrybooks.com

Frontispiece: John Verney in his studio, c. 1950

First published 1955 by Collins

Printed in the United States of America

ISBN 978-1-58988-131-0

To the memory of my son
Julian Comus Ralph
July 1940–November 1948

AUTHOR'S NOTE

MODERN PAINTING, and the modern approach to all painting, might be described as a quest for those pictorial values which are permanent or, to use the fashionable if misleading term, Abstract. In this spirit I have approached the facts of my own life between 1937 and 1945. Although the story, as it concerns myself, is true, I have allowed myself freedom, to the point of fantasy, with everyone else. I could find no other way of saying what I wanted to say.

Parts IV and V are based on a narrative written ten years ago in the Army's time, soon after the events described and during an illness which followed upon them. In the subsequent excitements of rediscovering civilian life, the manuscript was shelved, almost forgotten. I am indebted to Robin Denniston for encouraging me to finish the story backwards, so to speak, and for much invaluable advice; as I am also to John Grey Murray for permission to reprint five chapters which have already appeared in the *Cornhill Magazine*; and to Mrs. C. E. Montague for permission to use the fine poem by her husband.

CONTENTS

PART ONE

Prelude & Fugue

CHAPTER ONE

"We Never Smoke During Battle"

THE BATTLE HAD BEEN RAGING since dawn, Northland chasing Southland over the Quantocks, like the flying cloud shadows which clung to the oak scrub and modeled each subtle combe. With the smell and sound of horses close by my head I had bivouacked the previous night in the heather, the sea breeze off Bridgwater Bay nipping me in my blankets. Now, though dirty and sleep-eyed, I rejoiced to be riding over wild country in early morning sun and wind. There was something, perhaps, to be said for Army life after all. Even my uniform, uncomfortably new, added a pleasure by identifying me, through wearing it, with other cavalry exploits in the past. I thought of Tolstoy's description of the young Nikolai Rostov riding into his first action. "There was not only nothing terrible about it, but it seemed ever more and more jolly and lively."

It was a pleasure, too, to escape for a day from the many social and military pitfalls of the camp. The effort of pretending to be someone I was not was proving a strain. I hated the ritualistic dinners and the long hours of horseplay which, by tradition, followed them. My brother officers were squires, farmers, land agents, and the like, born and bred in the country and sharing a hundred tastes and acquaintances from childhood. In after years, drawn together by the boredom and the exile of war, I came to love them. But on first acquaintance they struck me as formidably different from myself, a Londoner whose chief interests, priggish though it sounds, were modern Literature and modern Art. None of my brother officers had ever heard of Proust or of Picasso. Nor did this gap in their education trouble them unduly.

As a supernumerary officer with no "command" of my own, I had been attached for the Battle to a Squadron Leader to be "shown the form." He was a fierce Major called Victor Bone and as I jogged along beside him, hoping that I looked more at home on a horse than I felt, he attempted some conversation.

"And what's your line of country in civvy street?"

"Well, um—as a matter of fact, I'm an assistant film director, sir."

"Oh. What does all that mean?"

"Well, it's a bit difficult to explain really, sir. I have to see that the actors are ready to go on the set when they're wanted and that sort of thing."

"Good God!" snorted the fierce Major.

After that we rode on in silence and for my part, so far as the Battle went, in mystified ignorance, though I tried to pick up such clues to the confused military situation as Victor Bone let fall. For military tactics, even of the simple Boer War variety used by a Yeomanry Regiment training in 1937, were as yet unintelligible to me. Two rival kingdoms, Northland and Southland, were supposed to be at war. A Squadron, with two troops of C Squadron, represented the aggressor, Northland, and wore distinguishing blue bands on their caps. B Squadron and H.Q. Squadron represented Southland, with the two remaining troops of C Squadron attached to them in the guise of a Mountain Battery with pack mules. We were now, it was to be assumed, picking up the threads of a battle that had begun the week before and in which, by 0500 hours this very morning, the opposing forces had reached positions—there had followed a fantastically complicated string of map references.

To digest even this initial hypothesis required, I felt, prodigious feats of memory and imagination. I glanced enviously at Victor Bone's red neck, considerably awed that above it should exist a brain capable of performing these feats. He was a soldierly-looking figure whom I rather feared and whom, because he had shown me a gruff kindness, I was prepared to idolize. It was thus a shock to discover later that he had in fact no military qualifications—unless a permanent state of inebriation at the yearly camp for the past ten years could be called a military qualification. In "civvy street" he himself was an insurance agent with sporting tendencies and he enjoyed these battles in the spirit of a day's foxhunting in midsummer.

For the moment the hounds, so to speak, had lost the scent. The squadron huddled together on horseback under cover of a wood. Tense with the excitement of the chase, Victor Bone sat erect on his horse, his heavy cavalry moustache stirred gently by the morning breeze. He sniffed the air as if to sense from it the whereabouts of the missing enemy. Then, with a few curt orders, he sent a patrol forward to reconnoiter. I wondered whether the time would ever come when I would attain to a comparable grasp of these complex matters.

The patrol assembled itself without seeming haste; and without seeming haste trotted off ahead. Obviously we had some time to wait before fighting could recommence. I took out a packet of cigarettes and offered one to my idol.

"Have a smoke, sir?"

His prominent, rather red-rimmed blue eyes stared at me in outraged astonishment.

"We never smoke during battle," he said angrily.

Later in the morning, the enemy or some of them having been located on the ridge of one of the Quantock hills, he gave me the chance to redeem this unfortunate lapse by sending me on a desperate mission.

"It is vital, absolutely vital," said Victor Bone, "that we should know how many of them are up there. Gallop off, young what's-your-name, and try to work your way up to them from behind. Then report back to me with the names of any officers you can identify. That will tell me all I want to know."

Horsed cavalry operations, it had been disillusioning to discover, are seldom conducted at more than a trot. The excuse for a legitimate gallop came rarely and though I was not confident of being able to identify any of my brother officers by name, I set off lightheartedly on my mission. For a happy and breathless twenty minutes I galloped across streams, through beech woods, into and out of combes. Then tethering my horse on the edge of a coppice I crept on my stomach through the heather. I could hear the enemy just ahead of me firing blanks, presumably at the squadron I had left. I spot-

ted their blue-banded caps on the skyline and crawled very stealthily forward. It was a situation that I found I enjoyed and the whole
episode would hardly be worth mentioning except that it made me
aware, for the first time, of a latent and unsuspected Red-Indianism
in myself. The episode foreshadows, perhaps epitomizes, much of
the story that is to follow. Strangely, the real thing when it came was
not much more real than the make-believe.

Peering round a bush of golden broom I came face to face with
another officer of my regiment. He was pale and very tall, and I
knew his face though not his name. He was eating his sandwiches
and looked rather astonished. I was unknown to him, but he must
have guessed that I was the enemy for he drew his revolver and
snapped it at me.

"Clicketty-click, you're dead," he said.

"No, I'm not!" I shouted, and dashed away, completing our re-
semblance to small boys playing cops and robbers.

A mounted patrol came after me and I ran down the hill as if my
life depended on it. They gained on me, and too exhausted to run
farther, I hid in a bush. The patrol captured my horse and then with
drawn swords prodded the bracken all round me.

"It's too thick," I heard the N.C.O. say in the rich burred voice
of the West Country. "You could hunt all day for the bastard in this
stuff."

So, leading my horse away, they abandoned the search—to my
relief, for I hadn't fancied being prodded.

There seemed to be no point in attempting to return on foot
to Victor Bone. Even if I reached him, which was unlikely as the
sounds of battle were receding, I had nothing worth while to report,
and it would be shaming to admit that I didn't know the name of
the officer who had killed me. So I wandered around for a time in
the sun on the hillside and then, bored and exhausted, sat down
beside a road and waited to be caught. Soon afterwards some enemy
cavalry including the patrol that had chased me came along, an
umpire with them. I was restored to my horse and the umpire, pro-
nouncing me *hors de combat*, advised me to return to camp.

My sword and other accoutrements jingling from the saddle, I
rode peacefully away from the battle down a wooded grassy combe.
The larks were singing, clouds and sunshine appeared in patches

between the trees with glimpses of the blue Bristol Channel beyond. My first battle had ended more happily than Nikolai Rostov's and, as I reflected on the strange new experience of the past few days, I wondered what my friends in the film studio where I worked would say if they could see me. For I had kept this particular activity a secret from them.

It happened that a group photograph of the officers of my regiment in their summer camp appeared some months later in an illustrated paper. By a most unlikely chance a copy of the paper turned up in the studio and by a still more unlikely chance my presence in the group, looking every inch an officer and a gentleman, was spotted by Butch, one of the barbers in the makeup department. As, unable to shave, I had grown a ragged beard the difference in my two selves was the more striking. For I suffered then, as I have suffered ever since, from a delicate skin and had contracted the "barber's itch" from this same Butch's razors and brushes. The photograph provided the simple studio staff with jests at my expense for a long time; in fact, I never quite lived it down, no one laughing louder or longer than Butch himself.

One of the pleasures of middle age is to find, looking back, how many past episodes begin already to complete a pattern. Everything seems to have occurred by plan, nothing to have been wasted, and friends forgotten for twenty years re-emerge suddenly at a fitting moment. I ran into Butch the other day working in the hairdressing shop at Waterloo Station. He remembered I used to wear a beard, though not the reasons for my having to wear it, and he seemed offended when I declined his cordial offer to shave me. The skin trouble, an isolated occurrence in Denham in 1937, recurred more persistently and with more dramatic consequence to my life in Cyrenaica in 1942, leading me to a fateful meeting in Jerusalem with the skin specialist, Doctor Katzenellenbogen, which I shall relate in due course.

And then the unknown officer whom I encountered behind the bush of golden broom . . .

I shall call him Amos. I saw him again in the anteroom, where the officers, smartly dressed in blue patrols with chain mail on the shoulder and clinking spurs, assembled before dinner. The anteroom was a draughty marquee adjoining another draughty marquee, where we ate. You could smell the damp grass under the threadbare, alcohol-stained Persian carpet. A pressure-lamp hung on the tent post, vividly lighting up the faces and the chain mail, but casting eerie shadows over the rest of the scene, the flapping canvas roof and walls, the dilapidated basket chairs, the old piano, the thirty officers . . . The lamp hissed and began to fade.

"Muggs! Come and fix this bloody lamp!" shouted Victor Bone who, as P.M.C., organized the comforts of the Mess. Muggs was the civilian waiter provided annually by the messing contractor, along with the carpet and the basket chairs. White-faced and undersized, he seemed to live in a permanent state of hardly-repressed insubordination, always muttering as he went about his work what I assumed to be threats. "You wait, you bastards. When the day comes . . ." I imagined him to be saying under his breath. My social conscience, in those days, was highly developed. It was intolerable that Muggs should be kept up serving glasses of port or beer night after night till 2 A.M. and then be expected to serve breakfast at 8 A.M. Years later I found out what it was that Muggs muttered. He was memorizing the innumerable drinks to be charged to the different officers' accounts. Now he tinkered with the lamp till it burnt brightly again.

"Stop mucking about with that light and fetch me another pink gin."

Doubtless Victor Bone suffered many humiliations as an insurance agent, so that not the least of the pleasures he derived from this yearly masquerade as a cavalry officer was that of, in turn, humiliating Muggs.

"Bloody civilian," he growled as Muggs left the anteroom to fetch the pink gin.

My sympathy for Muggs was probably uncalled for. When war was declared, Muggs voluntarily traveled all the way from Bermondsey to join the regiment. I heard Victor Bone say, "Good show, Muggs," when he enrolled him. Muggs became my batman. He grew quite fond of me, I think, but I always remained, with my sniveling humanitarianism, a poor sort of creature in his eyes compared to Victor Bone, whom he regarded as the embodiment of everything he himself would have wished to be.

Amos, when I entered the anteroom, was standing alone, a detached, sardonic expression on his pale face, which contrasted with the bucolic health of the others. He looked rather bald, I thought, for a Second Lieutenant. Actually he was thirty-three, ten years older than myself. He recognized me as I walked up to him.

"Clicketty-click. You were dead but you wouldn't lie down," he said, grinning.

We chuckled over the absurd incident. Then, with becoming diffidence, we followed our seniors into the dining-tent. Dinner in camp was treated as a formal occasion, perhaps to hide from ourselves the fact that we were merely amateur soldiers. Various cups were ranged down the long tablecloth, on either side of the Regimental trophy itself, a monstrous facsimile in pure silver of a cavalry officer mounted on his charger, with every detail of saddlery and equipment accurately rendered. The effigy was quarter life-size. The Padre, Hilary, said a Latin grace. Then we took our places, the Colonel in the center with senior officers like Victor Bone or the "regular" Adjutant, near him, while newly-joined officers such as Amos and myself huddled in outer darkness at the ends. Throughout dinner the Regimental brass band, stationed by its impresario R.S.M. Burge just outside the marquee, played "The Overture to William Tell" and other pieces suitable to the occasion. Conversation at this stage of the evening was necessarily restrained.

Life has few excitements to offer compared with that of making a new friend. As, through dinner, Amos and I talked in subdued voices about ourselves, I could hardly believe my good fortune at having found in these unlikely surroundings a congenial spirit who shared my enthusiasm for Proust and who had not only heard of Picasso but even possessed several of his paintings. Amos was a businessman who built roads successfully. He also owned a half-share in a London Art Gallery, he told me to my astonished delight. I was deeply impressed. To build roads at all seemed much. But to own half an Art Gallery as well . . .

"I make the tar pay for the Art," he said, for he always refused to talk seriously about his business affairs. But Art dealing was only one of many such sidelines in Amos's life. In all the years we were friends I was never able to piece together the whole picture of his business ramifications. Nor have I been able to since. That side of him remains slightly unreal and fabulous, like a character in the *Arabian Nights*. Perhaps he preferred it so and I am not surprised.

After the war, as one of his executors, I spent many hours attempting to make sense out of the financial muddle he left behind. Certainly the tar paid for the Art. But what precisely paid for the tar we were never able to discover. At the time I first met him, he must have been heavily in debt, although he possessed an immensely valuable collection of modern French paintings. Unfortunately they vanished, literally in smoke, one night in February 1944.

I don't know why Amos joined the Yeomanry. He had never ridden; he disliked horses; his exceptional height made it difficult for him to master the technique of riding and although his heroic antics won the admiration of the Regiment, they must have been as painful to perform as they were grotesque to watch. Like many cynics he was perhaps a romantic at heart. Among us geese he stood out as a sort of quixotic swan. When I asked him once why he had joined he refused, apparently, to be serious.

"I love leather and brasswork. Also, I want to get in on the ground floor of what may soon become an expanding racket." I think, now, both reasons were literally true.

Perhaps at this point I should say something of my own reasons for joining the Yeomanry, so far as they are discernible. How I managed to join this particular Regiment—I shall call them the Barsetshire Yeomanry—was always a slight mystery to my brother officers and remains so to me. I had no family connection with the county and the Yeomanry was a rather snobbish county institution. For an outsider to be commissioned into it was almost unheard of. Yet somehow or other I was. My brother officers, if they looked at me askance, politely concealed their misgivings.

Why I applied for a territorial commission at all is also a mystery. I remember that De Vigny's *Servitude et Grandeur militaires*, with its picture of the army as an austere ideal, made a strong appeal to me when I read it in my first year at Oxford. Like many undergraduates, I was inclined to remodel my life on whichever hero, in fact or fiction, I was studying at the moment. But surely I had grown out of that phase by twenty-three and I had no obvious leanings towards militarism; on the contrary. I soon found, as I had suspected, that the outward forms of army life were totally uncongenial. I disliked from the start marching in step, calling people "sir,"

and being called "sir," saluting and being saluted. Nor could I reconcile my egalitarian principles with the glaringly unequal privileges
and comforts enjoyed by officers. Admittedly I was often, at a later
date, glad of the privileges and comforts; as of the opportunities
afforded by a commission for sightseeing. But the guilt-feeling that
began with my first innocent meeting with the army in a Yeomanry
camp continued throughout our long association, poisoning it, until
at length I found peace, as did Amos too, in a unit where officers
and men shared their hardships on a more nearly equal basis. To
have such qualms of conscience at all was, I supposed, a fault that
lay somewhere in my own personality. I envied, even admired, those
officers like Victor Bone who accepted their commissions without
a moment's misgiving, who indeed looked upon them as their due.

In the autumn of 1936 when I applied for my territorial commission, the Italo-Abyssinian War was recently over, the Spanish Civil
War had recently begun. Even a self-absorbed and politically half-
baked young man could not fail to be aware that world catastrophe
was impending. To join the Territorial Army was the easiest and
most obvious course open to anyone who felt he should make some
effort to avert it. But, no. That sounds altogether too patriotic. I am
sure my own motives were less worthy. Obviously I might before
long be called upon to soldier compulsorily. Would it not pay to
make a small sacrifice, a propitiatory offering to Fate, in the mean-
time? As things turned out, it did pay. Like Amos, I got in on the
ground floor of an expanding racket.

But wars and rumors of wars, I fancy now, cast only a faint
shadow over my life then. Shadows there were, but they came rather
from an inherent melancholy. Quite simply, the prospect of a fortnight's riding in camp every year had probably more to do with my
joining. Introspective, shy, tormented with most of the inhibitions
of that age, I was passing through a period of various self-imposed
ordeals, imposed for the good of my "soul," and of these riding,
which frightened me, was one. No ordeal could have been greater
than that of appearing for the first time before my Regiment dressed
up as a Second Lieutenant and painfully ignorant of every detail of
the military life that lay ahead for two weeks. I knew how to stand
at attention, and that was all. If I tried to turn smartly to the left or

right, I tripped over my spurs. As to the latter, the Adjutant, giving
me a quick critical glance before I went on parade, pointed out that
I was wearing them upside down.

"We seem to be a little untidy about the neck this morning," he
added facetiously. He was probably right. I was then and, alas, have
always been "a little untidy about the neck."

But on the whole, my worries, like the apparent refusal of my
Sam Browne belt and riding-boots to shine, were of my own imag-
ining. A week passed, anxiously but without disaster, and I was
allowed to take part in the battle I have described. Now, as dinner
and the pleasantly secluded conversation with Amos drew to an end,
I awaited a further ordeal. The Senior Subaltern, a jovial ex-rugger
blue called Alan, had warned me of it on the first evening of camp
and I anticipated it now with that sick pit-of-the-stomach feeling
to which English schoolboys are, perhaps fortunately, accustomed
from childhood. Amos, I learnt, had not been warned. I glanced
down the table to the other newly-joined officer, Fergie Deakin.
Dark and wiry, he was a well-known amateur rider, about half-way
in age between Amos and myself, who already knew most of the
other officers intimately from the racecourse. He was enjoying a
joke with Victor Bone and was not anyway, I suspected, the type
of person to be troubled by the performance that would shortly be
required of him. Lucky Fergie Deakin!

The Colonel tapped the table and stood up. We all stood up.

"Gentlemen, the King!"

"The King, God bless him!" we toasted.

The Regimental brass band, tipped off by Muggs when to start,
played the National Anthem and thereafter, to my relief, held its
peace. The conductor, according to custom, was invited into the
Mess and drank a glass of wine with the Colonel without evident
enthusiasm. Cigarettes were lit, the talk livened up, Amos smoked
a cigar. I wondered at his calmness. The ordeal I awaited with so
much misgiving was not, in itself, so very severe. Each newly-joined
officer had to stand on the table and sing the tongue-twister, "She
sells sea-shells on the sea-shore" through to its end, drinking a
pint of beer for every mistake he made before starting through the
song over again. But as with any ordeal, the degree of severity depended simply on the temperament of the victim. For myself, a self-

conscious young man who loathed beer, the prospect was appalling. The intensity of the pit-of-the-stomach feeling is oddly invariable. On this trivial occasion it was not noticeably less than it had been six years previously before being flogged at school or than it was to be, six years later, before jumping out of an aeroplane at night into a country occupied by the enemy. And on that occasion too, Amos appeared unmoved.

Outside the Mess the sound of a thunderstorm blowing towards us across the Quantocks from the Bristol Channel replaced the noise of the band. The tent poles creaked, cold gusts of air swayed the lamps, rain pattered depressingly on the canvas overhead. "Plip, plip, plippity, plip . . ." Water, seeping through a rotten seam in the roof beat out a little tune in a puddle behind my chair. The dread moment approached. I noticed Victor Bone lean across to say something to the Colonel. The latter smiled and nodded.

"Muggs," Victor Bone shouted—or rather neighed, for his voice, by some distorted process of wish-fulfilment, sounded more like a horse's than a man's. "Bring twelve pints of beer."

He then made a short glib speech to the effect that tradition was the string which held together the parcel of regimental pride and that no tradition was more hallowed than that of newly-joined officers singing "sea-shells" to prove their mettle and drinking pints of beer when they stumbled. He himself, he concluded, accepted his own traditional role, as P.M.C., of paying for the beer. The speech was greeted with hilarious applause and cries of "Good old Victor!" "Come on the new officers!"

"Your turn first."

At least I was grateful to Victor Bone for giving me the chance to get the ordeal over quickly. I clambered on to the table and stood among the Regimental silver, with what I hoped looked more like devil-may-care *insouciance* than sheer pink embarrassment. Then in the guttural moaning sound on one note which serves me for a singing voice, I chanted the ditty. With cowardly cunning I had memorized the words very thoroughly beforehand. Even so I sung by mistake "the sells she shells are sea-shells I'm sure." I drank a pint of beer, started again, sang through it this time without a slip, and was allowed to sit down.

"Thank God that's over," I muttered to Amos.

"This is a menagerie," he replied quite loudly.

The applause for my effort was kindly, if half-hearted. The performance, I was sadly aware, had been dignified and dignity is a cold dull sort of virtue. Give me the man who is uninhibited enough to make an uproarious fool of himself. Fergie Deakin, who followed me on to the table, was such a man. He had a good voice and a loud one. He sang with gusto, made several probably deliberate mistakes, drank six pints of beer in as many minutes without turning a hair, and sat down again amid wild cheering and laughter. I wished I was more like Fergie Deakin.

Outside the rain pattered more loudly on the marquee, the water plip-plipped more insistently in the puddle behind my chair. A clap of thunder drowned Victor Bone's voice as, the self-appointed Master of Ceremonies, he gestured to Amos to rise.

Slowly, deliberately, Amos climbed on to the table. He stood there like a blue beanstalk, puffing unconcernedly at his cigar and reaching with his head almost to the roof. The last living member of an old English family, he called to mind some French aristocrat at bay, humoring the mob from a tumbril. But there was also a glint of menace, a cornered look in his eyes, which seemed to say "All right, have your piece of foolery at my expense. Only, beware . . ." I saw a similar look in Amos's eyes again, once, when an excited and angry German officer prodded his stomach with a revolver.

Holding his cigar gracefully with two fingers, Amos spoke. "With your consent, Colonel, I will drink pints of champagne. Beer doesn't agree with me, I'm afraid."

The laughter and the conversation round the table stopped suddenly. The Barsetshire officers waited for a cue from the Colonel whether to take this remark as a joke or as an insult. For the first time I noticed the Colonel closely. In appearance, he seemed to have stepped straight out of Gilbert and Sullivan. "I am the very model of a modern Major-General." A cross between that and the silent Colonel Bramble. But the red peppery face, the grey bushy hair and moustache were a mask from which two very intelligent very blue eyes twinkled with—was it great amusement or great irritation? Would he now administer some awful snub? I feared for Amos.

But the Colonel roared with laughter. "Excellent! Victor must buy Amos a bottle of bubbly!"

"Muggs, open a bottle of champagne." Victor Bone took his line, not with a very good grace, from the Colonel.

"Better make it two bottles," Amos said quietly.

"Ha! Ha!" laughed the officers. "Two bottles, very good that. Good old Amos. Poor old Victor." The bottles being opened, Amos began.

"She sells sea-shells on the sea shore," he said in a flat tired talking voice.

"Sing! You must sing!" yelled Victor Bone and several others.

Amos paused. "I never sing." He glanced politely at the Colonel.

For the moment, as if possessed of some ancient hereditary power, nameless yet undeniable and demanding obedience, Amos had become his own Master of Ceremonies, supervising his own execution. The Colonel, I discovered when I came to know him well later, regarded this particular Regimental tradition with even less enthusiasm than did Amos himself. It was the sort of boorish joke which could be made amusing by a natural buffoon like Fergie, but which, with someone like Amos, fell rather flat. The Colonel was secretly delighted to watch the tables being turned now on Victor Bone.

"Oh all right, Amos, do it your way," he said.

So, for what seemed to me a long ten minutes, Amos ploughed laboriously through the tongue-twister, slipping up, drinking a pint of champagne, beginning all over again, slipping up again, and so on. By the time he had finished he had drunk the two bottles—no mean feat—amid general laughter which was the louder for hiding general embarrassment. Swaying slightly, or did the lamps and the storm outside create that effect? the blue beanstalk descended at last to our earthier level still smoking his cigar . . . His attitude throughout had been magnificently debonair and arrogant, I thought. But if the ordeal was designed to test each new officer's potential good fellowship, Amos had come through it the least creditably of us three. As the officers thronged back into the anteroom, leaving Muggs to prepare the dining-tent for breakfast, I found myself pressed behind Victor Bone and the Colonel.

"Good chap, Fergie," said Victor Bone.

"Yes," grunted the Colonel.

"That new fellow Amos is a bit of a shit," said Victor Bone.

"I dare say. But an amusing one, don't you think?" replied the Colonel.

I disentangled myself hastily lest I should overhear a further unflattering assessment. All the same, I wondered, how did I fit into the only two known sub-divisions of male human being in the Victor Bone universe? Certainly I did not qualify, like Fergie Deakin, as a "good chap." Was I therefore in Amos's category? Hardly that, either. I supposed I was just dim.

Back once more in the anteroom most of the officers were determined to make a night of it. There was cause for celebration. The day's battle had been well fought and the visiting General had given the Regiment a good "chit." Besides, who wanted to flounder back in the dark to his tent through the mud and rain to find, most likely, when he got there that his bed was soaked? To keep the party spirit alive Alan stood on his head and in that position drank two pints of beer off the floor. To make liquid flow upwards into your stomach seemed at the time a superhuman, indeed a metaphysical achievement. We removed our spurs and organized a game of rugger. "Don't spoil the carpet," protested Victor Bone, unaware of the irony in such a precaution. So the carpet was rolled up and Fergie, doubling up on the grass floor, offered himself as a football. During the ensuing mêlée I noticed Amos fast asleep in a basket chair in the corner. The rain dripping through on to his face had extinguished the cigar which still stuck out of his mouth.

Drink, or perhaps relief at having put the "sea-shells" ordeal behind me, began to melt my natural reserve. To my satisfaction I found myself accepted as part of the Regiment for the first time. Officers who before had been anonymous now acquired names, even nicknames. "Bubs" Tregunter, "Boy" Harland . . . The rugger gave place to a sing-song and the carpet was put back. Alan played the piano, surprisingly well. Victor Bone sang.

I touched her on the toe and said what's that my dear—O
It is my toe tumper, my old bandolier—O

Successive stanzas progressed, anatomically speaking, upwards.

Inflamed by success Victor Bone followed it with other songs, each more splendidly obscene. Arm in arm with Bubs Tregunter and Boy Harland I joined manfully in the choruses, though, to tell the truth, my young mind was deeply shocked. For one is curiously pure at twenty-three. Bawdiness, I reflect now, is an aphrodisiac which middle age more and more needs to compensate for its flagging powers. After one particularly lurid ditty, the Colonel was heard to remark, "Old Victor gets nearer and nearer to the bone."

Amos, still asleep in his corner, began to snore. The wet cigar had disappeared and his mouth was wide open. The officers gathered round him. Victor Bone, to pay off his own earlier discomfiture, took a glass of beer and poured it slowly into Amos's mouth with a glug-glug noise. Amos spluttered and woke up. No one could ever quite remember what happened after that. One moment Amos was staring wildly at us. The next he and Victor Bone were locked in each other's arms rolling over the grass. They crashed against the tent pole. The pressure-lamp fell and spilled burning paraffin over a pile of Regimental Orders on a table. The pole itself caught alight. We stood round and shrieked with laughter. Amos was the first to react sensibly. He seized a siphon of soda water and played it on the tent pole. We followed his example with other siphons. Beer bottles were smashed and the contents hurled at the flames. Alcohol which had started the fire, extinguished it. The crisis past, we ordered drinks all round and then we plunged out of the anteroom into the deluge, to visit the Sergeants' Mess. As we left I noticed Muggs, muttering to himself, begin to clear up the debris with a bucket and a brush.

"The Sergeants' Mess is the heart of the Regiment," R.S.M. Burge was fond of saying to young officers like myself, putting them wise, in a fatherly way, to the wrinkles of Army life. He had another favorite dictum, on the care of horses. "Always see the rug is well forward. Keep your horse's heart warm and you keep all of him warm." There may have been some unconscious connection between these two maxims for certainly, by comparison with the chaos of our own, the Sergeants' Mess was always snug and tidy and well lit. No swinging paraffin lamps for R.S.M. Burge. One of the sergeants had rigged up electric light from a car battery. A radiogram blared in a corner and was switched off politely when we entered.

The happy relationship between officers and sergeants was an endearing, in fact an essential feature of pre-war Yeomanry camps. Many of the N.C.O.s were successful businessmen who looked upon this brand of soldiering as a fortnight's escape from responsibility, with free riding thrown in. Between them they could have bought up the impecunious squirearchy, from which the officers were mainly recruited, without feeling it. R.S.M. Burge himself came from a very different social background. With the Adjutant and the Quartermaster he was the third of the triumvirate of regulars, seconded from cavalry Regiments, who ran the Yeomanry. The son of a Northumberland miner, he had risen in the Army the hard way, and the Army had left its mark. In such an environment every man grows a protective skin. The more sensitive the feelings underneath, the tougher the skin. R.S.M. Burge's skin was very tough indeed. His present job was a cushy one, the reward of a twenty-years' struggle. Lesser men might have relaxed. But Mr. Burge, as he was called, carried it through with a tireless zeal, which reached its climax at each yearly camp when he was never seen to sleep. By day ruthless military efficiency; by night, equally important to the Yeomanry "spirit," relentless debauchery. Much of his success lay in his sense of showmanship. A good Regiment, it cannot be denied, is a smart Regiment. To watch Mr. Burge mounting a guard, particularly when there were women in the audience, was to watch the Great Barnum reincarnated. Altogether he was an exceptional man. Given an easier start in life he would probably have become a Bishop. As it was, many of us younger officers were sure that if war came Mr. Burge, with his apparently encyclopedic knowledge of Army matters, his Napoleonic brow, his incredible vitality, would certainly rise at once in it to dizzy heights. He was always kind to me, though I was aware of falling far below his standards of what a cavalry subaltern should be, standards based on long years of experience with cavalry Regiments in India and Egypt.

Now, drinking beer with him in the Sergeants' Mess, the libidinous flow of his anecdotes as always fascinated me. They illustrated the brutalizing effect of the Regular Army on what was, basically, a sensitive temperament.

"Christ! How he bled! God! How I laughed!" said Mr. Burge, describing some accident that had once happened in Quetta.

I staggered back to my tent as daylight was breaking. The storm was over and my bed, I was thankful to find, was dry. I put my hand under the pillow and pulled out the diary in which I had intended, hitherto unsuccessfully, to record my impressions of Army life. It was a new diary, all its paper still a blank. I sucked my fountain pen for a moment, pondering. Then, in the semi-darkness, I scrawled across the front page the first cryptic entry.

"My brother officers. Are they human?"

So ended a fairly typical day with the Yeomanry in those years. If there was little in it of military solitude and grandeur, still there were moments, like riding over the Quantocks, which compensated for the tedium of the rest. And there was much, visually, that delighted me. The horse lines, the groups of marching men, the white tents diapered with mathematical regularity on the hillside, were all very beautiful if you detached them from their implications. Certainly it was all a new experience—and I was greedy for new experiences. "Perhaps I shall write about it some day," I thought, as I settled down to sleep for the two hours left before breakfast.

A fortnight passes all too quickly nowadays, but to me then the three camps I attended seemed interminable bad dreams in which, as in dreams, I lived in terror of being exposed. It was always with surprise and relief that I emerged from them at the end without Victor Bone or some other officer having pointed an accusing finger, saying while the others closed in to stare, "Who is this?" With Amos, there was someone in this strange and hostile Army world whom, in the distance, I could smile at and be understood by; there was someone I could exchange just the faintest wink with.

He was older than I so that his friends and interests, apart from the Art Gallery where I occasionally saw him, were very different from mine. Inevitably we met seldom in the next three years except at camps and other Yeomanry occasions; and not always then for Amos, unlike myself, who was too scared of the Army to disobey it, turned up only when it suited him and the Adjutant was for ever writing him "rockets." But the war with one stroke reduced us, if not to the same age, to the same plight. Through the greater part of it we clung together, by accident as well as by design, united primarily by a common sense of humor. When, a day or two before September 3, 1939, I arrived desolately in Bath where I had been called up, there was Amos grinning by the bar. I felt much happier at once.

John and Lucinda, circa 1939

CHAPTER TWO

Lucinda

I HAD KNOWN LUCINDA vaguely since childhood, regarding her with that particular brand of suspicion and dislike which children reserve for the children of their parents' friends. Antipathy was mutual. I tweaked her hair once or twice at young people's parties. She kicked my shins on a memorable occasion getting out of a taxi in her 'teens. After that we lost sight of one another for several years until, one evening in May 1938, we met again by chance in Venice. I was on a month's holiday between films, had finished a fortnight in Italy and was about to return, reluctantly, to my second Yeomanry camp. I paid a last visit to the Carpaccios in the Chapel of San Giorgio before walking back to the hotel to pack. As I crossed the Piazza, thinking of the very different surroundings that awaited me within twenty-four hours, I came unexpectedly on some acquaintances of mine called Prendergast sitting outside Florian's. Talking to them was a young woman with long dark hair. I was startled to recognize Lucinda whom I had last seen as a leggy schoolgirl.

The two Prendergast brothers, I was brought up to take it for granted, were brilliant. If abundant evidence of their brilliance was sometimes lacking, Ma Prendergast, as I called their mother, stressed the point insidiously until it came to be generally accepted. "I am afraid my sons are different, too different, from other boys," she used to sigh complacently to my mother. As she and my mother were old friends, by "other boys" she meant commonplace hairy-heeled boys like me.

Mrs. Prendergast always wore an air of unassailable superiority. Possibly it was no more than a protective skin, grown in self-defence like R.S.M. Burge's coarseness, but it weighed oppressively on her sons, I think. Certainly in our schooldays her more devastatingly foolish utterances caused them great suffering. To one of their friends, a victim of haemophilia, she once said, "Is it true you're a bleeder?" Still less fortunate was her remark to another boy who collected bugs.

The war changed most people, but few so completely as it changed Matthew. A tall dark remote person, whom no one even at school came to know well, he was at this time, 1938, a morose young man of no particular occupation, except that of living with Mrs. Prendergast. Matthew was my contemporary. Luke, a year older, and outwardly more successful (he was a barrister), always struck me as cold and pedantic. I think we disliked one another equally.

Now, on the Piazza, the Prendergasts saw me as I saw them. There was no escape for either of us, so I joined them at their table, feeling unaccountably pleased to meet Lucinda again. She seemed pleased too. We laughed over our last encounter in the taxi.

"How I used to loathe you," she said.

The others looked on gloomily while we gossiped about the old days. I began to wish, more than ever, that my holiday in Venice was beginning, not ending. We got on too well together. A malicious gleam in Ma Prendergast's eye warned me I was intruding. At length the conversation, interrupted by my arrival, was resumed. The Prendergasts had been telling Lucinda about Art.

Their attitude and mine to the subject were basically antagonistic. I considered the art of any period from the point of view of the present, to them it was essentially something at least two centuries old, to be read up in books or to be studied behind glass in museums. I approached all works of art through feeling; the Prendergasts through learning. Now they laid on their factual knowledge of Venetian painting pretty heavily, I thought, for Lucinda's benefit. It astounded me how eagerly the girl swallowed the stuff. My own, much more perceptive, contributions to the talk were peremptorily brushed aside. I resented being snubbed when I particularly wanted to shine.

"But all this must be awfully boring for you. I believe you don't care for the Old Masters," Matthew said unpleasantly, implying, "Why not go away?"

"Oh, don't you?" Lucinda looked at me as if golf, perhaps, was more in my line.

"Of course I do. He only means I'd rather own a Picasso than a Tintoretto. Which indeed I would." Sitting there under the shadow of St. Mark's the statement did not sound at all daringly modern, as I had hoped, but merely silly. The Prendergasts, zealous custodians of the Past, were easily able to turn it against me. Ma Prendergast and Matthew threw up their hands in mock despair. Luke delivered the *coup de grâce*.

"Ah well, it's a matter of taste. Some people like to drink old wine, others prefer fizzy lemonade."

After that I made to leave, explaining aggressively that I had to be in a Yeomanry camp by the next evening. Only the Prendergasts could have changed me, for the moment, into a militant Yeoman.

"The Yeomanry? What a curious old-fashioned word! Do tell us what it means," they all cried.

Perhaps I could still turn the situation to my advantage. I made the most of my adventures with the Army. Lucinda, I was glad to see, laughed twice. But the Prendergasts listened with supercilious boredom.

"It all sounds rather a waste of time," Ma Prendergast murmured dryly.

Matthew and Luke concurred.

"Of course he's very nice, dear, but not really quite your cup of tea I would have thought," Ma Prendergast said to Lucinda, when I had left.

Luckily for me she proved to be wrong. In London, where I was better able to choose my ground, I met Lucinda again. The meeting led to what I once saw described as the commencement of warmer feelings. Rivalry with Luke and Matthew was not precisely a spur to my wooing, but I dare say their discomfiture added a flavor to victory. Lucinda and I were married in the spring of 1939.

(Lucinda, having read thus far, says I make it sound as though I only married her to spite the Prendergasts. She wants more space devoted to our long and beautiful courtship. But this, as I have tried to explain to her, is a war book. Maybe I will write about our courtship some other time.)

We settled in our first home above a greengrocer's shop in Chelsea. Emboldened by the success of one plunge, I made another. More truthfully, Lucinda, abetted by Amos, gave me the courage to make another. I threw up my job in films to become a painter. It was what I had always wanted to be and I had for many years been painting diffidently in my spare time.

Lucinda and I both knew we could probably only expect a few months together. We made the most of them. Even so our happiness was interrupted twice during the summer by camp and by a further fortnight in the Army Equitation School at Weedon. With the nearing prospect of war, training had become a more serious business than in those distant Quantocks. When, in 1939, Northland gave battle to Southland, the troops, in addition to the rest of their iron-mongery, were realistically encumbered with gas masks and anti-gas capes.

Before the war my friends, those who knew of it, looked upon my Territorial commission as a sort of practical joke I had played on myself, inexplicable except in terms of perverse eccentricity.

"Perhaps you're an unconscious homo," said one, to whom I had told my experiences.

But the investment over three years of many weeks apparently wasted, paid an immediate dividend when war started. The racket, as Amos had called it, expanded at once. The Barsetshire Yeomanry, brought up to strength with "reservists," joined the Cavalry Division which was concentrating in the Midlands and which began to move after Christmas to Palestine.

Lucinda and I were shattered by the prospect of indefinite separation. But Ma Prendergast, whom I met in London on my embarkation leave, seemed to think I had shown a rather discreditable forethought in joining the Territorial Army. The pathos of my being torn from my young wife and dispatched to foreign lands, there to be cut off in my prime as likely as not, did not trouble her at all. It was simply monstrous, she said, that I should be dressed up as a Lieutenant in dashing blue patrols while her Matthew, who had joined up, kicked his heels as a Private in Aldershot.

"Imagine the waste!" she wailed.

To avoid further waste, Luke, I learnt from his mother, had joined the B.B.C.

A sense of impending doom hung over the sordid pub in a Nottinghamshire mining village, in which a dozen officers, most of them with their wives, awaited the Regiment's departure. The snow lay thick on the ground, the plumbing had frozen up, nerves were on edge, the males glowered at one another, while the females bickered. Amos, not currently married, had the laugh on all of us. Some resented his mockery, but Lucinda and I found his dry humor more consoling than Victor Bone's sing-songs.

To escape from the terrible pub on Lucinda's last evening, we drove with Amos to the Black Boy at Nottingham. There we ran into Oliver Bomfrey. He was a friend of Amos and had known Lucinda in a previous period of her London life, so we all dined together. Bomfrey, full of charm and up-to-the-minute information, was the sort of flashy and successful Tory M.P. I disliked, if only because his self-assurance accentuated my own awkward shyness. I came to reassess him, like Matthew Prendergast, differently later.

Through dinner he amused us moderately. Wearing the uniform of a Second Lieutenant in the Household Cavalry, he seemed an unlikely subaltern even for that delightful and eclectic Regiment. However, he was only with them temporarily over the Christmas recess.

"I needed a military disguise to wear in the House," he explained, with disarming frankness. "The war will be over in a few months anyway, but don't quote me as saying so."

The Tories in both Houses of Parliament were liberally represented in the Cavalry Division when it sailed.

"If the Germans sink us there will have to be a change of government," Bomfrey predicted.

But Oliver Bomfrey did not sail with us. We heard later that he had left, in the opposite direction, on some mission or other to the Finns.

In many ways I regret that, unlike Matthew Prendergast and others of my friends, I never served as a private soldier. I should like to have known for a short while the hardships and the intimacies of the barrack room; an experience, I note, that few sought to prolong who could avoid doing so. Still, my own less arduous experiences were worth having and I was fortunate, I think now. But I did not think so when the time came to say goodbye to Lucinda. At that moment I would gladly have changed places with Matthew or with anyone, if thereby I could have remained with her a few weeks longer in England.

"It will be for six months," we said.

"It will be for a year," we thought. In fact, it was to be for over four years.

When she had driven off into the snow, I returned to the bedroom and tried to brace myself for Regimental duties by swallowing half a flask-full of brandy. Only Anglo-Saxons, so far as I know, are ashamed of tears and are taught from early childhood to hold them back. There were many times later when a good cry might have helped, but as an Englishman I lost the knack early in life and cried only once again in the war, at the end of a sad day's battle against the French in Syria.

If the fortunes of war prevent Lucinda featuring personally in the rest of this book, she must be understood by the reader to stand behind every page of it as a Presence. Or rather as an Absence. For the vast correspondence addressed to her, and which, miraculously, she has preserved, provides the raw material from which I attempt to compound my story—the story of a young man torn from his own Lucasta by war and of his efforts in the end to rejoin her.

PART TWO

Amateur

"Palestine soup!" said the Reverend Doctor
Opimian . . . "a curiously complicated mis-
nomer. We have an excellent old vegetable,
the artichoke, of which we eat the head;
we have another of subsequent introduc-
tion, of which we eat the root, and which
we also call artichoke, because it resembles
the first in flavor, although, *me judice*, a
very inferior affair. This last is a species of
helianthus, or sunflower genus of the *Syn-
genesia frustranea* class of plants. It is therefore a girasol, or turn-to-the-sun. From this
girasol we have made Jerusalem, and from
the Jerusalem artichoke we make Palestine soup."

Thomas Love Peacock, *Gryll Grange*

CHAPTER THREE

Zion

AS WE BOARDED the boat at Southampton Alan stooped to tap
England with his stick, a gay little gesture of farewell, unsentimental
and appropriate. There was something of the bulldog breed about
Alan. A natural soldier, he had been appointed our first "Territorial" Adjutant to allow the "Regular" one to rejoin his own Regiment in France. He believed, or appeared to believe, in himself, in
the Army, in the rightness of war, and he inspired a welcome confidence into all of us.

In the four months already spent together I had grown fond
of most of the officers with whom I now embarked; the Colonel,
Tom the Quartermaster, Fergie Deakin, Bubs Tregunter, Hilary the
Padre, Boy Harland, and the rest. Even Victor Bone, I had come to
feel, was potentially human. As the ship sailed out of Southampton, each of us chose his own way to endure the solemnity of his
mood. With whisky and laughter; or with silence. Often in the past
I had sailed this route for holidays in France. Now, gliding down
the Solent on a calm wintry evening in January 1940, I leant on the
hand-rail and gazed at the familiar landmarks as they passed. Below
decks, R.S.M. Burge had organized a game of housey-housey for the
men. His voice, bellowing the time-honored numerals with relish,
could be heard all over the ship. Amos came and stood beside me.

After an hour darkness hid the last of England.

"Let's go down and get an enormous drink," Amos said.

Our train, the horses peering out of cattle trucks, chugged and
shunted for three days across France towards Marseilles. My diges-
tion must have been enviable for I tried to subdue my sorrows with

a tin of *pâté de foie gras*, washed down by a bottle of Benedictine bought in Cherbourg on the way through. Most of us in the smoky carriage were newly married and suffered the same emotional strain, though, in our English way, it was not a matter we discussed. Tom the Quartermaster, a veteran of the First World War and in appearance a Silenus by Rubens, kept up our depressed spirits with a flow of ribald anecdotes.

"And what happened to you after that?" I plied him with Benedictine anxious at all costs to avoid the necessity of silent thought. Besides, the picture he painted of another war might shed some useful light on this one. But he needed little pressing.

"Well, after we came back from Bapaume I was billeted on a farm. I was only a strapping young corporal at the time, and the farmer was away in the French Army. One evening, the farmer's wife . . ."

The train drew slowly through Martigues on the Etang de Berre. From the window I could see the little hotel where nine months before Lucinda and I had spent some of our honeymoon. At Marseilles, numbed by a freezing mistral, we led our horses off the train and reloaded them on to the ship waiting to carry us across the Mediterranean. I sought out my charger, Caesar, a large Roman-nosed chestnut hunter from Leicestershire. He shivered and looked little pleased with this change of environment. His rug had slipped back and hung round his hindquarters like a skirt. Remembering R.S.M. Burge's maxim, I tugged it well forward to cover his heart.

Life on board was quickly organized, as nearly as was possible, along Army lines, and the ship became a sort of floating Yeomanry camp with Orderly Officers, "stables" routine, and formal evenings in the Mess. After dinner the old songs were sung and Victor Bone blew his hunting-horn.

"We have been away from England ten days," I wrote to Lucinda as we neared Haifa. "Among these same chubby English companions it is hard to realize we have left at all. Their insularity and utter inability to adapt themselves to any change amounts to genius. They carry their own little England about with them, plant it wherever they happen to stop and then sit down in it."

The letters contain many similarly bitter and disparaging remarks. If I quote them occasionally it is not because I agree with them still or because I feel they have any special validity. My life, like the lives of Amos and the others, had been wrecked. A wounded dog bites any hand however friendly and to bite at something, at everything, became for me too often the means of relieving my feelings. A few weeks later the contrast between my own state and the sight of happy civilians leading a normal life in a modern Jewish colony provoked the following outburst:

"The spring is fully upon us in a blaze of sunny days and sprouting grasses. The red mud everywhere has turned to green, the birds sing as never before, the anemones grow out of the concrete and the young repulsive Jewish male casts a furtive suggestive look at the young repulsive Jewish female as they walk together beside the plough."

In the mood I was then in, I am sure I would have written the same words had I found myself in Scotland instead of in Israel. For the Army does and always has done ugly things to people, pushing them out of shape and giving them a different outlook and mentality. My skin, like R.S.M. Burge's, had begun to thicken.

Haifa. I look back upon the town now with nostalgic affection, recollecting many a good meal at Prosse's, or the Lev Hacarmel Hotel, many a good concert by the Palestine Symphony Orchestra. First impressions were disappointing. From the sea, the modern box-shaped buildings terraced on the slope of Carmel were pretty enough in the bright sunshine. But I had expected clusters of domes and minarets, as drawn by Edmund Dulac, set against the Mountains of Rumm, as described by T. E. Lawrence. My naïve enthusiasm for the latter's exploits led me to ask a captain in the Scots Greys, who had been in Palestine for two years, whether he enjoyed riding camels. He looked stunned.

We moved south by rail into Sharon, along the narrow stretch of coast between Carmel and the sea, the route taken by the Crusaders on their march to victory at Arsuf. The sight of their Castel Pelerin at Athlit, silhouetted against the evening sky, raised hopes in me of another truer Palestine ahead. Victor Bone, staring moodily out of the window, livened up too.

"H'm. Not bad-looking country for foxes. Do you think they've got a pack of hounds out here?"

We arrived in Hadar-le-Zion, a colony reclaimed from waste land on the coast by hard-pressed and industrious Zionists.

"I've just come in from visiting a sick horse by moonlight," I
wrote after a few days. "The moon is extra large here and casts extra-
mysterious shadows, in which, like Tartarin, one hopes may lurk a
lion—or something. By day the blue hills of Samaria beckon to us
from the south-east and soon, I hope, we shall be there. Meanwhile,
I would have preferred fewer European Jews sunning themselves in
purple pyjamas on concrete balconies, more Arabs in fancy dress;
less imitation Le Corbusier, more castles like Athlit; less suburban
back garden, more desert—Lawrence's desert. This place is nothing
but a sort of exotic Hampstead, with a mixed crowd of film extras
from *The Four Feathers* thrown in for local color."

Perhaps I was still homesick. Or perhaps I was deliberately playing down any delight I felt—that I can remember feeling—in the
country, in the hope of pleasing Lucinda. For it is an open question
whether a wife likes to think of her absent husband as happy or as
unhappy.

An inexperienced and therefore too-busy Troop Leader, I fussed
over my thirty horses and men, checking and re-checking their
thirty complicated sets of arms, saddlery, and equipment, always incomplete in some trifling particular.

"You try and do your Troop sergeant's work for him," Alan, my
mentor in the ways of the Army, scolded me. "Why keep a dog and
then bark yourself?"

Alan understood by nature the boundaries dividing the duties of
an officer from those of his N.C.O.s. He understood how to make
people work willingly for him and was somehow born a soldier,
whereas I was not. Amos called him "our best type of Public Schoolboy." The definition was not meant wholly as a compliment. Amos
himself, though he detested both the war and the Army, was efficient
as a matter of course from long business experience. He watched my
own efforts with ironic amusement. "Can't think why you take so
much trouble," he said. "You're a painter, not a professional soldier.
Why not just be yourself instead of trying to be Alan?"

My own tenuous efficiency sprang not from any particular military or patriotic enthusiasm but rather from an instinct of self-preservation. It was part of my private war against the Army, begun in
a desultory way at the first camp, and in which I was now fully involved. The Army was an implacable external force which I feared

and hated, yet in some respects also loved, but which in either case I knew I must either conquer or be conquered by.

"The question is how, while fighting this private war, to preserve some vestiges of personal integrity and inner life."

Personal integrity, inner life . . . whatever they mean. A young man's words, high-sounding and vague.

In February 1940, we were no longer a light-hearted band of solicitors, squires, farmers, butchers, and businessmen playing at soldiers, but a cavalry Regiment on active service overseas preparing itself—for what? Where was the enemy? We could not tell. If the Germans came to realize the futility of ever hurling themselves against the Maginot Line as, we were led to believe, they surely must, the war in the West might fade out. We were not so ingenuous as to suppose that if that happened we should be allowed to return home. The transportation of a cavalry Division, complete with horses, across three thousand miles of land and water costs a lot of public money. "They," that anonymous and malevolent power which controls the destiny of soldiers in wartime, would surely see that the money was not wasted. We might have to stay on indefinitely in Palestine to hold down a resurgence of the Arab rebellion.

Or a rebellion by the Jews? Tin-hatted and armed, we lined the streets of Hadar-le-Zion while a procession of Jewish youths "demonstrated" against the recent British White Paper restricting their purchase of land from the Arabs. The youths booed and jeered at us standing silently along their route and we ourselves, though we had only the faintest understanding of the reasons for their resentment, became restive and angry. The feeling that a "situation" of some sort was developing which might at any moment take a more dramatic turn was most unpleasant. But the procession, after breaking the Officers' Mess windows, dispersed.

Was this the enemy? I wondered afterwards. There had been a moment in that street when, being booed at, I felt a sudden surge of hatred towards Jews, but little remained of it on reflection. What of the Jewish Palestine Symphony Orchestra? Was that the enemy too? I could not imagine any satisfaction in trampling the Jewish violins under my horse's feet, in kicking the Jewish double basses to bits with my riding-boots, in thrusting my sabre through the Jewish drums.

The war against Hitler seemed far away as, early every morning, we exercised our horses among the tall silvery trees of the eucalyptus forest grown to drain what had been a malarial swamp; or splashed them in the sea. Although the bedouin we met camping on the dunes were about as near to Lawrence's or Doughty's bedouin as are English gipsies, I found them infinitely mysterious and exciting. With Baldwin, my groom, a "reservist" whom the Army had failed to brutalize, a gentle lover of horses and, like myself, an expectant father, I rode back to visit them at my leisure one afternoon. The cattle, poultry, children, and grown-ups were all together in the black tents sheltering from the sun. The bedouin were friendly and consented, with much giggling, to be photographed.

"I wish I could live with them for a while, when my Arabic is better," reads the inevitable letter. "They would probably murder me very soon when they found how useless I was and who could blame them? Though I might become quite popular by drawing their portraits and I imagine I would be good at amusing the children." In parenthesis, the presumption of the last statement flabbergasts me now.

Children . . . Lucinda, alone above the greengrocer's shop in Chelsea, awaited our own child. The Squadron Office in which Victor Bone daily scolded his Troop Leaders overlooked a backyard. There the antics of an infant, who grinned and gurgled at us from a sort of hencoop, did much to enliven the tedium of his admonishments. Furtively I made faces back at the child until Victor Bone's eyes were turned on me, glassy, uncomprehending, and hostile. He was unmarried, was enjoying the war, and had become wonderfully military and self-important. Amos and I collected, sometimes invented, "Victor Bone stories." The best at this time originated with Alan, who had accompanied him on a camp inspection. As they walked through the men's latrines they passed by a seated Trooper. "Don't stand up," Victor Bone had said, taking it quite seriously for granted that any Trooper, so situated, would pay him this deference.

If, in my war against the Army, Victor Bone as my immediate superior drew my fire, there were deeper causes of discontent.

"I begin to sympathize with Lawrence who preferred to remain at the bottom if he couldn't be at the supreme top of the Army, so as to avoid passing on orders he disagreed with. That's all officers and N.C.O.s do—pass on orders. Eventually some miserable bank clerk who joined up to fight for his country, who spends the whole day cleaning his horse, his saddle, his sword, his rifle, his equipment, his billets, and half the night on guard of something or other, is found with a dirty button, cursed high and low, placed under arrest, given a dozen duties and fatigues, so that he forgets to clean a button again, is cursed high and low, placed under arrest, and so on and so on . . ."

My distaste for this aspect of soldiering was a recurrent theme at the time, a theme that later was dropped as experience revealed a basic common sense in the system or as, more probably, the Army blunted my sensibilities. This particular grumble was occasioned by an extra Church Parade, imposed on the Regiment as a punishment for a poor turn-out. The idea of the Army using the Christian faith as a stick to beat itself with was faintly comical.

Church Parades were always an ordeal for me, and more of an ordeal for Muggs, whose incompetence in making my belt and boots shine I privately condoned. I blamed the Padre, Hilary, for them; unjustly, for he loathed, far more than I did, the subordination of religious observance to the requirements of military pomp and circumstance. Now, his essentially good face grimly set, he warned the troops in a pure voice about unspecified dangers lying in wait for them in Jerusalem. Like the missionary in Somerset Maugham's *Rain*, he had a sharp nose for sin. When he himself left the next day for Jerusalem, to arrange for the baptism of some Barsetshire Yeomen, I asked him if he was intending to reconnoiter the dangers.

It was the start of a feud between us which developed in the next eighteen months with growing bitterness; a silly feud, for we had many tastes in common. Perhaps I was conscious that Hilary preserved more successfully than I did "some vestiges of personal integrity and inner life." Or was I jealous of his freedom? For he roamed about Palestine at will, visiting the Biblical sites in a car provided for the purpose by the Army. The Baptism episode was typical of his endearing innocence.

Learning that some of the troopers and one of the officers, Boy Harland, had never been baptized, he obtained the Colonel's permission to take them all to Jerusalem for the ceremony. Bubs Tregunter and Fergie Deakin joined the party as godfathers. When R.S.M. Burge announced that he had never been baptized and asked to be taken too, even Hilary's suspicions were aroused. But Burge persuaded him his case was genuine and Hilary remained convinced afterwards that he really had redeemed the old sinner. Much envied, the baptismal party left happily. They were away for two days. On their return R.S.M. Burge went sick. It took him a further two days to recover from the effects of baptism. The excuse given was that he had caught a bad cold at the font.

Religion and politics were subjects traditionally debarred from discussion in officers' messes, but not so in ours, greatly to its credit. Presided over by our intelligent and amusing Colonel, many a theological tussle took place in which the unfortunate Hilary was called upon to defend his faith to the last orange. For evenings in the mess at this time often ended in orange battles. Victor Bone blew on his hunting-horn, while electric bulbs, crockery, glass, even tables and chairs were recklessly smashed; a nostalgic survival of past customs. Muggs, no longer muttering under his breath, helped to sweep up the debris. He seemed to enjoy it.

"Quite like the old days," he grinned.

The serious-minded inhabitants of Hadar-le-Zion, whom the Army paid for the damage to their requisitioned property, must have wondered how effectively we would protect them against Hitler, if the time came to do so. Relations between them and us, never friendly, had not been improved by the street incident. There were faults on both sides. We grumbled that we were robbed in the shops; they complained, too often with justice, that the British were arrogantly anti-Semitic. Only R.S.M. Burge openly declared his Zionist sympathies. With Amos, I attended one evening a production by the Habima Theater Company. The play was given in the same cinema where on Sundays Hilary drew us towards his God.

"The only other soldier in the audience was R.S.M. Burge. He sat behind us with his latest girl-friend. He seemed to be known to everyone there and was kept busy greeting his acquaintances, particularly among the women. A remarkable man in many ways, he has a great gift for getting on with people. I overheard most of his conversation. It was impressively refined, sympathetic, interested, interesting. Probably he had an ulterior purpose in making himself pleasant but then, who hasn't?"

A palpable "ulterior purpose" lay behind the party given by the Mayor of Hadar-le-Zion for the officers of the Barsetshire Yeomanry. The hospitality was lavish; so was the propaganda insinuated into the evening's entertainment. Led by the Colonel, a dozen of us walked down to the Mayor's house after dinner. The Mayor, the Mayoress, and about twenty prominent citizens of either sex, mostly of German origin, greeted us in the small, stuffy, hideously over-furnished drawing-room. None of the officers, except myself, could speak German. None of the prominent citizens could speak English, except a predatory matron, the living image of Ma Prendergast, who acted throughout as official interpreter. Most of us were ready to further the *entente cordiale* though I noticed, uneasily, that Victor Bone stared truculently around him, a sure warning that he was already half-drunk.

To open the proceedings, the Mayor recited a long written speech in Hebrew, which Ma Prendergast translated sentence by sentence. Apart from a preliminary welcome to the officers of the Barsetshire Yeomanry, the whole speech was an attack on the British Government's policy in Palestine for which, the Mayor implied, we were ourselves responsible. His compatriots applauded the various points while we listened with growing embarrassment.

"What cheek!" Victor Bone growled.

The Colonel made a brief and brilliantly incoherent speech in reply, with many references to milk and honey and oranges. God knows how Ma Prendergast interpreted it into Hebrew. The tension eased as cakes and Palestinian muscatel were handed round, but increased again while Ma Prendergast declaimed a poem she herself had composed on the same theme as the Mayor's speech. More cakes and muscatel and then another poem. After that we danced to the gramophone. Everyone by now was slightly drunk and talking loudly. Music and drink overcame the barriers of language, but Victor Bone's voice saying "Bloody Jews" was audible above the general din.

Dramatic entertainment followed: a two-act play with songs, acted by Ma Prendergast, Ruth Draper fashion, alone. I remember nothing about it except a love scene between a Tommy leaving for the wars, and his wife, both of them more articulate than Lucinda and I had been. The scene was very emotional. Amos and I sat together in the darkest shadow, handkerchiefs pressed to our faces, trying desperately to hide our helpless laughter.

The play over, the Mayor and Ma Prendergast conferred. What next? we wondered. Ma Prendergast addressed the Colonel:

"The Mayor asks, will you British officers please some of your famous national songs sing?"

The civilians clapped expectantly. There was no escape. Victor Bone, by now aggressively drunk, rose to the occasion. Without accompaniment he began: "I touched her on the toe and said, What's that, my dear O," while the rest of us, a Barsetshire version of the Don Cossack choir, stood solemnly round him and joined in the chorus. Other famous national songs followed. The Jewish audience was deeply moved. Only Ma Prendergast looked puzzled. The Lady Mayoress begged me to translate the songs for her. As best I could, I paraphrased them into German. Victor Bone, enjoying himself, was set for the night.

He had started on "Hey ho, Gethusalum, the harlot of Jerusalem . . ." when the door opened suddenly and R.S.M. Burge came in. Inhibited by his presence, Victor Bone stopped singing at once. He had never got on well with the R.S.M. Now he glared at him. The latter had not been invited, but as a personal friend of the Mayor there was perhaps no reason why he should not have joined the party. Nor should it have mattered that he did. Certainly he had seen us all drunk and singing in the Sergeants' Mess often enough. Still, to have come uninvited to a party given for the officers was foolish of him. Discretion was not one of R.S.M. Burge's strong points. Perfectly aware that he was intruding, I suspect that he was unable to resist the temptation to show off to his Jewish friends, by putting himself on a footing with the officers of the Regiment. Like myself in front of Lucinda on the Piazza, he wanted to shine. To that extent he had himself to blame.

"Ah, good evening Mr. Burge, glad to see you," said the Colonel, not very cordially.

The Colonel handled the situation gracefully and contrived to leave soon afterwards without affronting either R.S.M. Burge or our hosts. Victor Bone showed less tact.

"Never knew you were an officer, Burge," he said pointedly as, bidding a gruff good night to the Mayor, he left the room. Two or three other officers, ignoring the R.S.M. completely, went with him. Victor Bone was drunk. Even so his remark was unforgivably boorish. The R.S.M. never forgave it.

A few of us stayed on to try, like Muggs, to clear up the shattered fragments of the evening. In vain. Amos and I talked to Mr. Burge for a while. He was sour and very sorry for himself. Indeed, we were very sorry for him. "For the first time in five years I am ashamed to be a member of the Barsetshire Yeomanry," he said. When we, too, said goodbye to the Mayor, Ma Prendergast handed each of us a printed pamphlet to take away. The pamphlet elaborated, in violent terms, the Mayor's speech.

The *entente cordiale* gained little on either side, I fear, by the Mayor's party.

CHAPTER FOUR

Araby

THE ANGELS, so the tale went, carried the supply of stones destined for the whole world in a sack. But while they flew over Palestine the sack burst . . . Unlike the nimble Arabs ridden by the police, our horses stumbled painfully—none more so than Caesar with feet the size of soup plates—when we rode forth daily on "schemes," equipped with sabres and Hotchkiss guns. For Northland once again pursued Southland, this time across the fields of Esdraelon. Or, for the sake of variety and by some wilder flight of fancy in the Orderly Room, R.S.M. Burge would be dressed up as an Arab bandit, Abdul el Fukr, to be chased at night into the wild hills behind Megiddo. Under whatever name the military hypothesis was disguised, the same familiar mock-battle followed. The tactics struck all of us as monotonous and archaic, though boredom was tempered by a vague uneasiness. Might there be a connection between Armageddon predicted in the Book of Revelation and our presence on its supposed site?

As Intelligence Officer Amos seldom rode if he could escape it, but his huge ungainly mare was kept in my Troop, and on the occasions he had to mount her she was like a mother to him. Our horses, before their hurried requisitioning by the Army, browsed peacefully in English pastures and many foaled after arrival in Palestine. Amos's mare, I suspected, was in the same state and everybody with experience of such cases was called to give an opinion. If the old mare had any modesty it must have been monstrously outraged but she appeared flattered by the attention. The experts agreed with me. The mare, they guessed, would foal at the beginning of July, when

Lucinda expected our own baby to arrive. The subject of maternity much occupied my thoughts at the time and I took a special interest in the mare's progress, keeping her beside Caesar who, if clumsy, was at least placid.

Our camp, lying under the hills on the edge of Esdraelon, was a heat trap. In the sun you seemed slowly to lose your identity and to be diminished until you were no more than another shadow in the white dust. To step back into shade was to step back into yourself again. But for the horses there was no release. They stood in the sun on flinty terraces cut out of the rock, ceaselessly tossing their heads and stamping against the flies. They were shackled to prevent kicks, but accidents happened. One day I heard a sharp "crack" and, turning, saw Amos's mare standing on three legs, the fourth dangling. Caear, aiming at a fly with one of his soup plates, must have caught her hind leg. The bone below the hock stuck out, broken. She made no sound and was not apparently in pain, but waited quietly for what she perhaps knew was the only end. We half-dragged, half-carried her away from the lines. I shot her with my revolver. What had been a precious living creature, in fact two living creatures, became instantly a carcass, loaded on a lorry and deposited in some dry wadi to be devoured in a night by the jackals.

Victor Bone was furious with me. Accidents gave the Squadron a bad name, he said. What was Amos's mare, which belonged to R.H.Q., doing on my lines, anyway? In my overwrought state, I wished I could have substituted Victor Bone for the mare.

Amos bore his loss philosophically. "Now I shall have to ride in a truck," was all he said.

In the welcome cool of evening, you could look from the Mess across the green Plain of Esdraelon towards Gilboa and Tabor; towards Nazareth, a faint whitish cluster cupped high in the hills of Galilee. Beyond Nazareth you could just see the snows on Mount Hermon, pink-flushed in the evening light, a hundred miles away in Lebanon. Beside Hermon, somewhere to the East, lay Damascus which I might at that time have visited, for the French were still allies and Vichy had not yet closed the frontier.

At dinner, when I could, I sat next to the Colonel, drawing on myself a baleful glance from Victor Bone. To his hierarchic mind Lieutenants did not sit beside Lieutenant-Colonels. I was starved of good company and the Colonel was a delightful companion who gave a humorous twist to each turn of the talk. More than any of us, not excepting Hilary, he found Palestine a gold mine of exciting new knowledge and experience.

Now, in a mischievous mood, he was telling Alan and me beside him of a Biblical tour, arranged by Divisional H.Q., he had just returned from. Possibly the details of the Bible story really were confused in his mind or possibly he was teasing Hilary, listening in further along the table. At any rate, he recalled his tour with witty irreverence, pretending to have forgotten, for instance, whether Jesus had changed the water into wine or the other way about.

"Which *actually* was it the fellow did? I can never remember," asked the Colonel, with an expression of perplexed innocence.

The talk, as always with the Colonel, switched suddenly. From Biblical topics we discussed more mundane matters concerning the morale of our own soldiers. Most of the officers owned or jointly-owned private cars. They had ample opportunities to visit, if they wished, the Jewish fleshpots on the coast. At week-ends an Orderly Officer from each Squadron remained and the rest could slip away to Haifa or Tel-Aviv. But for the men, sweating in barrack huts and with no diversions beyond darts or housey-housey in the canteen, life was less pleasant. Was there anything more we could devise to amuse them? The French Army, one had always understood, arranged these things better.

The Colonel invited Tom into the conversation for the benefit of his long experience. Hilary, uninvited, offered the opinion that more games like football should be organized to fill the men's leisure. Idleness bred the unhealthy broodings and desires from which they were said to be suffering.

"Satan finds some mischief still for idle hands to do," he added sententiously.

This from Hilary, who did no work at all, apart from Church Parades, and who spent half his time in Jerusalem! But before I could say so, the deep-voiced deep-chested Quartermaster, second only to myself as a Hilary-baiter, had sailed in to the attack.

"Nonsense!" he bellowed. "A man's a man, dammit, and you can't tomfoodle him with a football!"

After this Hilary slipped away obtrusively to bed and for the next hour we debated the feasibility of a Regimental brothel, quarreling hilariously about the most suitable officer to command it. Victor Bone, doubtless brooding unhealthily on the Squadron's good name while he drank glass after glass of port, had taken no part in the debate. He emerged at last from an alcoholic haze.

"Don't you feel perhaps we should do something of the same sort for the men too?"

I hastened back alone through the dark camp to relate this new "Victor Bone story" to Amos. For dinner in the Mess bored Amos and he seldom appeared there, arranging with the Mess-Sergeant to send food to the room we shared together, behaviour that in any other subaltern would have been firmly disallowed, but which Amos typically got away with. Nearby in an officer's hut the racing fraternity celebrated one of their religious festivals—might it have been the Grand National in which most of them had sometime ridden? The silence of the camp was shattered by their singing. I stood and listened. The song was a simple one, consisting of two lines capable of seemingly infinite repetition.

Ooo . . . ooo . . . oooo . . . what a bloody song . . .
And what a bloody singer too . . .

After ten minutes they switched to a different song, also of two lines.

Why was he born so beautiful?
Why was he born at all?

The tune in both cases was the same.

I liked the racing fraternity. They were a gay self-contained band known as "The Spivs" with colleagues in all the regiments of the Division, who kept their own pre-war English world alive in Palestine. In the mess they formed the hard core of orange-throwers. More unfitted for Army life even than I was, they made less effort to become assimilated, for which I respected them. I wished that I, too, was now living like them among peacetime friends, with film technicians or with Chelsea artists. As I passed the hut Fergie popped his head out of the window.

"Come on in, Johnny boy, and join us. Having a party . . ."

But I waved and walked on. "Poor old Johnny boy . . . stand-offish sod . . ." Fergie's voice echoed after me in the night. The "Spivs" had no inhibitions about disturbing with their revelry the fitful sleep of six hundred soldiers in the surrounding huts!

"Just their bad luck, cock," Fergie would have said if you had tackled him on this ethical point.

". . . why was he born at all . . ." The yells of laughter rent the night and were taken up by a jackal. Then another jackal. A jackal chorus. "Come and get it," they cried, like the cooks shouting from the men's mess hut. Only by "it" the jackals meant Amos's mare. And the foal inside her.

In our room the light was on, the fan whirred, and Amos, misty behind the mosquito net, was asleep and snoring, his long, thin, white legs curled up under his belly. There was a faint lecherous smile on his lips. I wondered why. The Victor Bone story would have to wait till morning. The fan was our greatest pride and bent up and down as it whirred like a preacher. We called it Hilary. Now it stirred a pile of my Troop's letters awaiting censorship.

Before creeping under my net, I finished my own letter to Lucinda. "Everything is hopeless nowadays and I feel like a sun-dried camel pat inside." I examined the sheets and my own naked body for bed-bugs. Then I lay awake considering the list of girls' and boys' names that Lucinda and I exchanged. There were two and a half months still to go.

Sabrina . . . or Comus . . . Which would it be?

At our distance the Norwegian campaign sounded unreal. In these hot listless days we donned absurd sun-helmets and settled down, with Indian contractors to manage our laundry and messing, to the peace-time routine of cavalry Regiments in the East and Near-East for the past hundred years. Though I passed for an efficient Troop Leader, my mind had not enough to bite on. I was becoming bored and what Victor Bone called "bolshie." "Bolshi-ness" was one of his bogies. He regarded it as an infectious disease of which any symptom in his Squadron must be stamped out at once. A message being handed to him at dinner one evening he rose hastily and left the Mess, his lips quivering with anger. Asked what the trouble was, he muttered, "There's a case of bolshiness in the Squadron lines." Later I found he had sentenced my groom Baldwin to seven days C.B., for cheeking the Corporal of the Guard. There was nothing I could do except fume helplessly.

To escape from Victor Bone I thought of trying to join the Trans-Jordan Frontier Force; "that wog police force," as he called it. I loved the Arabs. Patrols with my troop to outlying Arab villages had provided the happiest moments in Palestine so far. Amos, in his capacity of Intelligence Officer, had taken me to several of their lunches, epic meals that lasted from midday till evening. I enjoyed the formalities and courtesies hardly less than the food itself. Why not join the T.J.F.F.? It would perhaps be more useful, certainly more amusing than life at present.

Amos was critical. "Don't be so bloody keen. You're deteriorating rapidly and I'm thankful Lucinda isn't here to see it. Try and do some painting." Compared to my own, Amos's life was a whirl of interest and excitement. Now he was leaving for Cairo on an Intelligence course. All very well for him to lecture me . . . As for painting, that was a distant dream and belonged to a part of me resolutely put aside in my war with the Army. The urge, never quiescent, expressed itself in embellishments to the text of my letters to Lucinda. Still, I knew there was justice in Amos's comments and I decided to wait a little longer.

Fergie and the other exuberant "Spivs" had a new song.

The First of May the First of May
Hedgerow loving begins to-day.

The First of May . . . A year ago exactly Lucinda and I had climbed high on to the ruins of Les Baux, capital of the old Courts of Love in Provence. Holding each other in the wind that threatened to hurl us off we had surveyed the hills below, the red earth patterned with vine and olive, the plain beyond stretching towards Aix and Cézanne's Mont-Saint-Victoire. "It will be like this always for us," we had said.

"The First of May the First of May . . ." chanted the "Spivs." But on the Tenth of May Hitler invaded the Netherlands and the "spivs" sang no more. Like all of us, they huddled round the wireless, constricted in the throat and sick at heart. As the German Armies rolled on, place names familiar from the First World War came to us over the air. Louvain, Charleroi, Mons, Lille, Dunkirk . . . News of friends killed in the fighting flashed round the Division, among them that of the Adjutant who had commented on my untidy neck-wear in camp three years before.

Lucinda had left Chelsea and waited now for our baby on the South Coast. I wrote and wired imploring her to move inland. It was her duty, I urged, to do so; even to sail to America where she had cousins. Of what use was an expectant mother to the country at such a time? But she had booked a bed in a Brighton nursing home. By telegrams and letters, in reply to mine, she declared her intention of using the bed, happen what might.

From worry or perhaps from Amos's Arab feasts, I started stom-ach trouble. A duodenal ulcer was suspected and the M.O. sent me, protesting, to hospital in Haifa. For fear of bombing if Italy joined the war, the hospital moved hastily and chaotically into a convent in Nazareth. There I drank Barium meals and listened, among the crowd, to the Dunkirk news on the only wireless. The chimes of the hundred Nazarene belfries tolling matins and vespers inflamed my ulcer, if it was an ulcer, with their mockery. Amos brought letters from Lucinda. She still had a month to go. What might not happen to Brighton and to her within that month? I complained of my dis-tended stomach.

"You're suffering from sympathetic pregnancy," said Amos. "I got it myself when my first wife had a child."

Then Alan arrived unexpectedly in the ward. He was paying me, I could tell, more than just a friendly visit. The expression on his kind and humorous face seemed fixed by some rigid purpose behind it. A formal, military, no-nonsense expression that I knew on Alan's face when he was determined to have his way about something.

"How's the tummy?" he asked briskly, tapping the approximate position of my ulcer, if it was an ulcer, with his little stick. My stom-ach felt as if it was being blown up by a bicycle pump attached to my navel, but I knew Alan was not really interested in my symptoms.

"It's getting on fine," I said.

"Good," said Alan. "Now, listen. One of the Squadron Leaders, not Victor Bone, has been 'promoted,' if you know what I mean, to command a transit camp in Gaza. The Colonel is giving the Squad-ron to me if I can find an Adjutant. I'm not strictly next in senior-ity, but never mind about that. The problem is to find an Adjutant. Whom do you think the Colonel wants?"

"No idea. Amos perhaps?"

Alan frowned. He did not share my admiration for Amos. Perhaps the latter's remark about the best type of Public Schoolboy had found its way round to him. If so, Alan was too sensitive not to resent the underlying malice in it.

"No, not Amos. You."

This was a complete surprise. I protested, sincerely, my unfitness for so much honor. I knew nothing of Army matters above the level of a Troop. Besides, I looked so unmilitary. An Adjutant had to be a paragon of correctness in all things, like Alan himself.

"You are a bit scruffy, but I expect you could smarten yourself up. Now be sensible about this. For a lot of reasons I can't go into, the decision has to be made today. It's a fascinating job with the nicest Colonel in the world. You'll pick it up in no time."

Alan had great charm. He was also openly and ruthlessly ambitious for his own Army career. I have never known anyone in whom the two things were so mutually compatible.

"Agree to come at once like a good chap, and I'll go and see the Commandant about getting you out of here."

There are people, I dare say, in everyone's life who seem destined to appear and reappear in it as agents of fate. Such a one was Alan in mine. We met in strangely similar circumstances two or three times again during the war and each time my life, if not radically altered—for I do not wish to exaggerate—was nevertheless deflected by the meeting into a new channel. So that when, too rarely, I meet Alan nowadays I experience always still a slight quickening of the nerves, a slight expectancy. But nowadays nothing happens.

I dressed, and drove away with him in his truck. Back at camp I had a short amusing interview with the Colonel. I apologized in advance for my inexperience.

"I expect we'll manage somehow," he smiled.

By that evening Alan was a Major and a Squadron Leader; I was a Captain and an Adjutant. I had won a victory in my war against the Army. But Amos shook his head sadly at me when he heard. To him the step-up in rank represented a further stage in my self-betrayal.

"I'm afraid that's the end of you," he said. "You'll get bloody now, like Alan. Poor Lucinda."

A price had to be paid for the victory. I worked hard, sitting at my desk late into every night. A Troop Leader, watching his men groom their horses by the hour, could afford to turn over in his mind what he would say to his wife that evening; indeed, was almost forced to do so by sheer boredom. But I do not think there was ever an Adjutant who daydreamed or who, if he did, remained an Adjutant for long. The letters in the next year make dull reading.

Paradoxically the Orderly Room sheltered me from the Army itself, at least from the Army relationship between officers and men. I was no longer directly responsible for seeing that orders I disagreed with were carried out. Mine was often the more congenial role of originating the orders. Although as an Adjutant, playing a part I could not believe in, I was a fake, the actor, perhaps the charlatan, in me much enjoyed giving the performance. Only Amos knew me well enough to be aware that it was a performance. To my annoyance, he clapped sarcastically from the wings.

Among the papers handed over by Alan for me to deal with, I discovered a note to the Colonel from Victor Bone. The note concerned myself, as a Troop Leader. He wrote that he was finding my attitude generally uncooperative and he suggested I should be transferred outside the Regiment. The newly-formed Jewish Pioneer Corps, he understood, was in need of British officers . . .

With the R.S.M. already against him, and now the Adjutant, Victor Bone had a poor time coming to him. His Sergeant Major, an experienced old soldier who really ran the Squadron, developed T.B. and had to leave us. There were several good sergeants worthy of promotion.

"If you are good enough to be a sergeant in the Barsetshire Yeomanry you are good enough to be an officer in any other unit in the Division—not excluding the 'Lumpers,'" R.S.M. Burge was fond of saying.

But, as it happened, the Regiment already possessed a spare Sergeant Major, a massive Yeoman farmer called Voles. He was a delightful man, quite hopeless as a soldier and bone-headed past belief. Created a Sergeant Major in peace time, since the war he had been carried around extra to Establishment, odd jobs being found for him in the Q.M. stores or with the transport. Partly because we were fond of Voles, partly for less worthy motives, R.S.M. Burge and I now worked on the Colonel to post him to Victor Bone's Squadron, instead of promoting the sergeant whom Victor Bone himself had nominated. It was only fair, we argued, to give Voles at least a chance of filling the job. In any case, 2nd Echelon, who supervised such matters from Cairo, would never allow the creation of a new Sergeant Major while a spare one existed on our strength.

"Won't it be rather a case of yoking the ox to the ass?" the Colonel said to me privately. He always hated what he called "these awful decisions."

In the end Victor Bone, despite frantic protests, had to accept Voles. The ox was yoked to the ass, but the ass knew whom he had to blame for the transaction.

"I'm not sure it really was the right decision," the Colonel sighed afterwards.

On the afternoon of 4th July I sat in the Orderly Room happily signing a rocket. I enjoyed any form of literary composition and Army jargon, I am ashamed to say, came naturally to me. "The Colonel directs O.C. B Squadron's attention to be drawn to the fact that . . ." etc. You could use the third person singular formula with devastating rudeness while remaining entrenched behind the frontiers of strict military propriety. Amos had been right. It didn't take long for me to get bloody.

"Just check that Major Bone acknowledges receipt of this, will you, please?" I said to the Orderly Room Sergeant who came in. The sergeant smiled and handed me a telegram. Instantly I forgot all thoughts of Victor Bone and everything else to do with the Army. The telegram was from my oldest friend. It read: "Bacchus rejoice Comus was born today Lucinda and child very well."

"Good news, sir, I hope?" said the Orderly Room Sergeant. Wonderful, wonderful news . . . I crumpled the "rocket" and threw it out of the window. Let it blow whither it might. Peace to Victor Bone and his horses. Peace to Hilary and his Church Parades. With less dignity than became an Adjutant, I ran from the Orderly Room and out of the camp to walk by myself for a while on Esdraelon.

Amos was right, too, about the sympathetic pregnancy. The ulcer, if it was an ulcer, vanished away and my distended stomach returned to normal.

CHAPTER FIVE

"Our Own Choice Yeomanry Division"

IT WAS OLIVER BOMFREY, I believe, who after watching our Divisional maneuvers, nicknamed us "Hitler's secret weapon." The ironic soubriquet neatly expressed our own feelings of being not merely useless, but faintly absurd. Though, as Yeomen, we threw ourselves into everything we did with enthusiasm, the anachronism of our equipment in a war of tanks and aeroplanes was disheartening. Our sabres belonged to the same era as the old gentleman who advocated the use of pikes by the Home Guard. While armored cavalry units in Egypt skirmished with the Italian enemy on the Cyrenaican frontier we forced unwanted help on the already adequate Palestine Police. We were aware, to the point of conceit, of being potentially a very fine Division. The long period of frustration marked every man among us with a sense of guilt which, in the course of the war, he expiated by whatever means lay open to him. When, in the late summer of 1941, the division was at last mechanized, the speed and efficiency with which it retrained could hardly be accounted for by mere "keenness." By that time, in any case, sun, flies, a sense of exile, the Army itself, had worn the edge off our "keenness." We were fighting by then to preserve our self-respect.

For the fortnight preceding the maneuvers I lived in a paper storm of unfamiliar Movement and Operation orders. The General, a victim himself of frustration, had let his imagination run riot and my mind, attuned to the Northland-Southland formula, had to grapple now with an initial hypothesis of cataclysmic dimensions, involving whole Armies and Air Forces; even Navies. After lunch on the afternoon before the maneuvers started, most of the officers having retired to sleep, I sat in the Mess browsing in a week-old copy of the scurrilously anti-British *Palestine News*. Amos snored on the Mess sofa. Noticing Oliver Bomfrey's name mentioned, I read the paragraph.

> Our correspondent reports that Captain Oliver Bomfrey, M.P., famous son of the more famous Cabinet Minister, arrived in Cairo last week. After a brief but tiring visit to Armoured units patrolling the Italo-Egyptian frontier, he is resting for a few days at the British Embassy, before visiting Palestine. It will be his second visit to our country. For Oliver Bomfrey, M.P., as he then was, flew out here in 1938 during the "troubles." Afterwards he expressed the opinion in the House of Commons that "the Palestine problem would be solved if all Jews were made to wear Arab headdress and all Arabs were made to wear blue bloomers." That, we suspect, is still about the extent of the gallant Captain's political wisdom. His presence now in the Middle East may have more military than political significance, if it has any at all. "In war even a Conservative M.P. must go where he is sent," Captain Bomfrey told us modestly. "I am a serving officer on my way to join my Regiment, the Blues."

I chuckled aloud at the malice and the chuckle woke up Amos. I showed him the paper. Hardly knowing Oliver Bomfrey, I was inclined to dismiss him as a bogus adventurer, but Amos, who knew him better, defended him crossly.

"You're too damned critical. Oh, I know he's rich and successful and a self-advertiser and much else that you resent. But the fact remains that Oliver is a clever amusing man who's done some remarkable things already in his life, and who will probably do many others before this war is over. He's got guts."

Back in the cool sanctuary of the Orderly Room the telephone rang. The Brigade Major was on the line.

"Everything under control for tonight? No worries?"

"None," I lied calmly.

"Good. Well, here is one. The General and that bastard Oliver Bomfrey have been lunching here. They'll be with you in about twenty minutes. Bomfrey bet the General a fiver you'd all be asleep, so I promised not to warn you."

"Thanks. What's Bomfrey doing? I've just been reading about him."

"That's another worry for you. He's on some sort of private mission and is going to watch the maneuvers. The General wants you to fix him up with a horse and look after him."

"But he's in the Lumpers," I protested. "Why can't he go to them?"

"Frankly, they won't have him. Anyway, he likes you better. It's your own fault. You have a reputation for obliging. O.K.?"

"Oh, O.K.," I said wearily.

There are only two sorts of General, the rugged and the smooth. Of the two the smooth is the more to be feared. Our own General was very smooth indeed. It was considerate of the Brigade Major to have rung. The Orderly Room Sergeant ran to warn the guard commander and to wake up R.S.M. Burge, while I ran to wake the Colonel, calling on the way at the Officers' Mess to see that tea was prepared.

"Hell's dust!" the Colonel muttered drowsily, jumping out of bed. "Still, it will be fun to see Oliver again."

Twenty-one minutes after the Brigade Major had telephoned, the Colonel and I sat at our desks in the Orderly Room looking busy. Through the window we watched the dun-colored staff car flying a red flag drive up to the gates. As the General and Bomfrey strolled towards the Orderly Room, R.S.M. Burge, with brilliant timing, happened to walk past. His hand, his arm, his whole body vibrated like a steel spring with the sheer dynamism of his salute. The Colonel and I giggled. The General walked into the Orderly Room unannounced. We leapt to our feet.

"Oh, hallo, sir," said the Colonel. "This is a surprise. No one warned us you were coming."

"Excellent, you're awake!" laughed the General. "Now Oliver owes me a fiver. Where's the fellow got to?"

I was sent to find him. He was standing joking with the R.S.M. outside the Orderly Room. In appearance they were curiously alike. The same powerful forehead and nose, the same jutting jaw, the same debauched pasty complexion. It was typical of Bomfrey to know R.S.M. Burge's name and to talk to him now as if he was the one person in the whole Middle East he had wanted to meet.

"There's a man for you," R.S.M. Burge said later. "I'd do anything for a man like that. He can talk with kings nor lose the common touch . . ." The R.S.M. had a passion for Kipling.

When the General had left, the Colonel went back to sleep and I entertained our distinguished visitor; or, rather, he entertained both of us. His ideas and opinions about the conduct of the war, global in their scope, bubbled out unceasingly in a stream of beautifully formulated English prose. Like the R.S.M., I succumbed immediately to the force of his personality and quickly forgot, both my former prejudices and the pile of correspondence awaiting attention in the Orderly Room, though I began to understand why the Lumpers had refused to have him for the maneuvers. Sublimely egotistical, he took it for granted that the pleasure of his company more than outweighed any inconvenience it might cause. The disarming frankness of his remarks did not always please. As we stood looking out of the Mess windows, he waved towards the splendid view across Esdraelon.

"How pleasant, how restful, to be up here—so far from anywhere that really matters!"

Conscious, perhaps, that he had not been altogether tactful, Bomfrey descended suddenly to my level and showed a flattering sympathy for my problems. He questioned me about Lucinda and I told him I was trying to persuade her to take the baby to America.

"Far the best thing she could do. I'm flying back to England as soon as the maneuvers are over. I'll take a letter and, if you like, I'll add my persuasion to yours."

It was a generous offer, more generous than the spirit of the letter I quickly wrote for him to take.

"If this ever reaches you, which I doubt, it will be by the hand of your old boy-friend. He has been amazing us yokels with stories of the great big world. By his account, he was the first man to step ashore at Narvik, the last to step into the sea at Dunkirk. For your sake, I have lent him Caesar to ride. Did ever husband do more?"

As a result of the last magnanimous gesture I had to approach Victor Bone at dinner for the loan of a horse. I explained the circumstances. "Bloody politician," he growled within Bomfrey's hearing. "Let him walk." However, he consented finally to lend me a mare from his squadron.

"I think she'll do for you nicely," he added dourly. The equivocal meaning of this remark became apparent later.

After dinner, aware of a plot by the "Spivs" to dump "the bloody politician" in a horse trough, Amos and I hastened him away from the Mess. In our room he continued to enthrall us with further accounts of the war, in which, so far, he had roamed about at will.

Bomfrey threw himself into everything he undertook with an infectious zeal. "What fun this will be!" he cried, mounting Caesar as the Divisional maneuvers began. "It is years since I rode on a gee-gee."

In the next days the columns of cavalry moving over the parched hills of northern Palestine, each column a black snake throwing off a white plume of dust, were a lovely sight to watch, but I had little time to enjoy it. Prompted gently by my patient Colonel and fearful of letting him down, I picked up the duties of an Adjutant in the field as I went. The maneuvers, among other things, were an exercise in Staff communications and an Adjutant is the ultimate and bottom link in the chain; a flustered and incompetent link in my case. Amos who followed in a map-filled truck smiled maliciously at me each time we set up our R.H.Q.

"Serve you right," his attitude implied. "Be a keen soldier if you must but don't expect sympathy from me."

I was harassed in other ways too. The horse Victor Bone had lent me was a vicious little creature and wouldn't walk. She jog-trotted, letting out an occasional kick and had to be "ridden" the whole time. And I was in no mood for equestrianism. I was in agony from the piles. Red-hot throbbing pains shot up my back and I finished each march of twenty or thirty miles standing in the stirrups and holding the front-arch of the saddle, my teeth clenched and the sweat pouring off me. Every step my horse took was a torment and I cursed every stumble. I longed for Caesar's comfortable gait. Passing Victor Bone, my horse in a lather, he shouted at me for the world to hear: "What's the matter? That little mare is as quiet as a lamb usually. You must be one of those chaps with an electric arse!"

I welcomed, therefore, the opportunities to dismount and, in the shade of a prickly pear, to decode the latest message from Brigade or to write out our own Operation Orders.

"For Christ sake get a move on with that map," I snapped at Amos, who was marking one for me to show the Colonel. It was unwise to try and bully Amos. He put the map down deliberately and lit a cigarette.

"You may like to think of yourself as Napoleon," he said slowly; "but your performance as Adjutant reminds me more of the Marx Brothers."

Oliver Bomfrey, on the other hand, enjoyed the maneuvers. Uninhibited by the usual military conventions and protected by his friendship with the General, he "swanned" about on Caesar, offering advice to commanders, sometimes with disruptive effects. He had attached himself at one point to Victor Bone. The latter's Squadron, riding into a defile, was confronted unexpectedly by a Troop of the enemy. Victor Bone wavered.

"Charge! Bone, charge!" yelled Oliver Bomfrey.

Drawing the sword I had lent him and flourishing it romantically, Bomfrey put his own advice into execution. Not unwillingly, half Victor Bone's Squadron followed his lead. In the subsequent confusion a trooper was spiked in the arm and a horse, breaking a leg, had to be destroyed.

That evening the Colonel, with his usual tact, suggested to Bomfrey that he might obtain a wider picture of the maneuvers from the General's car. Bomfrey saw the point. But he was quite unrepentant about the charge.

"You can't train troops for war without spilling a little blood," he maintained.

Amos drove him over to Divisional H.Q. after dinner. And I welcomed the prospect of riding Caesar again.

The maneuvers drew to their end. On the last day our own column, kicking up its cloud of dust, wound through the Musmus Pass. The Regiment was preceded as always by two troopers, known tactically as "points." They carried drawn swords with which presumably to prod lurking enemy tanks. You can see the same cavalry formation any day of the week when the Life Guards ride down The Mall. The Arab fellaheen, cultivating their little terraces of earth among the rocks, were impressed by our panache, but a more sophisticated Jewish onlooker gave us a skeptical glance. As we debouched, to use the Army word, out of the pass on to the plain by Megiddo we met the General sitting by his car. Oliver Bomfrey sat with him. The General beckoned us over. Bomfrey was refilling the General's glass with iced coffee. He winked at us from behind the General's camp-chair and made a rude sign. My eye, ever observant of such matters, noticed a cold chicken salad and other delicacies on the white tablecloth spread on the ground. The General swallowed a mouthful of smoked salmon before speaking.

"The maneuvers are over," he said genially. "There's a signal on its way to you somewhere, but don't bother to wait for it. Collect your Regiment up and march for home. I feel we have mortified the flesh long enough."

As we rode away I overheard a fascinating scrap of conversation.

"Yes, I realize that," Bomfrey said in reply to some inaudible remark the General made. "I'll send a wire to Winston as soon as I get back to Cairo tomorrow."

As I have said already, everything begins to complete a pattern if seen from a sufficient distance. I have wondered for fourteen years what Bomfrey's wire to Winston could have been about. Now, at least, I can guess. Glancing casually through *The Second World War*, I came upon a minute addressed by the Prime Minister to the C.I.G.S. The minute is dated 8-9-40, a day or two after Bomfrey would have reached Cairo.

> It has been heart-breaking to me to watch these splendid Units fooled away for a whole year. It is an insult to the Scots Greys and Household Cavalry to tether them to horses at the present time. There might be something to be said for a few battalions of infantry or cavalrymen mounted on ponies for the rocky hills of Palestine, but these historic Regular Regiments have a right to play a man's part in the war.

Youthful loyalties die hard. It amused me to notice a trace of resentment in myself, reading the minute, that our own historic but not regular Regiment was not referred to. In those days we prided ourselves that what the "Lumpers," as we called the Household Cavalry, could do, we could do as well—probably better. However, Sir Winston Churchill does elsewhere refer to "our own choice Yeomanry Division."

CHAPTER SIX

"Thumbs Up! Tiggerty-Boo!
Up the Bible Class!"

FAR FROM LEAVE-CENTERS, farther still from war, we wintered on the Lebanese frontier among wild hills shaped like elephants' feet. Forty miles away Mt. Hermon, fast gathering new snow, loomed above the Huleh marshes.

"At least," the Colonel consoled us, "we are on a frontier."

For Victor Bone, with some of the best duck shooting in the world at his front door, the winter passed pleasantly. Or, welcoming sport of any nature, he could ride after Arabs smuggling tins of kerosene into Lebanon.

"Amazing how fast the chaps can run," he said appreciatively. "One of them gave me a two-mile point."

He carried a shotgun in a rifle bucket attached to the saddle, so the Arabs' speed was perhaps understandable. One day, blazing with the same gun across the frontier wire at a covey of *chicor*, he browned an unseen French outpost. They returned his fire promptly and at close range. He rode back into camp unscathed, but with a bullet hole in his cap. "I gave them both barrels before retreating," he said. As, since Oran, political relations with the French in Syria and Lebanon had been precarious, the telephone wires between Jerusalem and Beirut fairly buzzed. Victor Bone, the stuff of which all "frontier incidents" are made, got a rocket from the General, but he was considered by the Division as a whole to have put up a good show. An instinctive Xenophobe, he mentally added "Frogs" to the list of those, like Jews, Wogs, Huns, and Wops, to be classified simply as "bloody." The Adjutant, of course, was also on the list.

Questionable though my advocacy of Voles had been, his appointment as Squadron Sergeant Major had proved a remarkable success. As so often in the Army, the local idiot, given the chance of responsibility, made good. Ox and ass ploughed together in happy unison. Even Victor Bone allowed me some grudging, if unmerited, praise for my part in the transaction.

"The bloody Adjutant seems to know more about people than he does about horses," he said to Amos, who gleefully repeated the remark to me. But, as Amos pointed out, perhaps Victor Bone did not mean it for praise.

For me, too, the winter passed pleasantly. After many adventures Lucinda and Comus had arrived safely in America at the end of October. So I was free from that worry. If I had wanted, once, to play more than a passive part in the war Providence seemed to have willed otherwise and I reconciled myself, without difficulty, to remaining uncut-off in my prime.

I slept and did most of my work in a tiny hut, a survival of some earlier, perhaps Turkish, garrison in Allenby's day. There, Muggs brought me tea in the early morning and hot rum at night, when I settled down to polish my Army prose style. The hut had been "condemned" by the Garrison Engineer and the flat roof was badly cracked, but I had seized it for myself when we arrived in the camp for the sake of privacy and quiet. Amos called it a womb of my own. I enjoyed, as Adjutant, my small share of power. "We seem to be a little untidy about the neck this morning, Catchpole," I said severely to the young officer sent to us from England. I had concerts in Haifa once a month; I had eight volumes of Proust still to read; I had two or three good friends and, hardly less important to a balanced diet, two or three good enemies.

If, as I suspect, all books are written in some degree to purge the writer of guilt, this might be a good moment to work Hilary out of my system for ever. Our many wrangles may have satisfied the combative impulse in him too. Indeed, I do hope so. He was a man who invited martyrdom and I did much, in a modest way, to furnish his crown of thorns. It is some consolation to me now that at least I seem to have been aware at the time of the Army's vitiating influence.

"I am frightfully rude, in a fairly polite way, to everybody. Otherwise, I find nothing gets done," I wrote. "And I regret that I am at my rudest with the two bodily representatives of the Church, Hilary and his R.C. counterpart Moody, when they badger me for privileges for their respective flocks.

SAYS MOODY: Of course I have nothing against Hilary himself. A well-meaning fellow and all that. But I don't see why he should have his own tent for Communion, when I have to use the N.A.A.F.I. pantry for Mass. I believe there's a hut being used to store saddlery. Do be a good chap and have it cleared out. Mass is hopeless in a noisy draughty hole.

SAYS HILARY: I hear Moody is after the saddlery store. When I asked for it last month you said saddlery came before Godliness. Of course Moody means well, but I must say it is typical of a Roman to come creeping to you behind my back.

"To both I am a Godless monster of obstruction. And you can guess that the role is not altogether uncongenial . . ."

On the last day of November an urgent signal ordered Amos to report immediately to G.H.Q. Middle East. Evidently he had made an impression on his Intelligence Course earlier in the summer. "A temporary attachment," the signal said. But the Colonel and I sensed, rightly, that we had seen the last of Amos as a Regimental Officer.

"Christmas in Cairo will suit me nicely," Amos chuckled. "I'll come back to you in Palestine in the spring."

A week later, with the news of Wavell's sensational advance in the desert, we knew where Amos was more likely to spend Christmas.

The horses, no longer on rock, stood often hock-deep in mud. The line guards, protected against the driving rain by that futile triangle of mackintosh called a groundsheet, floundered about adjusting rugs or tying up haynets. More adequately dressed, I strolled out from the warmth of my hut one stormy night to ease my conscience by visiting them. There I found Voles helping a line guard to pull a horse's rug forward. I held the lantern for them. Soaked to the skin and his huge frame shivering with cold, Voles tugged with all his might on the front strap. The strap broke, and Voles, falling over backwards, was submerged. By lantern light the trooper and I stared aghast at his shape wallowing, like a hippopotamus, in the slime.

He struggled back on to his feet. What had been a Squadron Sergeant Major was now a monster, murky as the night and glistening all over with black mud. The lantern light caught the gleam of teeth as the monster grinned at us.

"Roll on f—— death!" he said.

Mails were bad—most corruptive of all influences on morale. Letters from home when they came were full of the bombing and of understandable envy for soldiers idling safely in Palestine. The good-tempered resilience of Voles and his sort held us together at the time we most needed holding together. A greathearted man, without a trace either of vanity or of spite in his nature, he makes a brief and, alas, tragic appearance in these pages; the sort of man to whom absurd things always happen and about whom ill-natured people like me collect anecdotes. Voles, it was well known in the Regiment, had "trouble at home." The old, old trouble . . . When the Christmas mail at length arrived there was only one envelope for Voles. The envelope did not contain the sort of news we feared it might. Not at all. The letter—but I may as well quote again.

"To his disgust it was a printed circular, sent by the local Curate to the sons of the parish serving overseas. You know the sort of thing. Lots of hearty Christian ha-ha about cheer up, fight the good fight, etc. This one was headed 'Patronal Festival Greetings.' Some of the platitudes were not very happily expressed. 'The curse is stagnation. A change of life is a new experience, a new opportunity.' The final sentence printed in capitals read thus, 'THUMBS UP! TIGGERTY-BOO! UP THE BIBLE CLASS!' "

When, in due course, a letter came from Voles's wife, she announced in the same sentence that she had had all her teeth out and that she was hoping to marry a Pole. Voles took the letter calmly.

"It will save me money in the long run," he said. I never discovered to which piece of news his remark referred.

Early in the New Year Oliver Bomfrey visited us again. Returned from the U.K. in time to take part in Wavell's advance, he had come up to Palestine at the General's request to help raise morale in the Division with a series of lectures on the desert fighting.

"Up here on the Lebanese frontier, so far from anywhere that really matters . . ." he began the lecture.

But I had much to thank Bomfrey for. He had played some part in getting Lucinda to the States. In gratitude, I circumvented once again a plot by the "Spivs" to throw him in a horse trough. He gave me messages from Amos whom he had seen a few days before in Sidi Barrani and who, as I.O. with an Armoured Division, had "done awfully well."

"While I think of it, another friend of yours is there too," said Oliver Bomfrey. "Matthew Prendergast."

"Matthew Prendergast! I thought he was a private in Aldershot."

"Oh, that was ages ago. Matthew's out here in the Rifle Brigade. He needed a war to escape from that old bitch of a mother. As a matter of fact, he got a jolly good M.C. at Buqbuq. We shall hear more of Matthew. He's a fire eater."

I listened to the account of my old enemy's gallantry with mixed feelings. Oliver Bomfrey left at least one member of the Division's morale lower than he found it.

In February, Alan was summoned to command a mixed Yeomanry force being sent to Greece. We contributed some N.C.O.s and men too. When we had seen the party off the Colonel and I returned despondently to our desks.

"I know how you feel," the Colonel said quietly. "But, you know, your job is with me here. The war won't end this year, or the next, I'm afraid."

So I prosecuted my feud with Hilary. My attitude to Church Parades seems, as Adjutant, to have become shamelessly reversed.

"Hilary rebels against Church Parades because, he says, they stress the Parade at the expense of the Church. I reply that the object of a Church Parade is to make the men turn out in their Sunday best, which, without the excuse of a service afterwards, there would be no good reason for doing. Also, it is excellent practice for the Regimental band. Also, it gives a tremendous kick to all the people who have been lucky enough not to go on Church Parade . . . However, as an experiment, the Colonel has allowed Hilary to hold Voluntary Services on Sunday mornings instead. But there is no satisfying the fellow. Now he complains that Sunday morning football, which I have organized to keep the men happy, distracts his congregation.

ME: But if the men would rather watch football than go to Church, surely that shows they can't want to go to Church very badly.

HILARY: That's not the point at all . . .

"Oh, dear, how childish of me even to repeat these squabbles. How *pénible* of me to enjoy them. Let me hastily draw the curtain on the scene and change to a pleasanter topic. Spring, I believe, is really in the air. The valleys are green with young corn, the hill-sides are carpeted with anemones—scarlet, white, pale mauve. The weather is warmer and the officers show a definite restlessness to be off on leave to the nearest cities. What they hope to find or do there I don't know. Nor do they. Nature is stirring up the instincts in her own fashion but offers, out here, no assistance for their outlet. In a cavity outside the window of my little hut two sparrows have built their nest. I have watched their idyll with interest and amusement. Delightfully unselfconscious, they make love all day on the window-sill. The female sparrow, satisfied and complacent, grows visibly fat-ter. Her husband, a paragon among sparrows in his attentiveness, has begun to look worn and his feathers have lost their sheen. R.S.M. Burge comes often to watch them, fascinated by and perhaps envious of their antics. His own feathers are not as bright as they used to be."

The crack in the ceiling of my hut, made worse by the alternate heavy rain and hot sunshine of the spring, symbolized in a trivial way the other more important cracks threatening the whole fabric of our secluded existence, with its parochial squabbles and gossip. A thunderstorm drove me out of my little home on the same date that the Germans, after bombing Belgrade, marched into Yugoslavia and Greece; on the same night, as I discovered later, that Amos, taking part in the Desert retreat before Rommel, was wounded out-side Tobruk. In the early hours of 6th April 1941, I was wakened by water pouring through the roof on to my bed. I finished the night huddled on a dry corner of the floor. Muggs found me there when he brought my morning cup of tea.

"Cor," he said, surveying the chaos.

In my damp pyjamas, I splashed across to the window to see how my sparrows had fared. Their nest had vanished. Outside, the two dead birds floated in a puddle.

"My hut being no longer habitable, I have joined Hilary in what he calls 'the Church Tent,' whether because he sleeps there or because he uses it for Holy Communion, I am not sure. The action has surprised my brother Yeokels and has given rise to some speculative comment. It has surprised Hilary too. He is rather pleased, scenting my conversion. But the move was prompted by self-interest, pure and simple. I hate a noisy companion and Hilary, half the time on his knees, is quiet as a mouse. Also, if I feel talkative and want an argument before going to sleep, I have my favorite victim at my mercy. Also, as you may have guessed long ago, I like Hilary; if for no other reason than that he has a wretched time and I am sorry for him. Designed by Nature for tea-table conversation in a cathedral close, he has to uphold his faith in a bear garden."

In April, as the German armies pushed across North Africa and through Greece, we thought much of Amos and Alan. And, as more and more German agents were reported to have arrived in Syria, we wondered about our own fate. It looked possible that Victor Bone might some day soon have other things to shoot at than Arab smugglers and *chicor*. The Barsetshire Yeomanry was ordered to prepare itself to defend thirty miles of winding mountainous frontier; to our west, another Yeomanry Regiment defended the other thirty miles of frontier between us and the Mediterranean. The Colonel and I spent many hours improvising schemes to man the concrete pillboxes which R.E.s hastily constructed round us. R.S.M. Burge was sent on a "course" to learn how to convert an empty beer bottle into a "Molotov cocktail," a sort of home-made bomb to be hurled at tanks from five yards' range. Using my old hut as a substitute for a tank, the R.S.M. trained the rest of us. My winter's refuge became a charred ruin littered with broken glass. Defaulters, instead of perfecting the football field, were now set to turning out Molotov cocktails by the dozen till Tom grumbled there was no room left for them in his store.

We planned that a forward screen of mounted outposts, each man carrying two Molotov cocktails tied to the saddle, would first engage the advancing German armor. These outposts would then fall back behind the line of pillboxes, from each of which a corporal and five men (the remaining two men of the section holding the horses in some sheltered wadi) would blast the Huns with Hotchkiss guns and rifles. In theory, against such stimulating odds, we felt wildly gallant, even optimistic.

"I should think we might be able to hold them for ten hours," I said to the Colonel.

"At any rate, for ten minutes," he muttered.

Amos and Alan put it at ten seconds. Weary and battle-stained, they arrived together in our camp in the first week of May. Alan, with the handful left of his original force, had been evacuated at the last minute from Greece. Amos, recovering from a wound in the arm, had met him by chance in Alexandria and so on some excuse or other had wangled a visit to Palestine. With their more realistic experience of the German Army, they scoffed at the task we had been set and at our defence plans.

"*C'est magnifique, mais . . . c'est* bloody silly," said Amos.

Alan gave us a more orthodox appreciation of the situation. He scanned the large map, sparsely dotted with flags representing the positions of the two Yeomanry Regiments.

"If they really come through Syria, two Infantry Divisions would hardly be enough for your job," he said authoritatively.

We were cheered to see them both safe and to hear of their respective adventures. We fêted them appropriately. But somehow, as in the case of "old boys" visiting their late comrades still at school, there was no contact with them. They belonged no more to our little world.

"A Regiment, like a family, is something you need to get away from to appreciate it." Amos laughed dryly when, after a night or two, he left again for Egypt.

Alan's military future was uncertain. He spent much time between Divisional and Brigade H.Q., and smiled mysteriously when I asked him what he was up to.

"Just winding things up," he said.

Isolated from the rest of the Division by a mountain range, we had seen little of them for many months. "Blue lights," as we called rumors, had reached us recently of Regiments "losing" their horses, to become—what? Motorized infantry, armored cars, tanks? No one was quite sure. Victor Bone, an ardent rumor-monger, came back from a short Squadron Leaders' course in Cairo. The Division, he said, was to be disbanded, and he had met several Yeomanry Commanding Officers pushing their Regiments' interests at G.H.Q. Perhaps, he suggested, the Colonel should follow their example. "Or we'll be turned into bloody signallers." But the Colonel hated string-pulling and intrigue of any kind.

"Let's get on with the job we've been given," he said curtly.

Victor Bone proved to have been partly right. One day, about 10th May I think, the rest of the Division simply vanished. The Brigade Major rang me the evening before.

"As from tomorrow you'll come under O.C. Troops, Haifa, for administration. Otherwise, keep on doing what you're doing. We're off, can't tell you where. Alan is here beside me and wants a word."

"Hallo, you old bastard." As always, when he was pleased about something, Alan was inclined to be facetious. "Look after my kit, will you, for the next month or two?"

"Of course."

"One other thing."

"Yes?"

"I should make those cocktails of yours nice and strong. Ha, ha." Then he rang off.

The rest of the Division, we learnt later, had driven across the desert, Lawrence's desert, to fight Rashid Ali in Iraq. They captured Baghdad at the end of May. Alan, of course, was there. It must be something to tell your grandchildren that you once captured Baghdad.

But our time, or so we believed, was coming too. On the first of June a signal from Jerusalem put us under command "for forthcoming operations" of an Australian Brigade expected to arrive shortly in our neighborhood.

"Roll up the map of Palestine," grinned the Colonel. "I really do believe we are going up in the world."

The next day we greeted our new Australian Brigadier in the Orderly Room. He was in a harassed, indeed a bewildered, frame of mind. Rushed up with his Brigade from the desert, he had hardly heard a week before of Syria which he was about to invade. Certainly he had never heard, we were all too conscious, of the Barsetshire Yeomanry. Diffidently, we told him our strength, our equipment.

Above all, we told him, we wanted to help. He was impressed by our keenness, more so by the gleaming state of our boots and spurs and saddlery. For the rest, he was skeptical.

"Horses, huh?" he said, gazing gloomily round the camp. "We use them for rounding up sheep down under."

CHAPTER SEVEN

"Let Battle Commence . . ."

THIS IS NO PLACE to discuss the vexed political aspects of the Syrian campaign; to consider, for example, whether we might have marched unopposed, indeed acclaimed, into Syria the previous summer or whether, even in June 1941, Vichy French resistance would have been less bitter if Free French forces had not taken part on our side. I am concerned with people. For my purposes the tragic muddle is adequately summed up by the popular encyclopedia which I consulted recently to check a date. Having to cover the whole of World War II in fifty pages, the encyclopedia devotes a terse paragraph to the only war we have fought against the French for 135 years. But how much ironic understatement is contained in that paragraph!

On 8th June, 1941, the main Allied force, including a small contingent of Free French, crossed the frontier from Palestine. At the outset progress was slow; for Wilson, the Allied Commander, was anxious to spare his French opponents as much as possible. They, however, had no such feelings . . .

Volumes could be written round that last sentence. I like to imagine that the man who wrote it was one of those courageous officers in broadcasting vans, who crossed the frontier with the leading troops to implore our late allies to let us enter as friends. The vans were promptly blasted.

In the accounts of battles long ago, I have always felt much sympathy for the despised camp followers. Down-trodden by the

67

warrior class when things were going well, dragooned into action when they were not, there were many among them, I am sure, who secretly longed to be in the fray, but whom fate, or perhaps some flaw in their temperament, kept to the rear. Apart from a few bloodless and pleasant wanderings, which might be claimed as valuable patrol work, for nine-tenths of the Syrian campaign we played the part of camp followers, guarding Vichy prisoners-of-war or entertaining, in the best Yeomanry tradition, migratory Staff Officers. In mid-June Oliver Bomfrey, on a political mission to the Vichy French, spent some days with us in a Lebanese olive grove. We were glad to see him. His presence encouraged us to feel that, though inactive, at least we were somewhere that really mattered. Coming from Cairo, he brought news of a larger world. Matthew Prendergast, he told me, was with someone called Wingate in Abyssinia; and, of more immediate interest, the lorry-borne part of the Yeomanry Division, which Alan had accompanied to Iraq, was now advancing back across the desert on the French in Palmyra.

"What's the plan for all of us when this show is over? Or have 'they' forgotten us?" the Colonel asked.

In our parochial minds Bomfrey was to some extent identified with "them" and we credited him with all sorts of unofficial channels of information.

"I wasn't going to mention this, in case you're disappointed later. Anyway, it isn't my business—not that that ever stops me! But I *think* that most, if not all, of the Yeomanry Regiments will start to be mechanized within the next month or two; probably in Egypt, where the stuff is. It's a question of convoys." Bomfrey paused and looked mysterious. "In fact, I *happened* to see a scheme on someone's desk for attaching a few Yeomanry C.O.s immediately to Armoured Regiments in the desert."

This was fairly breath-taking news.

"Did you *happen* to see any names?" the Colonel asked.

But Bomfrey obviously felt he had been indiscreet enough.

"No names. The bumph just said that only the less incompetent C.O.s would be selected."

"Oh, well, that rules me out," the Colonel laughed.

In the cage we had improvised for them, we treated our Vichy prisoners as well as we could. One evening, to mitigate the bitterness of defeat and capture, we invited their officers to our Mess. While we gave them beer and whisky, Bomfrey addressed them grandiloquently in French. But they were in a resentful frame of mind. Most of them had already been many years away from France. Their Australian captors, furious at the heavy losses they had themselves suffered, had stripped them of their wrist-watches, their money, even their family photographs. Perhaps Victor Bone and Fergie Deakin, truculent at first, did more than the rest of us to further the cause. They made friends with a Major in the French Cavalry who had hunted in England before the war and who spoke adequate English.

"What do you mean by fighting against us, you old sod?" they asked. The question evidently put him at ease, and he explained that he had been ordered to fight us; so, as a professional soldier, he had fought us. *Voilà tout.* He seemed anxious to be assured he had "put up a good show." Victor and Fergie assured him. After which he became more communicative.

"You see, the Government of France, the government, that is, which pays me, is in Vichy. From my point of view De Gaulle is a traitor."

Oliver Bomfrey was not pleased with the evening. Knowing, better than we did, how important it was to win these prisoners over to our side, he complained that we had not treated them well enough.

"What's the use of giving them beastly beer and whisky? They must have wine!"

The next day, at the Colonel's suggestion, Bomfrey, R.S.M. Burge, and I set off in a truck in search of wine. We drove back forty miles across the frontier to Acre, where Burge knew the manager of an N.A.A.F.I. canteen. In the canteen store we found several cases of Palestinian hock. While Burge chatted with the Jewish manager, Bomfrey and I loaded the cases on to our truck. Discovering us at it, the manager protested.

"But who is actually going to pay for all this?"

Burge and I looked at one another blankly. Who was, actually, going to pay? But Bomfrey, once determined on a course of action, never had time for mere details.

"Oh, England will pay!" he cried.

For R.S.M. Burge's sake I did not want the N.A.A.F.I. manager to get into trouble. So, on behalf of England, I signed a formal receipt for the wine. Angry letters from the N.A.A.F.I. demanding payment followed me about for the next four years. I tore up the last one just before I was demobilized. By now, I trust, the bill has been paid—by England. Prisoners-of-war, it is one of their psychological symptoms, are never grateful for kindness shown to them. Ours merely grumbled that the wine, by French standards, was exceedingly bad. We were glad when some other unit came to look after them.

Damascus fell on 21st June and Bomfrey hastened off to be there. We filled in time visiting Crusader castles, feasting in Druse villages, and generally showing the flag. I recall with pleasure a glass of iced *arak*, supplied one hot afternoon by a Maronite Archbishop. Then, bathing near Tyre, we were ordered suddenly to report as fast as possible to a British Division in Damascus, a hundred miles to our east. Leaving one Squadron behind to continue patrol work with the Australians, we rode up to the outskirts of the city on the third day, 9th July. Caesar shied at the sickly scent of death emanating from one of the many graves made shallow because of the hard earth and piled over with stones. Those and a few derelict French tanks of archetypal design were the only signs of the recent bitter fighting. Though we were still keen enough, we doubted whether our 400 horses advancing across the desert in anti-aircraft formation and kicking up a dust storm, made an intimidating military display.

"I wonder what they think is coming?" I said to Fergie Deakin, pointing to the hills ten miles away, from which the French were presumably watching our approach through field-glasses.

"Fred Karno's circus probably, if they can see your animal."

Fergie always maintained that Caesar was the outcome of an affair between a cart-horse and an elephant.

Within a few minutes of arrival in our bivouac, the Divisional General himself drove up. He belonged to the rugged category of Generals.

"You've come faster than I expected," he said. "I'm jolly glad to see you." Then, over a map, he explained why.

"My Division is putting in an attack up the road to Beirut at dawn the day after tomorrow, 11th July. We've had casualties, as you've probably heard, and we can't cover our left flank—those hills you can see from here. I've no idea what's up there—rather less than a Regiment probably, but they've got some guns which could do us a lot of damage, unless they're given something else to think about. Frankly, I'm a bit vague what you fellows are trained to do, but the 'Yeomanry' sounds sporting. Could you leave your horses and climb up there tomorrow night—your objective will be that hill on the right with two knolls—so that you're on top before our attack starts? I'll give you more definite orders later, but I wanted to hear first whether you think you can do it."

The Colonel said, as every man in the Regiment would have wished him to say, that of course we could do it.

"And I am sure you will. I'll send one of my Staff out to you right away. Let him know what transport and other equipment you need. We'll do our best to lend it to you."

Before the General drove off, he added: "If, in daylight, you find more up there than you can tackle, pull out. I don't want you to have heavy casualties. This war is nearly over, anyway."

There was a great deal to be arranged in the next twenty-four hours. The orthodox-minded Staff Officer was amazed, when he came, both at our happy mood and at our lack of the most elementary tools of the trade. The one, he felt, should have precluded the other. We had no bayonets, for instance, and he assured us that bayonets were most necessary; tommy-guns, also, which none of us had ever seen. We gave him a drink in the Mess to help him recover. Our sense of inferiority asserted itself, as so often, in a rather silly arrogance of manner towards this helpful, if humorless, young man who had seen so much more of the war than we had. He overheard Fergie say caustically to Victor Bone: "Spurs had better be removed before battle, don't you think?"

"And what do you use spurs for?" he joked.

"Oh, don't be such a B.F.!" Fergie snapped. There was an unusual harshness in his manner that evening which jarred on me, and which, fancifully I dare say, I attribute now to some premonitory nervousness. But probably he was only tired, like everyone else.

Tom fetched the load of new weapons from Damascus the same night and issued them in the morning. The Regiment was in high spirits. The men tied the bayonets on to their leather belts with bootlaces and spent the day practicing with the tommy-guns and grenades. Soldiers, like children, love new toys and in the Orderly

Room, a tarpaulin slung to an apricot tree, our difficult work was made the harder by the ceaseless firing and banging that went on around us.

Inevitably a number of men had to be left behind to tend the horses, constituting a very unwilling band of camp followers. R.S.M. Burge had been ill for some days past with malaria. Yellow in the face and shivering, he spent this day wrapped in blankets and washing down quinine pills with what he told me was water, but which was more probably gin. When the time came to get ready, I saw him struggling into his breeches.

"Don't be a fool, Mr. Burge. You can't possibly come."

He grinned at me in a ghastly sort of way.

"I've been training, or supposed to be training, this Regiment to go into battle for six years. I know you and the Colonel wouldn't hold it against me if I stayed behind now, but there are others, believe me, who are less charitable. Anyway, I'm —— well coming."

I was always fond of the R.S.M., but at that moment I loved him.

About 10 P.M., just before we climbed into the trucks that were to carry us across the plain to the foot of the hills, a Divisional D.R. brought in an urgent signal which had come for the Colonel from G.H.Q., Middle East. He was to be attached, indefinitely, to a formation in the desert, was ordered to report to Cairo immediately and to hand over command of the Barsetshire Yeomanry meanwhile to Victor Bone. The Colonel stuffed the paper into his pocket.

"Don't mention this, will you?" he said. And then he chuckled: "I have always wanted a chance to do what Nelson did at—hell's dust, where was it?"

The Colonel was always spoiling his jokes by forgetting some obvious name or word when he wanted it. As we bumped along in the moonlight there was much that might reasonably account for his preoccupied and worried look; the Regiment's future and his own; and, immediately ahead, the tricky night attack up a mountain against an enemy we knew nothing whatever about. But the trivial has a way of obtruding itself into the serious. I guessed, though I knew better than to suggest it, that what really troubled the Colonel was his inability at that moment to remember the word Copenhagen.

The convoy threaded across the plain and, under cover of a wadi, approached the dark mass of the hillside. The plain, though we did not know it then, was an artillery range over which the French 75s and 105s, sited in the hills we were attacking, habitually practiced. A roaring wind drowned the noise of our engines and the wheels were muffled by the thick dust. R.H.Q. had attached itself for the operation to Victor Bone's Squadron. I glanced at him and Fergie Deakin sitting opposite me in the truck. You can only drive into battle for the first time once in your life and I was curious to see if they looked any different from usual. They didn't. Tom sat beside them. The old warrior glanced at me, perhaps for the same reasons, and we exchanged a smile. He was too old and too heavy to come climbing and was to remain at the bottom, in charge of rear R.H.Q. I was surprised that I did not feel frightened. The anticipatory pit of the stomach feeling was there all right. But not fear. That came a few minutes later.

The head of the convoy had reached the de-bussing point, and the rest were closing up, when the truck in front of ours ran over a mine, or possibly a live shell. The unexpected explosion and the black smoke, twisted by the wind into monstrous shapes against the night sky, were terrifying. Any martial ardor I had worked up in myself evaporated instantly, like the smoke, and my first thought was to leap out of our truck and run for my life. And yet, afterwards, Tom told me he remembered wishing he had felt at that moment as calm as I looked. Whereas I admired Fergie Deakin who exclaimed cheerfully: "Let battle commence..." But no more explosions followed and my nerves steadied. Hating the sight and sound of anguish, I helped to remove the casualties from the warped wreck. If this was battle, I wished someone might call the whole thing off. My old Troop Sergeant lay on the ground among the rest. His legs had been shattered and he was groaning a little, sweating much.

I only have a good memory for inessentials. "Oh, God, sir," he gasped, when I tried to comfort him. "I've fairly dropped a bollock this time."

The Sergeant recovered the use of his legs after some years, but that was the end of his war. I was thankful when an ambulance drove up to deal with the situation and when, leaving that ill-fated wadi, which cost us dearly the next day too, we started to climb.

"My last must have been dated 10th July, but it seems longer ago than that," I wrote to Lucinda on 13th July. (As the letter describes the battle better than I could now and has the merit, if no other, of immediacy, I shall quote it in full.) "It was a trifle ominous and, to reassure you, I sent a wire yesterday dating it 11th July so that when you get the letter you'll know that all came right. The battle itself— obviously I can't tell you much about it—has no great importance in the history of the war or even much in this campaign, but for us it was serious enough, and we are elated to feel we have really done something, suffered something real, at last. But underneath we are also sad. It was a bitter first taste of action and the Regiment did astonishingly well—anyway, the General was highly complimentary, which is all one is supposed to fight for. Nobody you know was hurt, by the way.

"The story was briefly as follows. We had to climb a mountain during the night and take the ridge on top—thereby protecting the flank of a large-scale attack below us on the right. There was a freezing wind as we scrambled up the rough hillside by moonlight and in the middle I suffered a violent attack of diarrhœa which was decidedly awkward though really rather funny (afterwards). After very little fighting we found ourselves on top as daylight was breaking, in possession of our objective, all except what appeared to be a small fort at the end. Later we discovered it was a pretty big fortress cut out of the mountain top and quite untakable by a force like ourselves. Luckily, we never tried, because the sun was rising in our eyes behind it and we had to wait. Darting about among rocks dodging bullets was at the time quite good fun and quite unreal—like some Wild Western picture. I simply could not believe it was *me* taking part and consequently felt moderately safe, as indeed I was, so long as I kept behind cover. At first we were quite happy up there on our ridge, looking at the finest view imaginable, munching biscuit and chocolate and playing at Red Indians among the scrub and boulders. We were, moreover, doing all we were supposed to do; the fort was firing at *us* and not at the infantry attacking below! Unfortunately, our ridge was overlooked by other higher ridges, hidden on which the enemy (too absurd to think of them, of all people, as enemy—even now I don't bear them any malice) were lying in wait for us with all sorts of unpleasant surprises. For about six hours we lay up there, practically unable to move a hand and without any effective means of hitting back. I suppose our position from then on might be called desperate, but again it all seemed so unreal, so impossible to believe, that I don't think anyone was frightened or even excited. Chiefly we were scorching hot and thirsty and dead tired. I saw men sleeping, literally sleeping, with bullets spattering round them. We had done all that was required of us and the infantry had been successful. The difficulty was to get out—a long clamber down the mountain under shrapnel and machine-gun fire and a still longer march across the plain in range of their guns. To cut the story short, we did get out—I can't think why or how—perhaps because we were too tired to want to, much. Personally, I kept falling down and cursing and drinking whisky out of a flask to restore my legs and dropping to sleep. *Quelle histoire!* When I got back I fell on to the camp-bed which Muggs, who arrived before me, had kindly put out, and burst into tears.

"The dear old quadrupeds, in case you wonder how they got on, were left behind with a party to look after them which reduced our numbers—we were already few enough with only two Squadrons. I can't think of anything else to tell you about the battle itself—like everyone else, I am completely recovered now with an increased zest for life! I had one lucky escape when a sniper's bullet (the snipers were the worst part of the day) went through my shirt under the left armpit—just grazing the skin. I am rather proud of that shirt and its hole, slightly bloodstained—sheer vanity, I admit.

"We are still in the lovely camp from which I last wrote, within view on one side of the mountains where we fought and on the other of that wonderful wooded plain like a calm green sea, in the middle of which the gleaming white domes and spires of the ancient city appear to be floating. The morning after the battle I went for a ride through the woods, seeing nature with newly-opened eyes, feeling like a figure in one of those Persian paintings, who gazes meditatively at the little animals and birds in the trees around him. Indian corn, melons, cucumbers, tomatoes, even a few hollyhocks grew thick in the shade round my feet and brown wild-eyed children washing in a stream darted through gaps out of sight as I passed. Everything, everybody, that morning, seemed part of the same beautiful silent picture through which I was a wanderer—the memory of it is fixed in my mind as though painted on a screen in golds and greens and blues and crimsons."

I forbear to record the many memories which transcribing that letter has evoked. Accounts of other peoples' battles, like other peoples' bombs, quickly pall. Perhaps I may be allowed just one, though, to tell the truth, I have not needed reminding of the episode. It has haunted me these fourteen years, another of the ghosts I am hoping to lay by writing of them.

In the earlier stages of the engagement, before heat and tiredness had worn the edge off enthusiasm, I crawled forward to an outpost to see what I could of our enemy. At dawn, when we had reached the mountain-top, we had seen a few unidentifiable figures silhouetted against the rising sun. Since then the enemy had been invisible, shooting at us through loopholes in the fort or from the neighboring hillsides. I lay down beside a trooper. More for the fun of the thing than because he had a target, he was firing a Hotchkiss sporadically at a low built-up stone parapet about fifty yards away. Suddenly, behind the parapet, two black French soldiers (Senegalese, I believe) popped their heads up. Their two faces, under steel helmets, grinned at us, and I can still see the whiteness of their teeth and eyeballs. God knows what they thought they were doing. Probably they had never been in a battle before and, like myself, they were childishly curious to have a look at their enemy.

Or were they attempting to do something more? If men are ever to cease destroying one another, if the everlasting tit-for-tat process is ever to be halted, it will perhaps only come by an individual, a simple black man for example, standing up suddenly in the face of bullets and crying out:

"See, here I am. I don't want to kill you. Why kill me? Let us stop the battle and be friends."

The trooper beside me was so astonished by the apparition of the two black men that he never thought of firing his Hotchkiss.

"Shoot!" I hissed at him.

He pressed the trigger and nothing happened. A cartridge had jammed. There was a simple drill for curing the stoppage, but now, in his excitement, the trooper bungled it. I pushed him out of the way, grabbed the gun and ejected the cartridge.

Over the sights, I saw my burst hit the top of the parapet. The two grinning faces vanished like puppets. A little dust lingered in the air where they had been. Thus, with the wantonness of a boy destroying some harmless bird for "sport," I contributed my share towards the never-ending story of man's inhumanity to man. But at the time I thought I had behaved rather splendidly and the trooper was impressed too.

Voles was very deaf. Sniping happily from a ledge of rock, he could not hear the bullets which a machine-gun began to spray on to the stone behind him. The grenades we had been issued with were Italian, captured in Eritrea. Made of some plastic substance, they gave a great bang, but were otherwise harmless. Fergie, whose energy that day, like Voles's, seemed tireless, threw one of the grenades so that it burst a yard from Voles's head. Much startled, the latter turned, saw us waving, grinned placidly and clambered down. He was killed a few minutes later by a mortar shell. No one saw Fergie die. He must have stayed back to cover our retreat, for his body, shot to pieces, was found afterwards beside a Hotchkiss gun and a pile of used ammunition.

The irrational, not to say poetic, uplift of the spirit which sweeps over men sometimes during a battle is a well-authenticated experience, from Homer's day to our own. I do not know why it should be so and I have no desire to find out.

> *And when the burning moment breaks,*
> *And all things else are out of mind,*
> *And only joy of battle takes*
> *Him by the throat, and makes him blind,*
> *Through joy and blindness he shall know,*
> *Not caring much to know, that still*
> *Nor lead nor steel shall reach him, so*
> *That it be not the destined will.*

As I sit in an armchair by the fire, my disbelief willingly unsuspended, the meaning of those famous lines strikes me now as exaggerated nonsense. No battle, after all, is bloodless and surely no one *joyfully* risks being killed or maimed. Yet I understood them on 11th July, 1941, and once or twice again during the war. I knew the poem by heart, recited it often to myself and gained much comfort by it. And there are many who could say the same. Fergie Deakin, the volatile steeplechase rider, and Voles, the solid farmer, would not have been among them, but they too perhaps had their moment of ecstasy, of inspiration, call it what you will. At least I choose to think they did. It makes their death seem less futile. We recovered their bodies from the hillside the next day when, as the General had predicted, armistice was signed. We buried them, with the others, in the Damascus Cemetery. R.S.M. Burge, producing trumpets and drums from nowhere, organized the occasion movingly.

Less grim, if hardly less moving, was the send-off which he organized for the Colonel. Though the signal had "detached" rather than "posted" him away, we knew that we were unlikely to see the Colonel again as our C.O. Sad at heart, I accompanied him into Damascus for a last lunch together, before a Divisional car drove him down to catch the Cairo train from Haifa. In the bar of the Orient Palace Hotel we ran into Oliver Bomfrey. The Colonel told him where he was going.

"Apparently you knew what you were talking about for once!" he added.

"Alan is here looking for you. Have you seen him?"

"Alan! What's he doing?"

"Passing through on his way to a good job in Egypt. But there he is. He can give you his own news." And Bomfrey left us to greet a famous French General.

And there Alan was, exuding strength and efficiency and giving us the broadest grin in the Middle East.

"Good morning, Colonel. You don't know it yet, but we're traveling south together. I arrived from Palmyra two hours ago and called in at the Division here to try and pick up a car to Palestine. They told me to take a lift with you—it was the first I'd heard you were all here."

I could tell from the flicker of pain which crossed Alan's face when he greeted me, that he disapproved of my corduroy trousers. I affected, particularly now that I had been in a battle, a certain exoticism of dress, something between Byron and a cowboy; whereas Alan, who had been in many battles, looked in all circumstances as if he had stepped out of a first-class military tailor, having had a hot bath there into the bargain.

Over lunch he said: "Frankly, I think you were asked to do too much and from what I have heard, you did still more. But from the point of view of the Regiment's future, it may be a good thing. You don't know what's happening?"

"We know nothing."

"The Cavalry Division, or most of it, is being mechanized. One Brigade is to be equipped and trained in the Delta at once; in fact"—and the smile came back on to Alan's face—"it's on the way there now. I'm the Brigade Major!"

Alan loved to be a jump ahead of everyone else and one could not help liking him for it.

"You're incorrigible! Go on."

"Well, the first three Regiments to be mechanized have, of course, been chosen already. Two Yeomanry Regiments and the Black and Whites. But there is going to be some stiff competition to get into the second Brigade. To put it bluntly, I think the Barsetshire Yeomanry should stand a better chance now than it did of being one of the next three. Though, God knows, merit has little to do with these things."

Before they drove away together, Alan took me aside.

"I imagine," he said casually, "you would not be heartbroken if you were posted suddenly away from Regimental duties with Victor and ordered to join a certain Armoured Brigade—I don't yet know in what capacity?"

"Not exactly heartbroken. Of course I should be awfully sorry to leave the Barsetshire—"

"Quite so," he interrupted me. "The feeling does you credit. But a change of life is a new experience, or whatever it was, in that scurrilous story you used to tell about poor old Voles. Between ourselves, I don't think they will mechanize a second Yeomanry Brigade for months. There isn't the stuff. But with luck our Brigade will be trained and up in the desert by Christmas. And it would be fun if you were there. By the way, I believe Amos may be joining us too. Well, I can't promise anything but I shall be surprised if I don't see you within a month."

"So it's goodbye for the present," the Colonel said as we shook hands. "I can't somehow say all that I'd like to. Anyway"—he smiled—"you usually seem to know what I'm thinking better than I do."

Alan poked his head out of the window as the car started.

"Don't look so bloody glum," he shouted.

But I felt glum. And I felt glummer, after a disagreeable scene with Victor Bone in the Orderly Room.

"I would like you to start training Boy Harland as your successor," he said brusquely.

He was in command of the Regiment and had every right to choose a new Adjutant. Still, he might have waited a day.

"Very good, sir," I said, with icy politeness, determined not to show that I was hurt.

A few minutes later he succeeded, not less effectively, in enraging R.S.M. Burge. One or two sergeants had recently been sent off to O.C.T.U.s, with the recommendation that they should be commissioned back into the Barsetshire Yeomanry, if we had vacancies. So that when Victor Bone, unexpectedly, told the R.S.M. he was putting his name forward for an immediate commission, the latter exclaimed delightedly: "Do you mean within the Regiment, sir?"

"Christ, no. I mean, of course, I'm afraid you're rather too old for that," Victor Bone corrected himself. But too late.

"Thank you, sir." The R.S.M. saluted smartly and marched off. But he was white with humiliation.

Victor became in due course a very gallant Commanding Officer and much loved. Nowadays we meet occasionally and are quite good friends. But at that moment I thought him the most insensitive, tactless, arrogant, and malicious man I knew. And the stupidest.

Yet I was grateful in a way to him. It is easier to part in anger than in sorrow and now at least I need have no qualms of conscience about leaving the Regiment. I was very fond of the Barsetshire Yeomanry. It had been my school and my home for two long years. Even the grotesque Bone was inextricably woven into my existence for ever, if only as a memory. But I was suddenly sick to death of them all. I wanted a change and Providence would surely bring one about.

To be on the safe side I gave her a helping prod. From Damascus the next day I sent Alan a telegram.

"Urgent. Dog gnawed by tasteless bone. Please hasten medicine."

If nothing came of it, I had at least carried the old paradox of man biting dog a step further.

The best way to train someone else in your job is to clear off and allow him to get on with it. On the pretext of having my flesh wound stitched, unstitched, or otherwise attended to, I devoted the next week to discovering Damascus. And since the food and wine in the French Officers' Club and elsewhere were all that could be desired and since there were some very agreeable people in the city at the time, I discovered Damascus pleasantly. Boy Harland, too, benefited by my absence. He didn't take longer to get bloody than I had. In fact, he picked up the idea so thoroughly that I returned late one night to find he had posted me back to Squadron duty. I was not surprised.

With as good a grace as possible I checked saddlery, filled in Army Pay Books, inspected the cookhouse, attended stables, tent-pegged, played polo, in short took part once again in the peacetime routine of a cavalry Regiment in the East or Near-East for the past hundred years. This, I felt, is where I came in.

The documents posting Lieutenant Burge to an R.A.S.C. Base Depot in Cairo and myself to Alan's Armoured Brigade nearby, arrived by the same post. A few hours later we drove away together towards our respective new horizons. Muggs, at his own request, came with me. He, too, was tired of grooming horses and polishing saddlery. There was much conventional hand-shaking and best-of-luck wishing to be done before we left. "I'm awfully sorry to be going," I said several dozen times. But I knew no one believed me and I never felt a bigger hypocrite.

PART THREE

Regular

Yes, of course it was sin
And no Christ would say 'Fight
For the right'—
But we *had* to win.

When the chaplain would bluster and blow
About laying the rod
Of God
On the back of 'His foe,'

I knew it was all just a form
And there was no fiery sword
And the Lord
Was not in the storm.

Yet—to have stood aside
Hoarding my fortunate life
With my wife
While the other men died!

Some sort of god, good or bad,
Would have kept me longing in vain
To be slain
As I am, if I had.

C. E. Montague

CHAPTER EIGHT

Desert and Delta

BEFORE THE WAR, to qualify for promotion, a Second Lieutenant in the Yeomanry had to spend a fortnight attached to a Regular Cavalry Regiment.

"You will be pleased to hear," the Adjutant wrote to me soon after my first camp, "that I have been able to attach you to the Black and Whites in Aldershot this September. Please confirm that you can manage the following dates . . ."

The Black and Whites epitomized the splendor, the arrogance, and, with their countless battle honors, the undeniable wartime excellence of the Cavalry tradition; a tradition to which the Barsetshire Yeomanry modestly adhered. Since the ordeal had to be faced sometime, I decided to get it over, though I wished the arrangement could have been made with some less exclusive and, I was sure, forbidding Regiment. Whether, like other ordeals undergone in those days, the fortnight spent with the Black and Whites did my soul any good, I do not know. Certainly the memory of it remains so vivid that, after nearly twenty years, I still cannot drive past the Cavalry Barracks in Aldershot without a shudder.

Captain Carstammers-Waghorn, the Black and Whites' Adjutant, to whom I reported on arrival, surveyed me grimly.

"I understand you have had little military training. I think, therefore, that the best thing would be to treat you as we would one of our own newly-joined officers. Do you agree?"

I agreed. Then he led me before the C.O. I never caught the Colonel's name and was too scared to ask. It was the sort of thing one was supposed to *know*. The walls of his office were hung with original water-colors, grotesque portraits of horses and dogs; or hunting scenes in the manner, but without the skill, of Lionel Edwards.

The Colonel, having expressed the hope that I would benefit by the attachment, asked me what work I did. By this stage in my military training the inappropriateness of admitting to be an assistant film director had occurred to me. Now, untruthfully, I claimed to be a painter. The Colonel's glower lightened.

"Then you'll be interested in these," he said, waving at the pictures on the walls. "Awfully good, don't you think? Bobo does them, you know."

Bobo, I gathered, was Captain Carstammers-Waghorn. I hesitated, wishing I had stuck to being an assistant film director.

"Well, go on," the Colonel said irritably, "tell me what you think."

Art was perhaps the only thing in the world about which I could accept no compromise. So I told him what I thought. The interview ended abruptly.

Beyond a perfunctory request for butter or salt, none of the Black and Whites' officers spoke to me for the next two weeks. But then, to be fair, they did not often speak to one another. They only snarled. They were all exceedingly rich, most of them wore heavy moustaches, more or less luxuriant according to the wearer's status. The atmosphere was charged with fear and hate and, above all, with boredom. One heard more yawns than conversation.

Newly-joined officers, of whom no others were present at that time, spent their days, I soon discovered, doing basic training with the ordinary recruits. P.T., the square, the riding school, sword drill, P.T. again . . . And they were expected, as a point of honor, to excel in these activities over the recruits themselves, beefy lads from the Lowlands. My own performance fell far below this expectation and must greatly have encouraged the rest of the class, if only for a fortnight.

The tormentor in charge of us was a short, square, red-faced, Rough-Riding Sergeant Major. He was the angriest man I had ever met, with the loudest voice. He always called me "sir," in deference to my commission and because it allowed him to be infinitely ruder.

"You there, sir, supposed to be an officer . . ." was his usual way of addressing me in front of the class. His name was Brunton. In

him, I came to feel, the brutalizing effect of the Army could be studied in its extreme form.

Such, briefly, had been my unfair impression of the Black and
Whites in September, 1937. Exactly four years later I came upon
them again. For reasons which do not concern us here, they had
been included with two Yeomanry Regiments in the Armoured Brigade whose H.Q., thanks to Alan, I had myself joined. Their personality, as a Regiment, had changed so completely that I almost
wondered whether the earlier interlude was dreamt. The truth was
that the subjective haze, often alarming in its distortion, through
which I had peered out at the world in 1937, had lost much of its
opacity by 1941. Even Carstammers-Waghorn, now their Colonel,
struck me as a gentle dreamy individual. In the next year I often
came across him sketching beside his tank, unselfconscious and
stoical in the face of dust storms, flies, and onlookers, annoyances
which deterred me from ever attempting to paint. And I was able to
show a polite, if rather insincere, enthusiasm for his pictures. Simply
by growing older I had acquired a little more tact, if little more tol-
erance. It was so admirable, I thought, to paint at all.

How exactly Brunton came to be an officer in the Black and
Whites was a mystery. He had not been popular with them as a
Sergeant Major and soon after I met him in Aldershot had been
posted away as an Instructor, probably to a Detention Barracks.
Early in the war he had been commissioned—by a clerical error it
was believed—back into the Black and Whites. They had forgotten
his existence, when, to their dismay, he arrived in the Middle East
as one of their officers. If their distaste for him was admittedly snobbish, it was also partly aesthetic. A fine leg for a boot was the first
condition of a passport to their company. Brunton's legs looked as if
they had come off a billiard table.

Apart from the Brigadier himself, the officers on the Brigade
H.Q. were all Yeomen and the Black and Whites were unrepre-
sented. When I arrived my second-in-command had not been appointed and the Brigadier felt that, as an act of courtesy, the Black
and Whites should be invited to contribute this officer. The choice
was left to them. When it came to jiggery-pokery there were no flies
on an historic Regular Regiment like the Black and Whites. They
contributed Brunton.

I was not sure enough of myself to protest. Besides, the coincidence amused me and, remembering my past experience, I thought Brunton would be preferable to some scornful and exquisite young millionaire. I was quite wrong. After the first few days I came to realize that Brunton, as a regular of fifteen years' service, had little respect for any Yeomanry major, none at all for myself. He personified the side of the Army I most hated.

But Muggs suffered more than I did. As Brunton could do little against me overtly, he persecuted me through my batman.

"The mucker has put me on a charge again. I'll be up in front of you in Squadron Office," Muggs announced, with my early-morning tea. "Think I'll apply to go back to the Regiment."

When, later in the day, we had had our formal and distasteful interview and Muggs, sentenced to seven days' C.B., had been marched out by the S.S.M., he returned unofficially, grinned, and said: "I've arranged for one of the other batmen to look after you while I'm on jankers. Same as last time."

I think Muggs rather enjoyed my embarrassment. It strengthened his hold over me. And he never carried out his threat of leaving; our friendship was too firmly based on self-interest. He cushioned my physical existence. I protected him, with more success than the foregoing anecdote suggests, from "being buggered about by the Army," as he would have put it.

But perhaps I have exaggerated the importance of Brunton. He was a small thing in my life at the time—as a pebble in one's shoe is a small thing. The metaphor is doubly apt. His ultimate triumph over me came about through a blistered foot turning septic.

"No one dies except by his own wish," Groddeck says somewhere. Or words to that effect. Ma Prendergast was run over by a bus in the black-out on 25th October 1941. With both her sons serving overseas, her house blitzed, and her world shattered, she may well have felt there was little to live for. I heard the news from Luke, and it made me unexpectedly sad. I had not liked her. But she had always been there, a familiar if unloved landmark.

Luke was working in Cairo for the B.B.C. To my surprise, he had written to me in Syria. I looked him up when I got to Egypt. We were both glad to meet someone from the pre-war days and too much had happened since for our earlier antagonisms to seem important. Perhaps, having grown older, I saw him now from a different angle than formerly. The intellectual arrogance, if it was that, which had so riled me on the Piazza, now seemed an admirable intellectual integrity. He had contrived to remain himself in spite of the war. For the next eighteen months he was my main contact with civilized, which means civilian, life; a useful friend in countless ways, from storing my possessions to persuading American journalists to take letters for Lucinda.

After Pearl Harbor our postal routes became increasingly devious and to our other difficulties were added the Censor's savage and irrational depredations.

> Such queer rock formations
> funny conical hills sprouting up in the
> Sea shells
> old petrol tins and
> alas the sordid remains
> military excursionists and
> our goal a 'depression'
> suddenly like the Jordan
> far larger, down great lava
> a salt marsh below sea level
> completely bleak, amazing
> bare with one green patch in the middle
> the remotest most desolate
> spoon, a hammer, and an electric
> Robinson Crusoe couldn't have been more surprised

There is a trick used by Cubist painters, of pasting a few random strips of paper on the canvas before starting work. When the jugs, the bowls of fruit, the guitars, whatever it may be, have been painted, the strips are pulled off, thus leaving the picture suggestively incomplete. My letters by the time they reached Lucinda often had something of the same effect.

Through Luke I first heard that Oliver and Matthew had formed a small hush-hush unit, a private army of their own, in which they wore odd clothes, lived at G.H.Q.'s expense in a Cairo hotel, and disappeared for a few nights every now and again by aeroplane or submarine to the Greek islands. It sounded a pleasant, if hazardous, solution to the problem of being a soldier.

During the winter, vague, obviously exaggerated stories of their exploits reached us and the subject cropped up one evening in our Brigade Mess, a tent slung to the side of a three-ton lorry, when Amos was dining with us.

"How typical of Oliver to start another racket!" Alan said. "Bomfrey's Boys! How can you take anyone seriously with a name like that?"

"At least they're *doing* something," Amos replied hotly. "I feel we're hardly in a position to criticize."

"That's a fine way for a Divisional Staff Officer to talk. We could go into the battle tomorrow if G.H.Q. would give us the tanks."

"They won't. We've been the laughing stock of the Middle East for two years. While we spend our time thinking up some good excuse for driving into Cairo, Bomfrey's Boys are . . ."

"Are already there. All right, I know that's not fair. But this is a war of big armies. It will be won by the biggest army. Bomfrey's Boys and organizations like them fritter away valuable officers and N.C.O.s in side-shows. Oh, I've no doubt they're very brave, but what does it add up to? A pin prick here or there in the hide of an elephant."

"Well, I'd join them myself if I didn't earn more money where I am." Amos grinned mischievously and refilled his glass.

"And you'd deserve to be shot if you did. You're a highly trained and experienced Staff Officer assisting the General to command a complex and important . . ."

"My foot. I do nothing for the General that an A.T.S. Corporal couldn't do. In fact, when you think of it, not nearly as much."

And the conversation as usual turned bawdy. Amos's familiar line that all Staff Officers should be replaced by the A.T.S., did not make him popular on the Div. H.Q.—except, of course, with the General. Much of his sourness, at this time, may have been caused by personal worries. His Art gallery off St. James Street was closed, his tar business neglected, and at least two cases in the High Court awaited his return to the U.K.

In the argument, which I have greatly abbreviated, between Alan and Amos I listened without taking sides, agreeing alternately with each. The little I knew of Bomfrey's Boys appealed to what I have described earlier as my latent Red-Indianism. With them, I imagined, you could have the war without the Army. But Alan was obviously right, too. I took my soldiering seriously at this time. I was very keen. As a Major commanding the Brigade H.Q. Squadron, I felt I should be.

With our usual enthusiasm we had set about re-training ourselves in three and a half crowded months. Told to be ready to go into action by the New Year, we were ready long before Christmas. All we lacked was tanks. The news, therefore, that another Armoured Division had been brought all the way out from England and had been thrown, on arrival, straight into the battle in January, filled us with indignation. What on earth were "they" driving at? What had been the point of our own hectic efforts? The old jibe about "Hitler's secret weapon" still stuck. Perhaps Amos had been right. Some prejudice against us existed, had always existed, at G.H.Q. To be held in a condition of permanent futility seemed the destined lot of the Yeomanry Division.

"They've made up their minds we're no bloody good," Alan said to me bitterly, "and they're damned well not going to give us the chance to show them they're wrong."

The other Armoured Division's immediately tragic experiences would have made us laugh, if they had been a laughing matter. Or did we perhaps laugh? That might account for the retribution which later overtook us.

Alan's genuine eagerness for the Division to play its part in the battle always made me feel rather a fraud. I paid lip service to the view in public. In private, I hoped we would stay on where we were. In our training camp at the junction of Desert and Delta west of Alexandria, we enjoyed the best of both worlds. The contrast between the two added much to the alternate pleasures they offered and a golden glow illumines the period in retrospect. Even Victor Bone was often affectionately referred to in letters of the time. For the Barsetshire Yeomanry had, after all, escaped the fate of being turned into signallers. Leaving their horses, they rejoined the Yeomanry Division soon after I did, in a different Brigade, and were later transferred into the same one.

There were many distractions. I recall a pleasant drive with Hilary across the salt flats of the Wadi Natrun to visit the Coptic Monasteries.

"I believe he misses me," I wrote afterwards with awful smugness, "the shadow of my disbelief removed, I suspect his lamp seems to burn rather less brightly."

And there were the usual personal frictions. "The flies are getting bad, some of them in human form. Your books, handed round the Mess and much appreciated, have caused one pair of malevolent blue eyeballs to bulge still farther from their sockets . . ."

What were the books? I wonder now. Henry Miller's name is mentioned elsewhere and I should like to believe that I lent a copy of *The Cosmological Eye* to Brunton. For his eyeballs, I fancy, were those referred to.

Our trouble, put simply, was that we got on one another's nerves; the trouble would automatically be cured by a move up into the desert. Since no one likely to read these pages will be much interested in the organization of an Armoured Brigade, it is perhaps sufficient to explain that in a base area Brunton and I sat together in an office tent, with such harmony as we could muster; but that once in the field our duties diverged, Brunton administering the Brigade H.Q. itself, while I remained farther back in charge of a complicated shuttle service of supply vehicles, known as B Echelon.

If circumstances spring out of character and if every individual, like a spider entangled in its web, creates the complications of his own life, I suppose I had only myself to blame for Brunton. But probably our relationship was doomed from the start. Once a man has been able to address you as "You there, sir, supposed to be an officer," for a fortnight, he has gained an ascendancy which even the reversal of your situations cannot eliminate.

Strangely, I had not met Matthew and Oliver in Luke's flat so far, though they must often have come there. I heard news of them and of Bomfrey's Boys, in a very different manner.

In February, after the second retreat from Benghazi, the front had been stabilized south-westwards from Tobruk, remaining static for the next four months. The Eighth Army was said to be building up supplies for an assault on the Afrika Korps in midsummer. Rommel, one presumed, was doing much the same. The Yeomanry Division accumulated tanks by degrees, and perfected its training.

During April there was little for me to do in our camp that Brunton could not do probably better, so I arranged an "attachment" for myself to another Armoured Brigade up in the Desert of which my former Colonel was Second in Command. Taking Muggs, I spent a happy time touring the battlefields and gossiping about the good old days with the Colonel himself. I could give him up-to-date news of the Barsetshire Yeomanry, of Alan and Amos and his other friends.

"What has happened to Burge?" he asked.

I felt a stab of guilt at the question. What *had* happened to Burge? Selfishly preoccupied, I had never troubled to keep in touch with him and assumed he was by now indispensable to the R.A.S.C. Depot where I had left him seven months earlier. I promised to make inquiries when I got back.

By one of those chances which so delight me there was no need to make inquiries. Driving back into our camp a few days later, I reported to Alan in his office. He waited, rather impatiently I noticed, while I gave him messages from the Colonel.

"Good," he said. "Now, listen to this piece of news. A week ago we had an order from G.H.Q. calling for officers and men to join Bomfrey's Boys, of all things. Vital work of a highly secret nature, physical fitness essential, only men with initiative need apply. You know the sort of balls. And—this was particularly stressed—any officer or man who wishes to volunteer must be allowed to do so."

"Do you think I could persuade Brunton—" I began, but Alan interrupted me.

"An officer from Oliver Bomfrey's bloody Boys is coming here tomorrow to interview the candidates and to pick any he thinks suitable. And who do you think that officer is? A very old friend of ours. Mr. Burge—or rather Captain Burge!"

Burge arrived the next evening. I hardly recognized him at first. For one thing, he was thinner and about ten years younger; for another, he was wearing a red beard, a pale-blue shirt, and a pink beret, on which the monogram B.B. was embroidered in crimson. He carried a horribly lethal pistol strapped to his thigh in a fancy holster and within the limitations of khaki drill uniform contrived to look both smart and exotic, a cross between a Guard's officer and a Greek brigand. The right to wear a beard was a concession to Bomfrey's Boys by G.H.Q.

"It's such a help to us when we're being Cretan peasants," Burge explained blandly.

Disingenuously, I had arranged with Amos that Burge should stay with me and use my office for recruiting purposes, instead of visiting each Regiment. I should be better placed to prevent him taking my best sergeants and I wanted to hear about Matthew and his exploits.

Amos came to dinner and we talked to Burge late into the night. I reminded him how he had once said to me, after first meeting Oliver: "I would do anything for a man like that."

"I still would," he laughed. "In fact, I am. Do you think that *I* wanted to come recruiting here? Oh, I can imagine very well what you've been saying about Bomfrey's Boys and about me too, in the last few days."

We made some polite protest, but Burge stopped us. "We're old friends. We may not meet again for a long time. And I'd like to talk truth. Oliver's got plenty of faults, but he's got one rare quality and I forgive him everything for that."

Talking truth can be embarrassing. Still the new Burge impressed us, and we poured him another drink waiting to hear what Oliver's one quality could be.

"I can't put a name to it quite. I'll explain it this way. For twenty years I've wanted to be able to walk into the bar of Shepheard's and order a drink. That may not sound much of an ambition, but it stands for more than it sounds. And it was the first thing I did when I was commissioned. There were crowds of officers in the bar and Oliver was among them. He was talking to a General. He recognized me and came straight over." Burge paused. "It's easy enough to make yourself pleasant to an R.S.M. when you're paying a call on his Regiment and when you're Bomfrey. It's quite a different thing to stop talking to a General in order to go and say 'hallo' to some obscure R.A.S.C. Lieutenant in the bar of Shepheard's. But I can see I am embarrassing you."

"Not in the least," we said, untruthfully. "Go on."

"Well, after we'd talked a bit about what I was doing, Oliver said, 'Come and meet a friend of mine. We're starting a new Unit. We need an experienced old soldier to run the thing properly, and you're the very chap.' Then he introduced me to Matthew. I've been with them ever since. We've got a camp on the Canal, for testing equipment and training and that sort of thing; a base for operations in fact. Matthew and Oliver are away most of the time. They leave me to run my own show and though I say so myself, it's a very good show. We're a mixed crowd, with a dozen nationalities, but we get along pretty well. After all, no one's there who hasn't volunteered, and if someone doesn't fit in we send him straight back to his Unit." Burge paused again and added reflectively: "Frankly, I've enjoyed the last six months more than anything in my life. If I was struck dead tomorrow I'd have no regrets."

"Have you been on one of these hair-raising expeditions your-self?" Alan asked.

"Only once. I felt I couldn't keep the men's respect at the Base, unless I had done something. I'm too old and heavy for jumping out of aeroplanes, so I went on a raid by submarine. Oliver was away at the time and Matthew took me. When Oliver got back he was wild. He said there were dozens of young fools wanting to break their necks, but only one Burge . . . But I've talked far too much and drunk far too much, and if you'll excuse me I'm going to bed."

Burge, it seemed, had at last found a Unit where his militarism, his showmanship, and his passionate belief in the natural equality of men—each in some degree mutually exclusive in a normal Regi-ment—could all blossom happily together.

"It sounds a preposterous outfit," Alan said when Burge had gone.

"Perhaps," Amos said; "but doesn't it sound fun!"

"By the way," he added to me as he left, "I've arranged for the candidates to start arriving at your office at ten o'clock, if you can see that Burge is ready for them. And let me have the list of names later."

The next day Burge chose two officers and twenty O.R.s, with-out causing much ill-feeling. In fact, the Black and Whites lost an officer they particularly disliked. And I kept my own sergeants.

Burge had finished by the evening. He wanted to drive back to Cairo the same night and would not stay for dinner. Alan and I were giving him a last drink in the Mess when Victor Bone called in unexpectedly. So the meeting we had hoped to avert took place. Considering he had lost six Barsetshire Yeomen, Victor was more restrained than he might have been; though he managed to call our guest *Mr.* Burge twice.

The three of us walked with Burge to his car. He shook Alan and me by the hand. Then he waved ironically to our companion.

"So long, Victor. Nice to have seen you again," he said as he left.

Two hours later, driving at seventy down the pot-holed Alexandria-Cairo road, he pulled over to pass a convoy of tank-transporters. The offside wheels must have run off the tarmac into the soft sand. The car overturned and he was killed instantly.

"Funny sort of chap," Brunton said to me afterwards. "You wouldn't think he could ever have been an R.S.M., even in a Yeomanry regiment."

"Brunton's only redeeming feature that I have discovered," I wrote to Lucinda, "is the minute female dog, round which his emotional life is apparently centered. At present she is in season and is followed by a crowd of local pie dogs, rather crudely expectant, who have to be beaten off from time to time. The bitch is comically torn between affection for her master and her own natural instincts. And Brunton, I suspect, deep in his mean little heart, is jealous."

CHAPTER NINE

The Back of the Front

LIKE THE LETTERS of most married couples in our situation, Lucinda's and mine were full of tragi-jocular self-pity for our fate. We talked of Holy Deadlock. We had been married three years, had been separated for more than two. Our moods alternated between resigned despair and rebellion. We were victims of circumstances beyond our control; or then again, were they beyond control? Many wives had wangled their way out to the Middle East; many husbands had wangled their way home. Good luck to them all. Lucinda wrote that she was planning to leave Comus and to come out to Egypt with an American ambulance unit. But as, at the time, I had asked a friend in G.H.Q. to bear me in mind for a mission to the States, I hastily wired to her to wait. It would be too absurd if we crossed one another in the air above Marrakesh. But neither project was more than a daydream. She was supporting herself and Comus with a job in Washington and, we both knew, must remain there. The onus of breaking the deadlock lay on me.

But even supposing that, by some wild improbability, an opportunity to rejoin Lucinda in the U.S.A. did come my way, could I really take advantage of it? Would I be able to face telling Alan and the others that I was walking out on them before the battle had even begun? Luckily, however, these heart-searchings never got past the hypothetical stage. The battle did begin.

On the 26th May Rommel attacked. The high-level policies which, on our side, lay behind the preceding four-months' lull are brilliantly and amusingly described in *The Hinge of Fate*. Sir

Winston Churchill summarizes them in a passage I cannot resist quoting.

> I have often tried to set down the strategic truths I have comprehended in the form of simple anecdotes, and they rank this way in my mind. One of them is the celebrated tale of the man who gave the powder to the bear. He mixed the powder with the greatest care, making sure that not only the ingredients but the proportions were absolutely correct. He rolled it up in a large paper spill, and was about to blow it down the bear's throat. *But the bear blew first.*

I heard the news on Luke's wireless. He was being transferred to a different job in Jerusalem and we were having a farewell dinner. Matthew was there. It was the first time we had met in the Middle East but we found little to say to one another, and talked conventionally about Burge, what a good chap he had been and so on. I hoped Matthew would expand later in the evening and tell me about his adventures in Abyssinia or about his present plans. But he switched on the B.B.C. and we heard that the next phase in the Desert had opened.

"I'd better hurry back. We're bound to be involved this time," I said.

"Well, goodbye," Matthew said. "I'm sorry we've not had a better chance to talk. Let me know if you're interested in joining us ever. I imagine you're pretty well stuck where you are for the present?"

"Pretty well. Goodbye, Luke. I'll come and stay with you in Jerusalem when I get leave."

Three hours later I drove back into our camp. The paraffin lamp was burning in Alan's office tent, so I called in. Alan looked very busy indeed.

"Nice of you to turn up," he said curtly. But I could see he was delighted about something. "The Brigade is moving at dawn. The rest of the Division starts soon after."

"I'd better go and do some work."

"Don't worry. Brunton has everything under control." Then Alan laughed. "This is where the Yeomanry Division shows Rommel—and a few other people—where they get off."

We had been ordered to move up slowly, to conserve our tanks.

Mersa Matruh, Sidi Barrani, Sollum, Capuzzo . . . In the next days we trundled past the famous place names. Little of the places remained. Then along the Trigh Capuzzo to Sidi Rezegh, the scene of such bitter fighting the previous year. Would we, too, fight there now? It seemed probable. The sounds of the "cauldron" battle came to us from the West.

We waited, accustoming ourselves to a pint and a half of water per day. Half a pint to wash and shave, half a pint for tea, and half a pint for whisky in the evening . . . Plus what dew you could lick up. Soldiers, I came to the conclusion, are only content when they are thoroughly uncomfortable for a sufficient reason. My own had grumbled unceasingly about their food for the past nine months. Now that they had nothing to eat but bully and biscuits they were perfectly happy.

With Brunton, I visited Tobruk to collect stores. Sweat and dust had started the old skin trouble, on my foot this time. To soothe the inflammation I bathed in the shattered harbor, while he exercised his little bitch on the quay. Brunton, for reasons I was to discover later, never bathed; at least, in public.

We went on waiting. The thirst, the heat, the knowledge of impending battle were a stimulus. We were a legion of mercenaries. In the day heaven was falling, our shoulders held the sky suspended. Or were about to. The Free French Brigade on their way back from Bir Hacheim drove past and we cheered them. Our General paid us a call. A pep talk. You are the finest Division in the world and you have been kept waiting all these years for this one moment, to strike the decisive blow which will turn the war. Any day now . . .

We waited, poised, to strike the decisive blow.

I scribbled a line to Lucinda. "At night and in the early morning the smell of the desert air is indescribably sweet, not that many a flower can be seen blushing there. Just an occasional bird like a plover rising up and hovering away. Everything is marvelously peaceful, a sort of terrestial eternity."

The cannonade grew nearer. We waited. Then it happened.

"I just can't believe this," Alan stammered, reading the signal. "It says we are to hand over our tanks immediately to another Armoured Brigade."

The Brigadier hastened to the General, the General hastened to

Corps. But the order stood. The Yeomanry Division must hand its
armor over to the battle-weary troops returning from the "cauldron"
and who had already been fighting incessantly for a fortnight.

"What's the matter with you chaps?" one of them said with understandable asperity, as he checked over his new tank. "Can't you
fight?"

A blow, of sorts, had been struck. But it had come from the
wrong direction. Eighth Army H.Q. had kicked us in the pants.

The great retreat before Rommel began. Still proud, but perplexed and humiliated and with our tank crews riding in their
ration lorries, we drove eastwards again.

"We are soldiers of fortune and drift about in a way no one
knows whom listeth. We have had a rather hectic fortnight and
what with that and an inflamed foot, and the present disappointing
trend of events my nerves are a bit on edge. I still carry my gramophone around, but I seldom get time to play a tune on it. One lovely
night, though, I shall always remember. A full moon, a clear sky and
the desert air cool and thyme-scented. I perched the machine on a
tin of petrol and played the Mozart clarionet concerto until all the
anger and worrying of the day had sunk to the bottom . . ."

The Army Postal Service is a wonderfully tenacious organization. In these days, when the heavens were indeed falling, a telegram from Lucinda pursued me all the way up to the neighborhood
of Tobruk and then back again, catching up with me at length in a
base hospital. The telegram read "Separation bloody hell. Don't you
think we are perhaps taking it all rather too much lying down."

She was right. But I didn't see what I could do about it.

My skin trouble, unavoidably neglected, had spread angrily. I lay
suppurating from head to foot. A month later, still in hospital and
with small prospect of ever leaving, I missed the Prime Minister's
morale-raising visit to the Division. Perhaps, once again, I may be
allowed a brief quotation from his own account of it.

I spent the 8th with the Yeomanry Division. These fine troops,
hitherto wasted and never yet effectively engaged with the enemy,
were camped along the Kassassin road. For two years they had
served in the Middle East, mainly in Palestine, and I had not
been able to have them equipped and worked up to the high

quality of which they were capable. At last they had reached *the back of the front** and were to go into action. Now, at this moment in their career, it had been necessary to take all their tanks from them in order to feed and rearm the fighting line. This was a staggering blow for these eager men. It was my task to go from brigade to brigade and explain to all the officers gathered together, two or three hundred at a time, why they must suffer this mutilation after all their zeal and toil. But I had good news as well. The 300 Shermans were already approaching through the Red Sea, and in a fortnight the division would begin to be armed with the most powerful armoured vehicles current at that time . . . They would become the leading armoured unit in the world. I think they were consoled by this.

They were consoled. Muggs visited me and told me about it. The sight of the scruffy little man, a yellow cigarette sticking out of his wizened face as usual, cheered me immensely.

"Christ, you look bad, sir," he said mournfully, dropping ash over my blankets. But Muggs, too, was browned off.

"The mucker Brunton has it in for me. I've been on jankers ever since you went sick. When are you coming back?"

When indeed? The Army doctors were doing their best with alternate applications of acriflavian yellow and gentian violet.

"It is pasted on half an inch thick with a palette knife. By my own request, I do it myself, using my skin as a canvas and recapturing the joys gone by."

Such joys, however, were not enough. Alas, I am not a patient man at the best of times; and never one, readers may have gathered, to view my fellow human beings in the most charitable light. Now, in a condition of itchy despair, hospital life exacerbated my natural shortcomings. My ward-mates, if there is such a word, brought out the worst in me, judging by my letters.

The hospital sapped my will, as hospitals do. They are like a prisoner-of-war camp. I wonder that anyone ever manages to escape from either. The bare Chirico-esque perspective of the ward, the perpetual background motion of phantom sisters and orderlies, the

*My italics.

huge electric fans revolving slowly on the pastel-shaded ceiling, all added to the hypnosis creeping over me. I knew that I must shake myself out of it or become atrophied like the rest; like the stammering missionary from Bechuanaland, like the Flying Officer whining that he ought to be sent home, like the fat Major always talking about the price of beer, or like my immediate neighbor who had not spoken for three days and whom we all thought must be dead—he certainly looked dead.

"Everyone gets the war he wants," Amos once said to a guilt-ridden Staff Officer in the bar of Shepheard's, who was telling us how much he would rather be up in the Desert, fighting.

Add "if he's an officer" and "if he's lucky," and the remark has as much truth as most generalizations. In war, with those two reservations, you have free will to this extent; you can make a paper boat of your hopes and launch it on one of perhaps half a dozen available currents in the main stream. After that it will be carried along by events. My own paper boat had been carried into what seemed a backwater in Damascus. Luckier than most, I had been able to relaunch it with the Armoured Brigade. Now I was in a backwater again. Was it all luck? I have never, in my heart, been able to disclaim all responsibility for the turn events take in my life. The Brigade, I knew, would be going back to the Desert at any minute. And I did not intend to be left behind.

A letter arrived from Luke suggesting I should stay with him in Jerusalem where the cooler climate would give my skin a better chance to recover. He knew a skin specialist, Dr. Katzenellenbogen, who might be more experienced in such matters than the R.A.M.C.

Very tactfully, I discussed the idea with the doctor attending me. To my surprise he welcomed it. "I've heard of Katzenellenbogen. If you can get up there and if you are prepared to pay for your own treatment, of course go. Much the best thing."

I was wondering how I could borrow a Brigade car to drive me to Jerusalem before they left, when Alan walked into the ward. He gave me unexpected news of the Colonel, who had been posted as Second-in-Command of our Brigade. That in itself was an incentive to try and return to them speedily.

"This moment in the world's history is hardly the time for sentiment, I think you will agree," Alan said briskly. "The Brigadier has had to give Brunton your job, there is no alternative. If you come back to us when you are fit again—and you know we want you—it will have to be as a Captain. Meanwhile, if you can fix yourself a job in your present rank, no one will blame you."

The next evening I was drinking sherry in Luke's flat, overlooking the garden of Gethsemane on the Mount of Olives.

"It's nice to be up here," I said, "so far from anywhere that really matters . . ."

But the flat, with its pictures and books and modem comforts was, in a subtler way, more demoralizing than the military hospital; and so was Luke.

Remote, scholarly, refined, he made me feel like a barbarian; or rather, patched as I was in yellow and violet, like a uniformed baboon. He had none of the vanity, the ambition, which spurred Matthew and which I recognized in myself too. Jerusalem, less vulgar, less tumultuous, than Cairo, suited him perfectly. He, if anyone, had got the war he wanted.

"Why not join us in Psychological Warfare? The Colonel who runs it is a charming person. You'd love him, and I am sure he would find you a job."

It was a tempting suggestion. Also, it might be easier to be sent to the U.S.A. from here than from the Desert. I thought of Alan, Amos, the Colonel, and the rest now up there again. And I thought of Lucinda and Comus. On which current should I next launch my paper boat?

Katzenellenbogen saved me. A German by origin, he had lived his life in Jerusalem and looked like Beethoven. His anteroom was crowded with sick Arabs, whom probably he treated free. He spoke a fluent, pleasantly formal English, and I believed in him from the first moment.

I gave him my case history and he examined me. He laughed derisively at the caked patches of acriflavian and gentian on my body.

"I will give you some injections so that you will think I am doing something for you," he said; "but, frankly, all that is wrong is that your skin is better designed for those smooth green lawns in Oxford and Cambridge than for the Western Desert. Up here in Jerusalem you will get all right again in a week. After that . . ." He looked quizzically at me and shrugged his massive shoulders. "It will be your choice."

I saw him only twice again and briefly, for he was a busy man. He was disconcertingly blunt. But he was one of the very few people whose respect, I felt, was infinitely worth having. On my last visit he said, "You are young to be a Major, are you not? Have you deserved it or are you one of those from the King David?"

Probably I gave him a false answer to his question. But I think he read my mind as easily as my skin.

"In war there are only two kinds of Englishmen," he said as we parted, looking hard at me, "those who do far too little; and those who do far too much. No, I don't want to be paid. The air of Jerusalem has cured your skin; not me."

Before leaving Jerusalem, I gave Luke a message for Matthew, when he next saw him.

"I'm sorry you feel you must go," Luke said when I thanked him for his week's hospitality. "I adore this place myself. I think I shall stay here all my life."

He did.

By a paradoxical twist of fate the adventurous Matthew survived the war; Luke was killed shortly after it when the Stern Gang blew up the King David Hotel.

Hitch-hiking my way, I reached the Brigade H.Q. in the Desert two days later. There I substituted three pips for the crown on my shoulder; unreluctantly. I had always felt rather pompous as a Major.

I greeted the Colonel and I greeted Alan.

"You're just in time," they said. "We need a dogsbody to run the Officers' Mess."

"Glad to see you back," Muggs said gloomily. "The mucker . . ."

But I refused to listen to whatever grievance he was about to voice against my superior officer.

Everything had turned out for the best. Some miles to the rear Brunton struggled with the Brigade supply echelons, whereas I had a ringside seat for whatever excitements lay ahead. The memory of Jerusalem, with its doubts and temptations, faded as the guns rumbled their overture to the Battle of Alam Halfa.

CHAPTER TEN

Beachscape

RECENTLY I VISITED a therapist about my skin trouble, persistent to this day. He had done a friend of mine much good by subjecting him to a system of relaxation, which I thought I would try. He did me much good too, but that is neither here nor there. One of the exercises he prescribed, as I lay relaxed on his table, was to imagine myself sunbathing on a beach.

"Now," he would say, standing above me, his fingers pressed lightly on my eyes. "Leap up! Run for all you are worth down across the sand! Plunge into the clear blue water! Swim, swim! You are a very fast swimmer. Swim faster! You have swum half a mile. You turn without pausing and swim back again. Faster, faster! There! You are on the beach again. You run up the sand. You throw yourself down. You lie panting, utterly exhausted, in the hot sun. You breathe, slowly . . . slowly . . . Great lungfuls of breath . . ."

In these acquatic episodes, the beach I always visualized for the heroic swimmer, so different from my puffing dog-stroke self in real life, was a stretch of sand near Mersa Matruh.

It was an amazing beach, like a snowscape contrasted to the metallic blue-green of the sea. And where the dunes and beach joined, centuries of wind had piled the brilliantly white sand up into hard pinnacles, faintly striated with ochre and sienna, some of them twenty feet high, their tops blunt or crazily overhanging and about to break off. And a fresh layer of new-blown white sand covered all. The beach was a giant tray of creamy *millefeuille* pastry floating in cream and with more cream poured over it again. I drove there by myself one afternoon in late November 1942, to bathe and to brood.

I had a hangover. The previous night Amos and I had drunk too much captured vino to celebrate, though that is the wrong word, his posting back to a Staff College course in Haifa. Change was in the air. Alan had gone to command a Tank Regiment, the Colonel and the Brigadier were both expected to be promoted soon. I had few friends left within the Brigade. Victor Bone, Hilary, and Boy Harland were the only officers alive or unwounded in the Barsetshire Yeomanry as I had known it. I could no longer feel content with my sinecure on the Brigade H.Q.

In the killing-match, to use our own General's grim phrase, which lasted nearly a fortnight and on which the war hinged, the Division had paid the price of being "the finest armored unit in the world." On several occasions the sight of the General himself, so calm and immaculate in the midst of flurry, had made at least one irreverent Captain revise his attitude towards Generals. Now we had been resting for a fortnight, somewhat disgruntled at being left out of the chase, as the field swept on towards Benghazi and Agheila.

Unconsciously, I have adopted Victor Bone's sporting metaphor. So far as one could tell, he had actually enjoyed the carnage of Alamein and the subsequent break through; had even blown on his hunting-horn as we raced across the desert to cut off the German armor retreating by the coastal road. The operation had been brilliantly successful.

"We picked them off like pheasants," Victor announced after one particular engagement. I saw the pheasants. The charred face-less corpses in the burnt-out tanks would have cured me, had I needed curing, of any romantic illusions about war. But I had seen enough of the ghastly business by now to have none left. Though there had been moments, too, of extraordinary beauty, all of them at night; moments when terror was fused with ecstasy, as in the unforgettably resonant artillery barrage, which heralded El Alamein.

Basking in the wintry sun on the beach, I puzzled over this age-old dichotomy, over the poetry and the pity of a battle. I remembered some last-seen and characteristic attitude or gesture of friends so recently dead; Bubs Tregunter waving light-heartedly from his tank, Bobo Carstammers-Waghorn folding his sketch-pad with a sigh as the light failed, the evening before Alamein. And I thought of tracer bullets curving in lovely parabolas through the darkness, of the slow-falling flares spraying light on the enemy positions for our bombers to aim. "How can men survive such bombardment?" we had said. But many survived, as we knew to our cost next day. And the next night their bombers did the same to us.

And I thought of that other more marvelous beauty still, the beauty of men's courage. There had been, to quote but one example, the sappers crawling ahead of our tanks through the minefields. All the time they were under machine-gun fire and their officer calmly reported their inch-by-inch progress to us on his wireless. He was a heavenly man—and how that description would have surprised him.

It is only the fact of death, I reflected, which gives to battle its intense beauty, which lifts it above mere fireworks; as it is only the beauty which ennobles a battle scene into something more than a slaughterhouse. Why else should it always have been considered *better* to die in battle, than any other way?

"Let us drink to our death in battle." The rascally old Arab warrior with whom Amos and I occasionally lunched in Palestine used to give us the toast. Winking at one another, we drank it. The old Arab himself died soon afterwards in bed—of syphilis.

My beach was deserted, though I could see hundreds of soldiers' heads bobbing in the sea a mile farther along. If one of them drowned, his family would be consoled that, at least, he had died "on active service." I took a quick bathe myself, wondering whether, if I drowned now, Lucinda would feel similarly consoled. What did it matter? Death was the same. Burge had died in a silly accident. So had Muggs.

"You must be proud of him," I had written to the latter's wife; "he has died for his country." The sentiment had been nauseous to write. Yet I could not think of telling her the truth. A spark from the cigarette habitually drooping from his mouth had ignited a tin of petrol he was carrying. His screams haunted me on the beach, as they haunt me still. Many a garage attendant, smoking while he fills my car, has wondered since at my furious protests.

After bathing, I lay on the white sand, sheltered by a crusty pinnacle from the breeze which always springs up when I bathe. And my thoughts, as they often did in moments of leisure, turned to my meeting with Katzenellenbogen. "Those who do far too little and those who do far too much . . ." Which kind was I? Or rather, which kind did I wish to be? For compared to Alan, to Amos, to many of my friends, I certainly had very little so far with which to bore my grandchildren. Was it my own fault I wondered? In my heart, I felt that it was.

However, the means of adjusting this state of insufficiency lay to hand; to be exact, in the pocket of my tunic. I pulled Matthew's letter out and read it again.

"I've only just received your message from Luke," he wrote. "We are reorganizing and will be delighted to have you, if you are still keen. Send me back the enclosed form with your C.O.'s written consent and we'll fix the posting as soon as possible. How's the skin? A sea trip in a *caique* might be just the thing . . ."

The opportunity to refloat my paper boat on a new current had come again. It was necessary, only, to persuade Brunton to sign the form. He would hardly be sorry to see me go, though he might raise difficulties, to spite me.

Unexpectedly, Amos had approved the idea when I had told him of my decision to join Bomfrey's Boys. Three years earlier, when the war was still young, he would have said, "Don't be so bloody keen." Now he had just said, "Very sensible. I may turn up there myself some day. I am sick of being a Staff Officer. We're a smug crowd."

Though he was a far better soldier than he liked anyone to think, his caustic humor was not generally appreciated and perhaps lay behind his posting to Haifa.

There were other reasons, too, why I wanted to join Oliver and Matthew, all of them concerned, albeit confusedly, with Lucinda. The reasons were not very creditable, nor even very credible. I had a hunch that I might return to her more quickly that way than by remaining with a normal formation. A short raid, less dangerous than it looked, on the Greek Islands, followed by a lecture tour in the States? Something of the sort, anyhow, was at the back of my mind. The thought had been brewing for several months, ever since Burge's visit. At that time I held a responsible job and there could be no question of leaving it. Now, Brunton did the job better than I had done it, as I once told him.

"Oh, well, I'm a professional," he said modestly.

Pondering all this on the beach I was interrupted by the sight of a small dog trotting across the sands towards me. Surely I recognize you, I thought. A few seconds later Brunton himself came round the corner. He was naked and wet. But that was not what chiefly startled me. The whole top half of his body was tattooed. Snakes, mermaids, anchors, foliage, and the word "Brunton" were entwined over his orange flesh.

So that was why he never bathed in public.

He was a few feet away before he saw me. Then he stood spell-bound, staring at me with his mouth open, while a deep blush suffused his torso and face, accentuating the extraordinary blue designs.

"A young soldier in India . . . done as a joke . . . regretted it ever since . . ." he stammered.

Before I could speak, he turned and ran off again. His back, I noticed, was similarly tattooed.

The advantage was too opportune to be missed. Feeling kindlier towards Brunton than I had for many a long day, I visited him later that afternoon in his office tent. I showed him Matthew's letter and asked for his written consent.

He signed the form eagerly.

PART FOUR

Irregular

Sardinia, which is like nowhere. Sardinia, which has no history, no date, no race, no offering. Let it be Sardinia. They say neither Romans nor Phoenicians, Greeks nor Arabs ever subdued Sardinia. It lies outside; outside the circuit of civilization. Like the Basque lands. Sure enough, it is Italian now, with its railways and its motor omnibuses. But there is an uncaptured Sardinia still.

D. H. Lawrence

CHAPTER ELEVEN

Let It Be Sardinia

WE REACHED A TRANSIT CAMP outside Algiers on 14th June, six officers and fifty men tired and dirty from hastening three thousand miles across North Africa in summer dust and heat. Oliver and Matthew, who had flown to Algiers a fortnight earlier to plan the operation, whatever it might be, met us on arrival. They were living in great comfort on a Submarine Depot Ship in Algiers harbor, where we should all join them in a week. Beyond that clue, they refused for security reasons to tell us what we longed to know.

"It's a tricky operation but a worthwhile one, I think you'll agree," Matthew said. "Take all the exercise you can here. After that you'll be cooped up on the Depot Ship for briefing."

"And after that?"

"Come on," Oliver interrupted, looking at his watch. "We've got to rush back for that cocktail party. See you in a week."

They had given us little enough to speculate upon. We knew nothing of the next Allied strategic move beyond the common knowledge that a combined force was assembling in Algiers and Tunis to invade—where? Greece, Italy, Sicily, the South of France even? Presumably a submarine would drop us in one of those places as part of the invasion. On the whole, I was glad I should be landing by submarine rather than by parachute. I had not greatly enjoyed jumping out of aeroplanes.

Whichever place had been chosen for us was, I felt, a step in the direction of Lucinda and Comus. It had been for this I had left the Armoured Brigade at Agheila, and though, it is true, I had then flown several hundred miles in the wrong direction and spent five

pleasant months training, while the Brigade fought its way west-
wards (I had that on my conscience), still it looked now as if I had
reculé pour mieux sauter. Slightly ashamed of our long inactivity and
of our present queer company, Amos and I had visited the Brigade,
resting outside Tunis, on our way past. We had dined with the Colonel, now the Brigadier. He looked older and was in a sad mood.
Boy Harland had been killed at Enfidaville, Victor Bone and Hilary
had been missing since Mareth, believed prisoners of war in Italy.
And there had been many other losses.

"There's no one left from the old days," the Colonel sighed. "You
don't make new friends easily at my age. I wish someone would give
me a bowler hat."

The story of how Amos had joined me in Bomfrey's Boys cheered
him up. For Amos, wearying of what he called the sixth-form atmosphere of the Staff College, had simply walked out, taken the night
train from Haifa to Egypt and arrived the next day in our camp
on the Canal, seeking sanctuary. Only our sudden move out of the
Middle Eastern Command saved him from court-martial, an experience he often regretted having missed. "It would have been good
practice for what's awaiting me," he used to say.

As we left, the Colonel said, "By the way, look out for Alan in
Algiers. He's a Colonel now on Alex's staff. Let's all arrange to have
dinner at the Savoy around Christmas!"

It was the last time I saw the Colonel.

With our unusual luggage and equipment we must have been an
uncouth contingent, even for a transit camp. Our uniform, designed
originally by Oliver, but modified by each man to suit his individual tastes, struck a note of piratical elegance and variety, but the
orthodox Camp Commandant found our appearance displeasing.
However, on orders from above, he grudgingly did his best for us.
Thanks to Matthew and Oliver, the legend that we were hush-hush
troops to be left strictly to our own devices had preceded us. We fos-
tered it. Pleading lack of time, we peeled no potatoes. And our habit
of spending the nights out of the camp on training marches, and
our days in it asleep, immunized us from the routine chores, though
not from malaria which most of us contracted then, with disastrous
consequences.

The Commandant was glad when, at the end of the week, Matthew and Oliver collected us with lorries.

"Well, good luck Bomfrey's Boys," he said with forced jollity. "I suppose your outfit contributes something or other to the war effort."

Not that we had given him much to complain about. Our discipline was strict. No one had been drunk and disorderly. I think he would have preferred it if they had. It was simply our "difference" which annoyed him; that and being called "my dear" by the fantastic Fizzy.

The latter's real name was unpronounceable. He was called Fizzy because the first two syllables of it sounded like Fitzroy, and Fizzy suited his ebullient personality. Before the war, we gathered, he had been a cosmopolitan playboy. He had come out to Africa with the Free French, had fought at Bir Hacheim, and had been enrolled by Oliver one evening at the Mohammed Ali Club. He claimed, when incited, that he was a Polish Count, but Kempster, the only one of us who could pronounce Fizzy's real name, told us privately that that was nonsense and that he happened to know Fizzy was of Armenian Jewish extraction.

Kempster was one who always happened to know. More intellectual, less flamboyant and amusing than Fizzy, his own prewar life had run on similar, if less exalted, lines and the question which of them knew Paris the better was a constant point of friction. Once Amos, who disliked Kempster, called him "a poor man's Fizzy— almost moussec." Kempster turned red and for a moment I thought he was going to draw the Luger which at all times he carried pretentiously strapped to his leg.

"Oh, you English schoolboys and your humor," he growled instead.

Kempster was half-German. Perhaps because of that, perhaps because hitherto he had worked in an Intelligence department in Cairo and had seen nothing of the war, he was neurotically obsessed with some personal military ideal. To those, like Amos and myself, who looked upon the supposed toughness of our training as a tedious necessity, Kempster's evident delight in it all, and his pride in belonging to such an extraordinary organization as Bomfrey's Boys, appeared exaggerated and irritating. In retrospect I find him a rather pathetic character. Probably his mother weaned him too early or something. Personally, I got on well with him. I liked, in those days, to talk endlessly about Art and so did he.

Two sunny-faced young men called Jim and Bryan, recruited from an Infantry Regiment, made up our complement of officers. Suspicious at first of Fizzy, they had come to accept having their cheeks patted and being called "beautiful boys" by him. I often wondered what they wrote in their letters home to Aberdeen.

Most of our N.C.O.s and men were cast in the same mould as Jim and Bryan. For Matthew, though he agreed with Oliver that eccentrics might make good officers in this sort of unit, insisted that the men should be first-class soldiers by ordinary standards. Many of our privates had been N.C.O.s with their own Battalions and had voluntarily dropped their rank to join, though usually they were soon reinstated. It was a measure of the prestige which Matthew's personal exploits, coupled with Oliver's high-level string pulling, had built up for the unit during 1942, that we were allowed a high proportion of officers and N.C.O.s on our strength. None of the officers and few of the men who had helped Matthew and Oliver in those days were now left. Most of us were untried as small scale raiders. Our initial success would have to depend on what I have called latent Red Indianism; and on luck. Mostly on luck.

Driving through Algiers, a brief glimpse of the large hotels along the front and of the overhanging *kasbah* awakened happy memories of watching *Pépé le Moko* in the Curzon Cinema with Lucinda; the harbor too, where, if I remembered rightly, Jean Gabin had stabbed himself to death, while his mistress sailed away. Ah, the Curzon Cinema . . . It seemed long ago—on 21st June, 1943. The hotels were now military H.Q.s and the harbor had changed no less.

In the crowd of bustling warships and landing craft, loading up with tanks, troops, guns, and what not, the Submarine Depot Ship, newly painted in cream with a dark-blue band round the top of her hull, stood out with an air of prim innocence. A layman might have wondered at first, as I did, what this luxury-looking liner could be, anchored at this time in this place. Until he spotted the two or three long black shapes in the water beneath her. The sight of them startled me unpleasantly. Of course I had expected to see them as, at the dentist, you expect, but are still always dismayed to see the drill. Now they were a not wholly welcome reminder of the price to be paid for the past five months. Or, to take a more cheerful view, the price to be paid for returning to Lucinda. In that light I was more prepared to face submarines or any other bogies in the path.

While our launch chugged slowly through the dense harbor traffic, Oliver described the comforts in store for us. "Silver and glass on mahogany dining-tables . . . spring mattresses and hot water in the cabins . . . toast and butter with every meal . . . real whisky and Player's cigarettes on tap . . ." Oliver catalogued the attractions, and even Matthew, aquiline, brooding, nervous, ascetically indifferent to what he ate or how he slept, agreed morosely that the Navy knew how to do themselves well.

So, for a few days—we did not yet know how long—we were to live with the Navy. What was the Navy *like*? I had always wondered. Avid, in a superficial way, for new experience, I looked forward to the taste of a different sort of life, if only as an anodyne to fear. The Army was stale enough. The R.A.F. I could imagine without wishing to experience it. Through books, through visits to their Messes and airfields, I felt I knew the R.A.F. Besides, there it was flying about overhead all the time. But the Navy was unknown and mysterious. The typical Naval officer, if such existed, must be a dedicated man, a Captain Ahab, turned out from himself towards the elements to the point where extraversion becomes mysticism. Yes, that was it. Airmen and soldiers were poets, they knew ecstasy but within the bounds of earth. Sailors were mystics. It sounded paradoxical, because airmen flew and sailors stayed on the sea. But I felt it was so and, tentatively, I outlined my train of thought to Amos beside me. He had a headache from the sun.

"Oh, stop talking rubbish," he snapped irritably.

We arrived alongside. The vast pile of our extraordinary baggage accumulated on the virginally pure and gleaming quarter deck. Cases marked "High Explosive" and "Handle with Care," floppy deflated rubber boats like monstrous fish, strange bulky rucksacks, and assorted firearms . . . The pile grew and spread across the clean surface, leaving stains of grease and grime. Soon, however, we and our belongings had been removed from public view to a more seemly inconspicuity below decks.

There, in the well-ordered interior, we set up immediately on arrival our own characteristic island of confusion and hubbub, in a small cabin allotted to us for an office. The shape of our future, which Matthew and Oliver now unfolded to us, was briefly this.

The Allied Army was to land in Sicily on 10th July. German torpedo-bombers, based on Sardinian airfields, might do great damage to the fleet of transports. The R.A.F. had attacked and would continue to attack those airfields but, to supplement this vital work, a submarine would put three parties of Bomfrey's Boys ashore on the west coast of Sardinia on the nights of 30th June, 1st and 2nd July. At the same time a second submarine would land a fourth party on the east coast to form a base, on which the others would converge and from which they would all be evacuated on 24th July.

The three assault parties, each consisting of two officers and twelve men, would split after landing to attack separate airfields, so that six airfields would be covered in all. The patrols, as we called them, to be coupled initially would be Bryan's and Kempster's, Amos's and mine, Matthew's and Jim's, and they would be dropped off the submarine in that order. There were, obviously, innumerable hazards; the submarine journey, the landing in rubber dinghies, the approach march across wild unknown country occupied, we must assume, by a hostile civil population, the difficulty of entering the airfields and of placing time-bombs on the planes, the still longer escape march across Sardinia to the R.V. on the east coast and, trickiest part of all, the eventual take-off by rubber dinghy and submarine again.

Having conceived the plan and committed us to it, Matthew and Oliver were anxious to hear that the rest of us approved.

"I think we should all look at it like this," Matthew said. "There are roughly two hundred German bombers dispersed over the half-dozen airfields we hope to attack. Each bomber is potentially capable of sinking a troop-carrier, that is of putting perhaps 2,000 men out of action before the Sicily landing. If, between us, we succeed in destroying only one German bomber, then the operation will have been worth attempting. And, of course, I believe we shall destroy many more than that."

Oliver and Fizzy, as the least athletic of us, were to form the base party on the east coast. They alone would have a wireless set and, scanning the Mediterranean from their hilltop, they might be able to send back priceless information of enemy fleet movements, while they waited for us to reach them.

"Why, even if the rest of you do nothing," Oliver exclaimed, suffering perhaps from a sense of inferiority about his own role, "it is conceivable that Fizzy and I might spot the *Scharnhorst* and get her sunk. That alone would justify the whole operation."

Anarchic though the organization of Bomfrey's Boys was in many respects, we accepted Matthew's and, to a lesser degree, Oliver's leadership unquestioningly. After all, they had done these things before, we had not. Moreover, they were not, like the Duke of Plaza-Toro, leading their troops from behind. They were themselves involved in the operation as much as anyone. In a way the craziness of the project was its attraction. Whatever each of us may have felt privately about the chances of success, we agreed with them now that it was well worth attempting.

The Captain of the Submarine Flotilla under whose orders we came, was known as Captain "S." The impersonality of the name added to the nightmarish Kafka-esque feeling that was growing in me. We only met him once, on the first evening, at a conference to go through the plans. As the details had already been worked out by Matthew and Oliver with the Naval and Military staffs, the conference was a polite formality to put Captain "S" in the picture. He was a tall gaunt man, like a mastiff dressed in white. Here, I thought, is my Ahab, my mystic. We sat on a row of chairs in front of him at his desk. A map of the western Mediterranean, showing Sardinia, hung behind. On this Oliver explained our military objectives and the two submarine commanders plotted the route they were proposing to take. Most of the time Captain "S" listened silently, the gloom of his expression intensifying. One felt that, with so much else on his mind at present, he could raise only moderate interest in our little venture. He exchanged a few technicalities about "danger spots" with the submarine commanders. Once, pointing to an area off the Sardinian coast we should have to pass through, he said: "Some nasty accidents there lately." It was like being under an anesthetic and listening at the same time to the surgeons discussing the geography of one's stomach.

Captain "S" rose, at length, to indicate that the conference was over.

"Well, gentlemen," he said; "good luck to you all. I'm sorry to say that I think you have a very slender chance of survival."

And on that cheerful note we filed out. The odd thing was that I felt more exhilarated than depressed by the interview with Captain "S." I was, I knew, entering on the crisis of my war. I had been away three and a half years. It was all or nothing now; the higher the stakes, the higher my claim to repatriation when the immediate battle was over. Or so the confused argument ran in my head. But it was not really a matter of argument, it was a matter of faith. I believed that I was heading at last for home, by whatever devious route. I continued to believe it, against much evidence. To amuse me, Matthew and Oliver had arranged with G.H.Q. in Algiers that the whole operation should be called "Swann." Superstitiously, I took that as a good omen. And if I was to go down, I was touched that I should be doing so in the name, so to speak, of Proust's most famous character.

A general in the War Office, one of the rugged sort, whose cooperation I was seeking to include two pretty A.T.S. sergeants on an Establishment, once told me that in his opinion all irregular formations and private armies like Bomfrey's Boys contributed precisely nothing to Allied victory. All they did was to offer a too-easy, because romanticized, form of gallantry to a few antisocial irresponsible individualists, who sought a more personal satisfaction from the war than that of standing their chance, like proper soldiers, of being bayoneted in a slit-trench or burnt alive in a tank. He went so far as to hint that Bomfrey's Boys in particular had caused more dislocation to its own side than it ever had to the enemy.

I never argue with Generals. This one was much bescarred with wounds and beflagged with medals for bravery, gained fighting like a proper soldier, so I felt he was entitled to his point of view. Besides, I thought he was perfectly right.

The theory, held by most of us, that so far from being tough little heroes, we were simply escapists, used to infuriate the militaristic Kempster. Nor did anyone on the Depot Ship, except perhaps Kempster again, delude himself that what we were setting out to attempt would make the smallest difference to the Sicily landing. Doubtless our presence in Sardinia would cause mild alarm in German and Italian circles on the island, but, at a tenth of the cost, a flight of Spitfires could do more damage in ten seconds on the air-fields than we were ever likely to do in three weeks. If we were eager, light-heartedly enough, to undertake Operation Swann, it was for the adventure itself rather than for its military significance. To keep our self-respect we had to do something and Sardinia sounded as nice a place as another to do it in. Let it be Sardinia . . .

As for the General's other charge, dislocating our own side was our favorite sport. "It is the peculiarity of small-scale operations that they appear to require more preparation and to cause more trouble all round than one of General Montgomery's full-dress battles." (I quote from the last letter I had time to write to Lucinda and which was posted to her after we had left.) "Weeks of careful planning pre-cede them, planning down to the smallest detail. Yet when the Day approaches everything has been altered—even, perhaps, the purpose of the operation itself; there is a hectic last-minute rush for different maps, new equipment, whatever the latest brainwave has discovered to be 'absolutely essential' to success; a new design in pistol holsters or boots, which can only be procured in the time by dispatching a valuable officer to G.H.Q. for the necessary Special Authority for their release or manufacture, and then to search exhaustively all the Ordnance Depots and Workshops in the neighborhood. Usually he is successful, and returns proudly with the fruits of his mission, to find they are already out of date. Another and still better design in boots or pistol holsters has been discovered meanwhile, and another valuable officer is even now at G.H.Q. demanding a Special Author-ity . . . The confusion in the small cabin where we all work is inde-scribable. Thirty sets of maps, each set of a dozen sheets covering the country we are concerned with in varying scales, are piled on the floor, the table, the bunk, in hopeless muddle. The patient Bryan, our map officer, sorts them into tidy, intelligible heaps every night, but by the next evening they have become muddled again. They must be kept in this one place and not taken to our individual cab-ins, for security reasons. Besides the maps, there are countless air photographs to be studied in the stereoscope; cases of special stores too valuable to be dumped with the rest of our kit in the ship's hold; binoculars, compasses, a new design in knife wire cutters; experi-mental rations which the unashamedly greedy Oliver insists on sam-pling; top secret Intelligence reports and old tourist guide books;

specimens of the latest idea in boots, weapons, hats . . . There are at all times six of us trying to concentrate on the work in hand while another six, visitors from the Army, Navy, or Air Force H.Q.s, offer help and advice. Alan, for instance, who sends his love . . ."

To be fair to Bomfrey's Boys, on this occasion much of the confusion was due to stroke upon stroke of unpredictable bad luck. Operation Swann seemed ill fated from the start. The first blow fell the same evening, after the conference with Captain "S."

Appropriately it was Alan, who had so often influenced the course of my life in the war, who brought the news. In planning the Army side of Operation Swann, Matthew and Oliver had seen much of him at G.H.Q. in the past fortnight, so that when, after dinner, he arrived unexpectedly on the Depot Ship, we assumed he was paying us a social visit. But he was not. And what should have been, for Amos and myself, a delightful reunion turned into a fierce quarrel.

"I'm afraid you're not going to like this a bit," Alan said at once to Matthew and Oliver in his inimitably direct manner. "But the C. in C. has decided that you both know far too much about coming events to be allowed to land in an enemy country ten days before 'Husky' starts. So I'm afraid you'll both have to stay behind."

No need to describe the general consternation, the storm of protests, that followed. The sudden decision, if somewhat late in the day, was reasonable. And it was, Alan assured us, absolutely final. I suspect he had had something to do with it behind the scenes. If so, it was characteristic of him to come and see the situation through himself.

Oliver, caught out at last by his own love of sharing in secrets of State, felt he had been made ridiculous. He rushed off to protest in person but was properly snubbed for his pains. Seeing protests were futile, Matthew recovered his temper quickly and set about briefing us for all he was worth. He worked himself to a ghost in the six days that were left. Amos and I understood exactly how he felt. As it happened we were soon to feel exactly the same.

The next morning three of our men went ill, complaining of severe headaches. And Fizzy, falling downstairs after breakfast, dislocated his knee. I visited him in the sick bay. To my embarrassment he was weeping, partly with the pain, mostly with vexation.

"My dear, two things are driving me mad!" he said. "One is that of course everyone will say I am glad of this excuse not to go on the operation. The other is that they will be right!"

Fizzy's self honesty was always delightful. Later in the war he redeemed this set-back, landing by parachute on the roof of the Monte Carlo casino. Which, for him, was home. I believe he is still there.

Each day more men, though no more officers, fell sick. We had been eating mepocrine pills for weeks, so no one diagnosed malaria. Their complaint was attributed to the richness of Naval food after years of an Army diet.

Among many visitors, I recall a native of Sardinia, who painted a gloriously over-optimistic picture of the food and water we should find there (for we would have to live off the land); and an American Major, who lectured us solemnly on how to behave if we were taken prisoner. Having stressed the importance of giving nothing away under interrogation, he went on to list a few of the pleasant methods, thumbscrews and that sort of thing, that might be used to squeeze further information from us.

"Ah, well," he concluded, looking round at us, "I guess you boys are tough. You'll take it, I'm sure."

I dare say he was doing his best.

"I'm beginning to feel I have a rendezvous with death after all," Amos muttered when he had gone. We liked quoting poetic tags at each other.

By the time we were due to sail, Operation Swann had virtually been replanned. All the original patrols had been reconstituted and only three airfields were to be attempted. Kempster and Jim would leave the submarine on successive nights to tackle one small airfield each. Amos and I would land together two nights later, farther north on the west coast, to attack a larger airfield near Alghero, with possibly a second one afterwards on our route south-eastwards. Bryan replaced Oliver and Fizzy in the base party.

Nominally, I was now in command of the operation. I say nominally, because as we all worked independently the question of one commander hardly arose, except on the submarine journey. But the fact that I was in command has some importance to the story later.

To top everything, Amos and I both developed septic feet. In an excess of zeal, we had blistered them badly during a training march in the transit camp. Amos's were not serious or so he maintained.

But my old skin trouble was at work and mine looked awful. At the last minute and as a precaution, in case Amos and I were unfit to land, Matthew borrowed a spare officer from S.O.E., a fiery Frenchman called Gaston. He was to be briefed in our role during the submarine journey.

We embarked—squeezed would be a better word—on our submarine, H.M.S. *Tiber*, on the evening of 27th June, five officers and twenty-four men. At the same time Bryan and his party left on their submarine. I remember looking back at the Depot Ship, before I, too, disappeared after the rest down the hatch. Matthew and Oliver were leaning over the handrail, watching. At that moment the ship's bugler sounded the dinner-call. In a few minutes they would be sitting round the mahogany table, with its china and glass and toast and butter, and I should have begun my journey. I waved to them.

For the only time in my life, I felt like a great tragic actor.

CHAPTER TWELVE

The Submarine

FOR THE LAST YEAR of the war, having no strong desire left for glory but a great urge to prolong my own life into the post-war epoch, I worked as a Staff Officer planning operations for others to carry out. So it was that, helping to clear up some old files in the War Office after the Armistice, I came upon one labeled "Operation Swann." On the premonition that I might some day wish to write about these things, I appropriated the file. Which accounts, perhaps, for the fact that no mention is made of Operation Swann by Sir Winston Churchill in the fifth volume of his book, where he deals with the Sicilian campaign.

It is a thick file, containing several drafts of Outline Plans, amended here and there in Oliver's handwriting; long lists of stores, in which Matthew's meticulous attention to detail is recognizable; reports by the submarine commanders and by an R.A.F. pilot; an appendix labeled "Lessons learnt for future use"; and then, inevitably, where information would be most interesting, silence.

The file has lain on my desk many days now, guiding me in my labors and reminding me, though I find it hard to believe, that I am the same person whose name is occasionally mentioned. It has been a curious experience to read it all again, like reading one's obituary notice. Without my letters to Lucinda to help me out, I shall perhaps quote from the file from time to time.

The captain of H.M.S *Tiber*, called Grigson, was, on a first impression, a different type to most submarine commanders. With surprise and alarm, we detected a feeling of tension between him and his officers; Chiefy, the engineer; Jimmy, the first lieutenant; and the two remaining junior officers, very young men indeed whose actual job I never made out, though they were always busy on watch or elsewhere, when not snatching a quick sleep in their bunks. One, tall and lugubrious, was nicknamed Death, because of his unusual pallor. In the other, Craps, I discovered a passion for music and he had on board a good collection of classical records which, for fear of detection, could not be played at sea. Enemy asdic apparatus was said to be particularly sensitive to the sound of Beethoven.

The tiny wardroom had now to accommodate six more of us; Kempster, Jim, Amos, Gaston, myself, and "Gruff." The last was a small-boat specialist, attached to us, with two sailors, by the Navy to help inflate the rubber dinghies and generally to speed us off the submarine, when, surfaced a mile or two off the Sardinian coast, every second would be precious. Gruff was a cheerful faun-like person who played the penny whistle.

Amos and I had come aboard with bandaged feet, armed with further dressings and medicine. We had four or five days on board in which to cure ourselves, before reaching our dropping-off point. Gaston meanwhile stood ready to replace, perhaps to accompany us, whichever we decided. Amos and I were determined he should do neither and that we should be fit in time.

Our twenty-four men were crowded in the fore-ends. Half-naked, sweating, unshaven, sprawled among the forest of meaningless tubes and levers and technical gadgets, they looked like part of a scene in any submarine-film drama.

The eighteen-hour day periods, spent submerged, were not unpleasant. We slept and read and listened to Gruff's penny whistle. Above all, we looked forward to the joys of surfacing after nightfall, to breathing the cool fresh air pumped through the ship, to smoking cigarettes, and to eating the excellent Naval food—dinner first and then breakfast six hours later before diving again.

More of our men went down with malaria, though we attributed their headaches, difficulty in breathing, and lack of appetite to their conditions of living. "Just claustrophobia, lack of air, heat exhaustion . . ." we diagnosed hopefully when faced on the first morning by the ghastly apparition of Guardsman Jones. In normal health and looking his best, Guardsman Jones, with his close-set eyes and low forehead, with his absence of front teeth except for two molar tusks, and his huge wrists, would have been well cast as one of the crowd in some melodramatized version of the French Revolution. Now his appearance was terrifying. He choked and retched, writhing pitifully on the deck. There was nothing we could do. The submarine could not be brought to the surface on his account and there were many hours still before nightfall. He looked as if he might die before then. His was the worst case. He grew better, returned eventually to port, where he was put in hospital with malaria. Others suffered less, maintained they would be all right once they got in the air and were allowed to disembark with their parties. They seemed to recover outside but later, on shore, succumbed again. The week in the transit camp had indeed been disastrous.

"Lithium hydroxide was placed throughout the boat after twelve hours every day," I read in Grigson's subsequent report. He goes on to say that "this freshened the atmosphere considerably but the general malaise of the troops, who were unaccustomed to submarine life, still persisted."

On the morning of 29th June, his voice on the loudspeakers announced to the ship that we were now lying at periscope depth one mile off the enemy coast. Any alteration in "trim" might result in the ship coming on to the surface by mistake; every man on board must keep absolutely still . . . There was no danger of anyone moving. Personally, I hardly dared to breathe.

After making his periscope reconnaissance and identifying the correct point on the coast for the first landing, Grigson turned back out to sea to wait for nightfall. After dark—there was a new moon which set early—we came in again on the surface, to two miles off shore where we anchored quietly.

Gruff and his two sailors went on to the casing first to inflate and lower the boats. When these were ready, the word was passed down to Kempster and his patrol who were waiting below. Tense excited faces under the American pith helmets (chosen finally as our headgear), brave attempts at joke-making, cheerful "so long's" and "good luck's" . . . Kempster and the others, hauling waterproofed packs, pressed their way past us, through the narrow bulkhead, up through the gun-tower hatch into the darkness outside on the casing. It was a calm starry night. The party "got off" all right, though Gruff told me when he came down again they had been slower and clumsier than he expected. "It was most marked when disembarking that the troops displayed an unnatural dullness and had to be shepherded to their boats, and seemed to have small mental grip on the situation." I quote Grigson's report again.

Within half an hour we were heading out to sea, all thinking, though nothing was said, of the others paddling slowly towards the dim unknown coastline in two small rubber dinghies.

Grigson, watching the shore from the turret, saw no lights or flashes. A good sign. As we enjoyed our breakfast we felt they must by now have landed successfully and unopposed.

The following day and night we repeated the same process with Jim and his party.

Amos and I would be dropped off two nights later—2nd July. Our feet had healed adequately and we wondered how to explain most tactfully to Gaston that he would not be needed. We liked him and admired his keenness and had no doubts of his ability. But this, we felt, was our "party," what we had trained and waited for many months. Two officers were enough for the job allotted to us—a third would be an embarrassment and, in any case, an extravagance. His own unit had generously lent him to fill a possible gap if we were unfit. Now we were fit, the gap needed no filling. But it was going to be difficult to persuade the blood-thirsty and enthusiastic Frenchman to return peaceably to port.

The problem solved itself unexpectedly. Amos and I sat in the wardroom discussing these matters in whispers, while Gaston snored in a bunk—he had an enviable capacity for sleep. We waited for Grigson and Gruff to come down with the news that Jim had been successfully launched into the dark night waters. Gruff came first. Yes, everything had been all right, though rather slow. The nervousness of a first operation. We felt the vibration as the submarine began to move out to sea. We poured drinks and thought of Jim and his men paddling, and how we, too, in forty-eight hours . . .

Suddenly Grigson appeared. He looked pale and serious. "I am afraid I have some bad news for you . . ." And we felt that chilly sinking sensation, which the announcement of some unforeseen and unknown piece of bad news always gives.

"The rest of the operation will have to be canceled. I'm turning straight back to port now. I'm terribly sorry, but it's out of the question to go on . . . Lucky if we can get her back . . . Shouldn't have risked coming so far, really . . . Just been talking to Chiefy, and he says . . ." (Technicalities about engine troubles I couldn't understand. His first sentence stunned me and I hardly listened to the rest, anyway.)

He finished apologizing and left to deal with the crisis and to signal our return before we dived. Gruff murmured sympathetically. Gaston, whom we had woken to tell the news, swore in a mixture of French and American slang. Amos and I stared at each other blankly and poured another drink to help us re-orientate our ideas.

I suppose we both felt secretly relieved. I did, among a turmoil of other feelings; shame, that I should be relieved; anger against myself for being a coward, against Grigson for having a submarine which broke down and thus betrayed me to myself; guilt towards Jim and Kempster who were now who could tell where, while I, their leader, was sailing safely homewards. A hodge-podge of thoughts and feelings, reason and will battling as ever with the more powerful instinct of self-preservation. Or perhaps it was primarily a struggle between a sense of relief and a sense of hurt pride; of lowered prestige. We had set off gloriously—now we were returning ignominiously.

I slept for a while on the wall-seat. I dreamt, I forget what, and in my dreams I heard music—strange pipe music that Pan might play, a watery tune without beginning or end, a merry brook-like tune entering my unconscious from some other world. I was half-awake and yet the tune continued—it was near and real and, as I adjusted myself back to my surroundings and recognized them, I puzzled over it. Until raising my head I saw the jolly faunish face of Gruff playing his penny whistle. It was a delightful noise and I shall never forget the strange experience of waking to the sound of that tune in the wardroom of a submarine. Gruff maintained he was playing the old song, "Dinah," but, to me, it sounded and still sounds quite unlike it—belonging to an age many centuries earlier. It could have been introduced into *L'Après-midi d'un faune* without Debussy himself noticing any difference.

Gruff's music so stimulated and refreshed us that, as we ate breakfast, Amos and I made plans. When we reached Algiers we would charter an aeroplane and carry out our operation by parachute. There was still time, if the plane could be managed. We could reach our objective quicker that way, without the long approach march from the coast. Then we could rejoin the others at Bryan's base. The take-off from there was not arranged until 24th July. If we attacked our objective on the 8th or 9th July, we should still have a fortnight in hand to reach the base. And what a triumph over Providence to succeed in spite of this setback! We infected each other with enthusiasm and the craven misgivings, though ineradicable, were at least properly subordinated to the greatness of the Idea.

By the time a tired and harassed Grigson came for his breakfast he found us wonderfully recovered from the shock of disappointment. Of course we still had to reach port. Grigson and Chiefy were worried. The trouble lay with the batteries, I gathered. We had dived as usual before dawn and had covered about thirty miles from the coast when something else went wrong. My technical knowledge is limited, but I believe that the electrically controlled hydroplanes aft jammed as a result of the weakness of the batteries.

Suddenly the klaxon sounded "diving stations" over the ship— always an alarming noise. "Diving stations" at this time of day, when we had only been "dived" an hour or two was particularly alarming, at least to the uninitiated. Amos and I were very soon wide awake and wondering. A sailor rushed into the wardroom and "stood-to" the many little gadgets along the wall, which red notices ordered no one to play with.

In the wardroom was a large dial face and a needle, showing the submarine's depth in feet. Normally it registered fifty when submerged. Now we noticed the needle moving slowly round—70, 80, 90 . . . It reached 150 after minutes which seemed hours. Grigson's voice barked orders on the loudspeaker—unintelligible technical orders. His voice—and how carefully we listened—was calm; but, we could tell, only just calm. We could easily detect the excitement underneath. The submarine, Grigson himself had told us, was not designed to go deeper than 200 feet. It might manage 250. The needle stayed at 150. And then it began to swing back, slowly. 140, 130, 120 . . . We sighed, very softly.

But at 50, it didn't stop. 40, 30, 20 . . . and then the unmistakable motion of being on and not under the sea.

And it is under, rather than on, the sea one would prefer to be in a submarine in broad daylight, thirty miles off an enemy coast, when that coast is known to be vigilantly patrolled from the air.

Everyone was busy, very busy, except ourselves. Amos and I pretended to read; Gaston, who had never woken up when "diving stations" sounded, continued to sleep and we decided to leave him in peace, much as we envied him. From time to time one of the ship's officers would rush by, a very dour Chiefy, a more-than-ever-pallid Death. Craps, suddenly old for his age and unusually quiet, came and asked me for any secret documents—he was standing by to destroy all the ship's papers. I gave him our Operation Order. Gruff, who slept in the ship's office, arrived in the wardroom. He was cheerful as ever, but he had with him a waterbottle and some emergency rations and was wearing his water-wings, deflated. Amos and I rather ineffectually looked around for our own. It was difficult to believe this nightmare was in fact reality. We decided to let Gaston sleep on a little longer. Except for occasional orders on the loudspeaker the submarine was very quiet. The engines had stopped. We could hear the sea lapping against the casing outside, just above the level of our heads. An hour passed.

Then the engines started again. How good it was to feel the vibration and how still more good to hear the rushing, sucking noise she made as she dived. We watched the depth-meter. The needle began to move round—20, 30, 40 . . . We held our breath. 50 . . . the needle quivered there and stopped. And continued to stop.

We sighed, but this time loudly.

Later the same day Amos sat reading a pocket edition of *Alice Through the Looking Glass*, his inseparable companion through the war.

"This really is an extraordinary book," he said suddenly. "There is something in it to fit every situation in life. The Red Queen is giving Alice her directions. She says 'A pawn goes two squares in its first move, you know. So you'll go very quickly through the Third Square—by railway, I should think—and you'll find yourself in the Fourth Square in no time. Well, *that* square belongs to Tweedledum and Tweedledee—the Fifth is mostly water—the Sixth belongs to Humpty Dumpty. But you make no remark?'"

"Do *I* make no remark or is that what it says?"

"Both. Doesn't anything strike you about the order of Squares?"

Nothing had struck me. My attention was elsewhere. Much pre-occupied at this time with the prospect of reaching thirty, I was try-ing to write a poem about Life. How little of my own could I look back upon with pride, with a sense of achievement! I had enjoyed every minute of it, of course, but nothing really worth doing had been done. Now it was going, in the Red Queen's words, faster . . . faster . . . And the dreadful climacteric lay only three months ahead—on 30th September.

"Well," Amos explained, "the first three were the Yeomanry, not that we passed through quickly. The Fourth—Tweedledum and Tweedledee—was the Armoured Division. I see us being now in the Fifth Square—mostly water. We have had a check but we shall over-come it and enter the next."

"The Sixth belongs to Humpty Dumpty, you said?" I asked vaguely.

"Yes. Sardinia . . . Mussolini . . . He hasn't had a fall yet, but he soon will. We're bound for the Sixth Square."

"Oh."

CHAPTER THIRTEEN

The Approach

When we reached the aerodrome at 5 p.m., 7th July, they told us the plane would leave at eight and not, as arranged, at nine. This meant that Matthew, who had gone to fetch some essential air photos arriving by plane on another airfield, would not be able to bring them to us before we left. We pictured him tearing on to the ground in a cloud of dust in his jeep, just as we roared over his head in our four-engined Halifax. However, it couldn't be helped and we discussed the question of our dropping zone with the pilot and his navigator. Without the photos, they would have to work off the map and use their judgment. We should have to trust to our luck.

While we had been away on the submarine, Air Reconnaissance had located a new and important German landing ground right in the center of Sardinia, near Ottana. With the combined string-pulling of Alan, Oliver, and Matthew behind us, Amos and I had been able to persuade the various authorities to agree to our attacking this new objective and to lend us a bomber equipped for parachuting. The Ottana landing ground had several advantages over our previous target near Alghero. For one thing, it was fifty miles nearer to our R.V. on Mount Alberu. For another, we could be dropped close to it, in the broad valley of the river Tirso, so that we should easily be able to carry out our attack before the Sicilian landings began on 10th July. In any case, the time of moon-set made the night 9th/10th July the last night feasible for such an attack.

The aeroplane could carry six of us altogether, so we had had to choose two men each from the available dozen still uninfected by malaria on the Depot Ship. It had been a difficult, because seemingly invidious choice, where every man, from the point of view of keenness and fitness, had an equal claim. So, inevitably, we picked our friends. I took Brown and Fry, who had been two of the Barsetshire Yeomen recruited from the Armoured Division by Burge. Amos took Cope and Morris. They had been bred within a few miles of his ancestral home. The feudal instinct, even in so liberal and bohemian a character as Amos, dies hard.

We filled in the three hours before take-off by practice-fitting the parachute harness over our equipment, now reduced to a minimum—or the maximum that we could safely drop with on us, for we had decided against containers. We stuffed our feather sleeping-bags between our seats and the harness—a useful precaution. An expert "despatcher," loaned to us for the flight, ran through the drill. We had never dropped "through the floor" before, having trained in the door method. The R.A.F. staff were very efficient and helpful and kind, like doctors and nurses before a serious operation.

We ate a scrappy dinner in the R.A.F. Mess—a bare depressing place with terrible food, which, though we knew we ought to eat, we yet had no appetite for. Nor did two whiskies help much. The pit-of-the-stomach feeling was intolerable. I privately cursed our enthusiasm and hoped that the plane would be canceled, miraculously, at the last minute. I wanted some adequate excuse not to have to go, to be allowed to return peacefully to my bed on board the Depot Ship. And yet I knew, too, that that was not what I wanted. I prayed that the suspense might end quickly, and that I might find myself on my feet in Sardinia with too much else to worry about to think of fear.

"For Christ's sake, let's get it over," I prayed, if that is a prayer.

After much hearty hand-shaking we were crammed on board the plane, six grotesque figures in American helmets, with rucksacks bulging through the harness on our chests, the packed chutes on our backs and sleeping-bags protruding like bustles behind. We settled down as comfortably as we could on the floor, wedged against each other and the fuselage. Our equipment served as cushions and some of us managed to sleep. When I wasn't asleep, I sat huddled in a coma of sheer funk, wondering how I should find the strength, when the time came, to move myself down the plane to that hole. The hole was decently covered with a detachable wooden lid. I kept peeping morbidly in its direction; my eyes were drawn towards it, in spite of

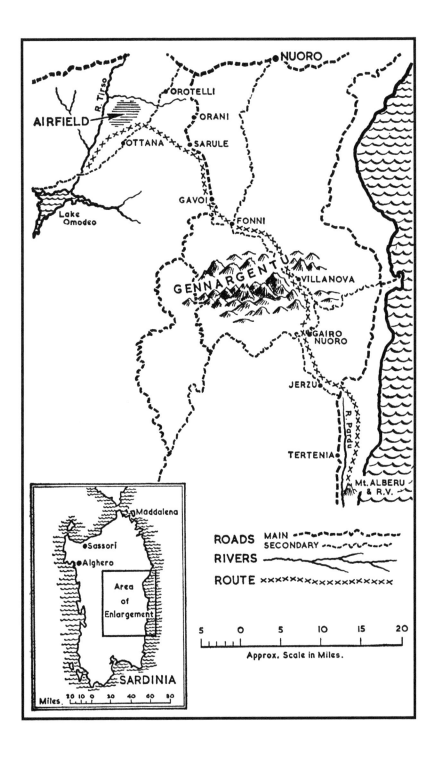

NUORO

OROTELLI

AIRFIELD

R. Tirso

ORANI

OTTANA

SARULE

GAVOI

Lake
Omodeo

FONNI

GENNARGENTU

VILLANOVA

GAIRO
NUORO

JERZU

R. Pardu

TERTENIA

Mt. ALBERU
& R.V.

Maddalena

Sassori

Alghero

Area
of
Enlargement

SARDINIA

Miles. 20 10 0 20 40 60 80

ROADS MAIN
        SECONDARY
RIVERS
ROUTE ×××××××××××××××××××

5   0   5   10   15   20

Approx. Scale in Miles.

my determination to pay no attention, to think of something else . . .
Inside the plane a dim red light outlined the shapes of Amos and the
other four. So far as I could see, they sat staring ahead at nothing—
or perhaps they were asleep. Brown, the next to me, I could study
more clearly. His eyes were shut, his very fair skin was a chalky white,
his features rigid, purposeful. He looked braver than I felt. Afterwards he told me he had not been scared in the plane, just bored.

10.45 P.M. The pilot told the despatcher, who wore earphones,
that we were now over the island. The plane shook slightly and
bumped—"a spot of flak," the despatcher explained, who had it from
the pilot.

Now the pilot was following the river which guided him to the
Dropping Zone. He said he could see clearly where he was. The despatcher beckoned us to our stations round the hole. When we were
seated he removed the lid. I peered down the short funnel. The earth
was quite clear in the moonlight, grey and flat and muddy looking,
intersected with dark lines, like an estuary at low tide. There seemed
to be no connection between it and us, no bond of gravitation.

The pilot messaged he was circling over the D.Z. now; it looked
deserted and suitable, the wind was 5 m.p.h. and he gave us the map
references. The despatcher nodded to me and I swung round so that
I was sitting over the hole, my legs dangling into it. I watched the
small electric panel for the signal lights, red for "Action Stations,"
green for "Go." The others were ready to follow in the order Brown,
Fry, Morris, Cope, Amos. I tried to smile at them, but I don't think
the smile ever reached as far as my face, it stuck somewhere between
my heart and my windpipe. The red light . . . I slipped forward over
the hole, my weight carried on my arms, waiting for green: Merci-
fully it came quickly—a few seconds.

I saw the light and the despatcher shouting "Go." A mighty rush
of air, the sensation of a piece of fluff in a whirlwind, and then a
great quietness and peace and exhilaration. It was always, for me,
a wonderful feeling of relief to find that the chute had opened and
that I was suspended safely, and apparently motionless, over the
earth. Many people, at that moment, break into song . . .

The ground below still looked a mud flat, a grey, dead color. It
was like floating down on to the moon—any place where no one
lived or had ever lived. After half a minute the earth began to rise

up at me and I could recognize the shapes of low bushes and rocks. I wondered, strangely without fear, if I should break my legs. I remembered "feet and knees together," the old maxim so emphasized in the training, and I strained in the harness to keep my weight well forward. I was swinging gently and I tried to gauge the distance, anticipate the moment of impact . . . Here it comes . . . Bump. The others, too, landed safely and we joined up.

It is always interesting, arriving in a new country which one has studied carefully beforehand from photographers, maps, and books, to see how far the mental picture tallies with the real one. In the past fortnight I had studied Sardinia very thoroughly in various topographical surveys and in air photographs. But what can you really learn about a country from such things? The landscape varied, so one guide book had said, between "high and wild mountain ranges where the only vegetation is 'maquis' or thorny scrub; undulating rocky pastureland for goats and sheep; populous fertile plains yielding rich crops of grapes, fruit, olives, corn," and so on. The only features common throughout the island appeared to be the "nuraghe," a prehistoric type of conical stone hut, and the Sardinian peasant in his long, black, woollen cap and white stockings. Now here we were, after so little effort, standing on Sardinian soil when three hours before we had been in North Africa.

By moonlight, the landscape resembled nothing I had imagined. We were on a plain, but parched, rocky, and barren, stretching away in all directions. Not a "nuraghe" nor a black-capped, white-hosed peasant to be seen. The landscape was so bare, we had difficulty in finding bushes thick enough to conceal our chutes.

The question was now to check our position. If we had landed where the pilot thought, the Tirso should be a few hundred yards north-east, and we set off to find it. Later we grew accustomed to walking calmly by night across enemy country. On this, our first experience of the sort, we stopped continually, fingering our pistols and straining our eyes to decide whether some lone tree was human. Then, rather foolish in our own eyes, we walked on.

We found the Tirso within a mile; a wide shallow pebbly bed between steep bushy banks and a small, half-stagnant but most welcome trickle of water. We rested and drank and meditated. The airfield, our objective, lay on the east bank, somewhere between one and five miles from us. We did not wish to stumble on it that same night and decided to continue towards it to the first suitable cover and there hide for the rest of the night and the next day, when we should be able to establish its position and our own more exactly. A short distance farther a large thorny bush offered the ideal hide-up and we forced our way into its center. The time was now 3 A.M., two hours before dawn, and the date 8th July.

The British soldier is a proverbial sleeper. I believe Brown, Fry, Morris, and Cope, with enviable indifference to their situation, slept through till the following evening. Amos and I woke at dawn from the light semi-conscious doze, which became our substitute for sleep for many days.

We peeped in turns out of the bush, comparing the landscape with our maps, identifying features, and plotting our position. In daylight there was more connection than by night between the Sardinia we could see and the Sardinia we had imagined. The Tirso plain was many miles broad, barren except for sparse crops of wheat. Wild mountains overlooked it from the two sides, east and north, visible from our bush. In the middle ground we identified, with delight, a conical pile of stones as a "nuraghe"; and in the foreground, with much less delight, a band of Sardinian peasants, complete with black headgear and white stockings. The peasants were threshing wheat by a stack, perhaps two hundred yards from us, though it felt closer. And there, busily employed except for a long nap at noon, they remained all day. In the early morning, and again in the evening, flocks of sheep and goats passed by us; we could hear their bells far away and the noise grew louder and louder, as they grazed towards us, until—the climax of the suspense—the beasts surrounded the bush itself and nibbled at it. A small boy was always with the flock somewhere and not easily distinguished from it. We could never, in all the following days, escape from the sound of sheep bells. In whatever remote corner of the island we hid, the bells followed and if there were no actual sheep, we still imagined them. Their tinkle-tinkle haunted us wherever we went, an insane, monotonous, and penetrating sound, which we hated and feared second only to the barking of dogs at night.

Lance-Corporal Morris, finding himself in a predicament which is never sufficiently recognized in accounts of this sort, solved the

problem in a hair-raising way, before we could stop him. While Amos
and I still watched the peasants nervously, lest they should suspect or
detect our presence, Morris strolled from the bush into the open. We
noticed him suddenly squatting there and could hardly believe our
eyes. Then, calmly, he came back again. The peasants never saw him.

The aerodrome, we could tell, lay about three miles north, in
the plain by the river. It was not directly in sight, but all day we
watched the machines landing and taking off, throwing up a plume
of dust in their wake. Transport planes, bombers, fighters . . . We
rejoiced in their number and that chance had given us this and not
the Alghero target. We decided we should be able to find the landing ground easily before moonset—0045 hours. If not, the following night would still give us time in the period of darkness between
moonset (0130 hours) and dawn—though not so much time. It was,
we had decided in Algiers, the last possible night when an attack
could be made.

By 10 p.m. it was dark enough to leave. We followed the river,
stopping to refill waterbottles and to drink. From the bush there had
been no sign of human habitation near the bank. But suddenly several dogs barked close to us and though we quickened the pace, the
dogs seemed to be chasing us. A man's voice shouted and then we
saw him, a peasant running to cut us off. He halted a few yards away
and leveled a shotgun, continuing to shout.

I suffered always an intense antipathy to the idea of killing anyone in cold blood, particularly a civilian, and a still greater antipathy, I confess, to the idea of being killed myself in the same way.
Now for a second or two both distasteful eventualities seemed possible. I shouted *"Tedeschi"* at him hopefully. It was a magic word
which helped us on more than one future occasion. The peasant,
who must have been a gamekeeper on the look out for poachers—
we had put up a covey of partridges shortly before—or perhaps a
poacher resenting the appearance of gamekeepers, now lowered his
gun at once. We said *"Buona sera"* to him several times heartily and,
in our anxiety to please, shook him by the hand with the few appropriate Italian words we knew—*"Soldati Tedeschi, Noi vostri amici."*

He seemed satisfied, even apologetic. Bidding him good night,
we disappeared out of his sight as fast as we dared walk without appearing too hurried.

Owing to thick scrub and steep intersecting ravines, our progress along the riverbank was slower than we had anticipated. The moon set and still we had not met the landing ground. We turned obliquely from the river to where the going was smoother, along a ridge. Then, suddenly, from the darkness below on our left towards the river, we heard German voices. I left the others and walked cautiously ahead. I found myself looking down, as from the top seats of an amphitheater, on to a wide plain, a sort of arena, bounded by the river on one side and on the other by the curving ridge upon which I stood. I could just see the silver glint of an aeroplane at the foot of the hill below me. And roaming about farther, I nearly walked into a guard tent.

I rejoined the others. We consulted and decided that it would be better to lie up in the neighborhood and attack the next night. The additional observation we should get would out-balance the loss in hours of darkness. If we went on to the landing ground now, in the dark, having no idea where to find the planes, we might waste hours accomplishing nothing. Keeping on the crest of the ridge, we made a detour around the guard tent and settled in two bushes about two hundred yards beyond it, which would, we hoped, give us a good view with daylight. Amos, Cope, and I buried ourselves in the center of one, putting Sgt. Brown, L./Cpl. Morris, and Fry in the other. The bushes grew on the side of a rocky knoll and were dangerously low and sparse, but the best we could find. It would be necessary to lie flat, and there was no room to stretch out.

When dawn broke, we realized the full advantages and disadvantages of our position. Of the former, we had—as far as we dared look out—a dress circle view of the landing ground. The runway across the center of the arena below was perhaps 1000 yards away. Half the planes seemed dispersed between it and ourselves, under the lee of our hill; the remainder farther off between it and the river. The disadvantages were that the guard tent was closer and our bush even smaller than we had expected. German soldiers were on the move to and from the guard tent all the time and occasionally would stroll over to our bush to take the air. Amos and I lay breathlessly, pistols drawn and cocked, wondering what on earth to do if one of them happened to look over the top. Shoot? We supposed so. But then what?

Cope, curled up in his sleeping-bag with his head covered, slept blissfully. When a German came close, I woke him in case he snored in his sleep. I felt sure the other three were asleep in their bush, fifty yards from us, equally near the guard, and also visited by them during the day. I hardly dared to hope they would escape discovery. L./Cpl. Morris would not, I knew, repeat his performance, but he or someone else might breathe loudly at the wrong moment . . .

When eventually I asked them if they had been worried by the proximity of Germans during the day they were genuinely surprised.

"Germans? No Germans came near us!"

In parenthesis, in case I have seemed to belittle our four men, I must mention that Amos and I never, for one moment, regretted our choice. It is, simply, a fact that when he is with an officer, any soldier knows, without meaning to take advantage of it, that the officer is responsible for him. And he forgets to use his own initiative. Such, indeed, has been his whole training in the Army. Left to himself, without the officer, he uses his initiative freely, and so did, in particular, Brown and Fry when eventually they escaped from a prison camp in Italy, reached our lines, and then returned voluntarily to rescue other escaped prisoners.

Planes came and went from the ground all day. By nightfall we reckoned there were about twenty fighters dispersed over the northern half and about twenty bombers over the southern half. It looked as if our job should be fairly easy. We could actually count on the ground about a quarter of that number. The rest were hidden from us because of the danger in looking over the top of the bush. We could guess their whereabouts.

In the cool of the night we waited for the moon to set, sucked a boiled sweet or two, drank a little water, and ate some of our dehydrated mutton and apricots. I had collected a few heads of wheat the previous night. During the day I shredded the ears and chewed the grain up into a paste, mouthful by mouthful, moulding the final collection of salivery lumps into one disappointingly small chupatee which I baked in the sun and now ate. It was not very stimulating. In the process of grinding I had chipped a tooth and I decided not to repeat the experiment.

Here we were then, incredible though it seemed, on the very brink of success. Our luck hitherto had been amazing. Would it hold? There were plenty of likely risks ahead; to reach the planes and lay the bombs could be troublesome in innumerable ways. We speculated, in whispers, on the unforeseen disasters that might await us. A prowling sentry . . . a sprained ankle . . . an accidental explosion . . . Somehow it never occurred to us that we would have difficulty in finding the planes in the darkness. There they had been in daylight, simply waiting to be picked off. So sure were we of success that Amos and I, before nightfall, took compass bearings on individual planes and planned which of them we would individually visit with our respective parties. In general, Amos was to make a circuit of the northern sector and I of the southern. We fixed a dividing line to avoid overlap. We would rendezvous again at our bush, distinguishable because of the knoll, at 3 A.M., and neither would wait for the other later than three-fifteen.

After that, independently or together, we would make for the hills overlooking the airfield on the east and hide there during the next day—always a critical time. Then we would march towards Mt. Alberu, eighty miles away to the south-east. We had heard, before leaving Algiers on 7th July, that the other submarine had landed Bryan's party successfully. Supposing they had been discovered before we reached them? But it was useless to plan so far into the indefinite future.

CHAPTER FOURTEEN

The Attack

RELIVING OPERATION SWANN over again as I have been, so vividly, in the past few weeks, I have perhaps taken for granted and left insufficiently explained one or two details of our equipment and methods. Let me clear the points up now before continuing.

Our headgear, for example. I fancy the idea of wearing the cork lining of an American steel helmet was one of those last-minute brainwaves I have already mentioned as complicating our hectic week's preparation on the Depot Ship. It was an excellent idea. The helmet was light; it was a protection in our parachute jump (though of course that was not foreseen); in darkness its silhouette enabled us to bluff, as we had done already with the peasant, that we were German or Italian troops; and if taken off and turned upside down, it could be used as a bucket.

Then the question of arms and explosives. Jim's, Kempster's, and Bryan's parties carried light American carbines, as well as pistols and grenades. In ours, more than enough encumbered already for a parachute jump, we left the carbines behind. They were, in any case, redundant. Mobility and stealth were better weapons for our purpose. On an island occupied by an enemy civil population as well as by enemy troops, and with a taking-off R.V. many nights' march away, the only hope of success lay in being able to steal unobserved on to the airfield and then, having laid the bombs and set the time-fuses, to steal very rapidly off again; to hide up by day and to march, swiftly but unseen, across country by night. If shooting started, it would be on our part at most a gallant gesture. And none of us were Japanese intent on suicide.

The bombs were a simple affair. They weighed one pound each and looked like small Christmas puddings with a length of detonating wire protruding from the top. Each of us carried six round his waist with a packet of detonating time-fuses in his breast pocket. The fuses, which could be tied quickly and easily to the bombs, were banded in various colors, each color denoting a different time delay—from ten minutes to three hours. Amos and I had debated, in a grim humorous vein, the best way of carrying these detonating fuses for a parachute jump. We had decided for the left breast pocket, on the grounds that if one did get broken in the fall, at least the man would hardly be aware of it.

We agreed, before parting at the knoll, that at whatever hour we succeeded in placing bombs on the planes, we should set the fuses to go off as near as possible at 4 A.M. That should give us time to get well away from the airfield, and it would give the Germans very little time, if they caught one of us or otherwise suspected what was happening, to search the planes.

The moon set at 1.30 A.M. We took some minutes to collect ourselves together, dump our packs in the bush, and arrange the bombs and fuses so that they could be reached quickly. At 1.45 A.M. we set off in the two parties.

With Brown and Fry in single file behind me, I began to walk down the hill, on the compass bearing I had made from the bush. It had seemed necessary in daylight only to follow the bearing down the hill till we struck our first plane, which would give us a guide to the others. But now, in the darkness, the ground appeared totally different. We descended the hill to the bottom only to find another rise. We were in a wide depression which, as dead ground, had been invisible from the bush and which now totally changed my conception of the airfield. In no time, we were badly lost.

The undergrowth and stubble made the noise of a forest fire under our feet. We had begun by walking slowly and as quietly as possible. But now the precious time was slipping away and we had to hurry regardless of noise, hoping that the guards, wherever they might be, would not hear us.

At 2 A.M. we reached the edge of the airfield where I had expected to find the first plane. There was no sign of it. We hunted around in vain and then turned south along the landing ground. The surface was dusty and silent for walking. Our rubber-soled boots made no noise. In spite of the clear starry sky visibility was only fifteen yards.

Where in hell's name had the planes disappeared? We hurried on until we had reached the southern end of the landing ground—still no sign of them. 2.30 A.M. . . . I began to feel a fool. If I worked back northwards, the way we had come, I would most probably overlap Amos. I decided to cross the runway and make a cast along the river. The runway was ankle deep in fine dust—soft almost snow-white dust which added to the ghostly effect of that silent, deserted plain. Beyond it, we could see the outline of bushes near the river. Then, with how much relief and excitement, the outline of a machine close beside us—we had nearly walked past without noticing it.

There was no guard near it. We placed two bombs on the petrol tanks, set the fuse apparatus to the appropriate time, and then slipped down to the river to fill our bottles and to drink. We were sweating hard and very thirsty. I knew the planes on this side were widely dispersed. We had been lucky to find one at all. 2.55 A.M. I decided to return across the runway in the direction of our bushy knoll and hope for some more luck on the way. We walked on to another plane, but found it had already been attended to by Amos, though I added a small contribution for the sake of the thing. But it meant we had overlapped after all. No good searching farther and, anyway, time was short. We made back uphill, running and regardless of the noise. We reached the knoll at 3.20 A.M.

All the rucksacks were still there. We waited for the others a quarter of an hour. I knew they wouldn't come now, but would make straight from the airfield to the hills east of it. Without their rucksacks, they only had one small waterbottle each, and emergency rations—no dehydrated mutton and fruit, no boiled sweets, no sleeping-bags, and in Amos's case, no boots, for he had changed into rubber-soled sandals for the attack, his boots being hobnailed. (His feet were outsize and he had never been able to find a pair of rubber-soled boots to fit him.) The thought of him and his party setting off on the long difficult march so ill-equipped made me very anxious.

We shouldered our packs and walked rapidly towards the hills. A German soldier appeared unexpectedly on a path, and shouted some inquiry about a lorry he was waiting for; he mistook us for his friends. I spoke to him politely in German, explaining we were

Italians on a night march. He seemed puzzled and then suspicious. To shoot him, or not to shoot him? I wished him good night and we walked away, changing direction as soon as he was out of sight, dodging among the rocks to put him off if he followed.

It was to prove a fateful meeting.

We began to climb, as in a race, over rocks and bushes, leaving all the distance we could between us and the airfield before dawn. It was hard uphill work. And as we climbed, we listened, above the sound of our heavy breathing, for the noise we expected to hear behind us at any minute. I had no idea how much noise there would be. Perhaps none at all. Supposing the fuses were dud? I wondered how much Amos had been able to accomplish.

The first explosion went off at exactly 4 A.M. We felt the blast. We halted half-way up the hill and looked back. Another seven explosions followed in the next two or three minutes. The noise and the flashes were terrific. The petrol tanks caught alight and went up with a sudden flare, illuminating the landscape for miles. We had to squat out of sight in the scrub. At least two big blazes and, besides the major explosions, the sound of ammunition crackling and a few minor bangs. A Very light shot into the sky. And then silence again. The machines went on burning, the blazes sometimes flaring up brightly, fizzing out sparks. And we hastened on towards the hilltop, where we thought we should find the best cover and observation.

Eight big bangs. I could account for four of them—two from the plane by the river and two from the other (one of mine and one of Amos's). Now, if Amos had only used one bomb in each plane, that might mean a further four planes—total six. And if the two other parties, Jim's and Kempster's, had each got six . . .

But I was worried about Amos. That machine-gun fire might after all not have been ammunition exploding. The several smaller bangs might have been grenades. I began to picture Amos staying too late on the landing ground, cut off, fighting a desperate last battle with grenades. The Very light seemed, in this respect, particularly ominous. The more I thought, the more certain I felt that Amos and his men were lost. And even if they escaped, they were miserably poorly equipped, particularly Amos himself in sandals. The elation turned quickly to bitter sorrow. I reproached myself for not having remained longer on the aerodrome, for having put our safety above the fuller accomplishment of the task. I should have continued searching for planes until daylight, at whatever cost. Amos had done the right thing, had been a hero. And we were here, unheroically safe. Dawn was about to break when we concealed ourselves in the usual bush near the summit of the hill.

CHAPTER FIFTEEN

The March

THE BUSH WAS TRANSPARENT but the surrounding cover was good and we had a fine view back towards the aerodrome. I watched sadly how many machines were able to take off from there that morning, though I found some consolation in the faint, soon dissipating, columns of black smoke which floated in the air over the ground for a few hours after dawn.

We had begun to feel the lack of sleep and solid food and took turns to look out for search parties. I was dozing after my turn on watch, about 10 A.M., when Brown clutched me. He had heard voices. Two Italian soldiers appeared among the rocks ten yards from our bush. We drew our pistols and lay watching them. They were evidently part of a body of troops searching the hills, but were themselves not taking the search very seriously. They wandered past us talking, and stopped near us for an interminable quarter of an hour looking vaguely in all directions over the hillside. If they had glanced at our bush, they must have seen us. Then they disappeared. We could not be sure how far they had gone and the rest of the day was too tense for sleep to be possible. In the afternoon we saw three horsemen, armed and in uniform, ride up the valley below us and then, later, return towards the aerodrome. They were *carabinieri*, though we didn't recognize them as such at this stage.

By evening we felt safer and brewed some tea in the bush over a tiny fire of twigs, carefully dispersing the smoke by fanning it with a map. The risk was small and worth taking for the boost the tea gave to our morale. After dark we continued eastwards over the hills until they sloped down to a valley, in which we had to cross the secondary road from Orotelli to Ottana. There was a bright moon. We feared pickets on the look-out for us. We stole along in the moon's shadow conscientiously when we could, and otherwise adhered to all the rules laid down for "concealed movement" and "use of ground and available cover."

The meager trickle of the Tirso had given me a falsely pessimistic impression of the local water supplies, which previous information had reported as plentiful even in midsummer. So that when we found a slimily stagnant pool we drank from our bottles and refilled them from it, adding a sterilizing tablet. We washed our faces and teeth in the foul water and combed our hair, and were much refreshed.

We came to and crossed the road in the approved manner; previous reconnaissance by the commander while the platoon remained concealed, and then a quick dash over its white surface one at a time into cover beyond; the platoon reassembled, it "proceeded" forward . . .

But my nerves were jumpy. Cattle bells were jingling somewhere close. We entered the mouth of a valley and from a bush beside our path a voice suddenly spoke. It said what sounded like "John," but that, I decided instantaneously, was only what it sounded like. A peasant asking who we were; a sentry telling us to halt; a dozen thoughts flashed through my mind but all suggested only one thing—DANGER—and prompted only one reaction—IMMEDIATE FLIGHT. The voice had hardly said whatever it had said when I was running wildly to the nearest hillside and scrambling up through the *maquis*, the others behind me. Breathless, we crouched and looked back to the valley below.

We compared our suppositions. The others were certain the voice *had* said "John." Brown said that he thought he had recognized Amos's voice but seeing me run had assumed he was mistaken. The cattle bells sounded closer. We saw three figures moving below us down the valley and I peered at them through binoculars. We had covered several hundred yards in our flight and it was hard to see the figures in detail. They were only in sight a matter of seconds and I took them first for peasants. They wore dark headgear, it seemed, and their clothing was white. My mind must have been tired for I particularly noticed they were not carrying packs and deduced from it that they could not, for that reason, be the other three. The next instant I remembered that of course the others would not be carrying packs. Their khaki drill would show up white by moonlight, their helmets might look like black caps. And surely peasants would not walk in single file? And surely the leader had been much taller than the two behind? I was appalled at what I had done.

We scrambled madly down the hill, tearing through the thorny scrub, until we reached the bottom of the valley where the figures had last been visible. They had perhaps five minutes' start, but they had been walking very slowly . . . (No water, no food, no boots . . . I cursed and cursed my nervousness in running like that.) A large spring became a stream and flowed down the valley, making a gorge. What path had they taken? Right or left bank? I shouted "Amos!" loudly two or three times. No answer. We hurried down the left bank. They couldn't be far ahead. Surely they must hear us? It was too cruel to believe that we could miss each other in such a way. I stopped and shouted again. Perhaps somehow we had overtaken them? We retraced our steps, in vain. And then hurried on again down the path along the right bank for miles until the valley bifurcated and the possible routes multiplied accordingly and I realized that it was useless wasting any more time in the search.

At least I knew that they were after all alive. But I nursed an awful sense of guilt and self-loathing in the matter for the next ten days.

There was excellent clean water in the gorge and we replaced the foul water in our bottles. The gorge turned north and to keep on our eastern course we climbed a small mountain. The country was wild, though sheep-dogs, lying in the open with their flocks, startled us by barking on one or two occasions. I shall never be able to be very fond of dogs again.

Near the top of the ridge we found a spring. Dawn was nearly breaking as we halted to wait for it and slept for a little. The daylight woke us. We were on a lonely range of hills and felt much satisfaction contemplating the distance we had come on the ground, though it was disappointingly little—about five miles—on the map. As the hills seemed deserted I decided to push on farther in the cool of the morning. The sun always became unpleasantly hot after 10

A.M. and the hours between noon and 4 P.M. were almost unbearable in anything except deep shade. After that the heat relaxed rapidly till the sun set about 7.30 P.M. The sensation of relief from the strain of the day was always delicious in the remaining two hours of twilight before darkness finally came.

Before leaving we shaved, for comfort but also for camouflage reasons. In our American cork helmets we could hope to pass for German soldiers among Italians, but with untidy beards the disguise would be less effective. We managed to shave every third day during our march—Amos's party of course could not. Razors had been a small but particularly important item in the preparation of equipment for the expedition.

We had only covered a few hundred yards when we met a shepherd and his flock. We told him we were Germans. To our dismay he left his flock and walked with us. The same old homicidal doubts I hated so much . . . We were debating in whispers what he could be up to when we came over a crest and saw the village of Sarule a quarter of a mile away. The shepherd stopped and pointing to it, told us to go there and people would give us cold milk and bread and cheese. We made a show of being delighted with the advice and started towards the village, looking back suspiciously to see if he was watching. But he had returned to his flock. We swerved away from the village and crawled into some low but adequately thick scrub, to spend the day.

The scrub gave very little shade and we spent a wretchedly uncomfortable day, dozing and sweating and wriggling ineffectually under the sparse foliage to escape the sun's rays. The date was now 12th July.

Amos and I, in planning this march, had originally decided to move "across country" the whole way—first eastwards as far as the coast and then south over the coastal hills, the summit of one of which, Mt. Alberu, was the R.V. But now, seeing how slowly we covered map-distances over those rough hills, I thought we should never reach the R.V. in time. Personally, I preferred to take the risk of using roads at night, for the sake of the extra speed. Brown and Fry agreed with me. (Afterwards I learnt that all the other parties had come rapidly to the same decision after a short experience of marching across country in Sardinia.) So we decided to strike the road south of Sarule and follow it via Gavoi and Fonni over the Gennargentu range till it joined the main coast road, when we would consider the question again.

By the evening I felt alarmingly weak with hunger. The others admitted to feeling the same. We brewed tea on an inconspicuous fire and boiled up some dried mutton into a broth, but it was bulk we needed. Brown and Fry recalled every large meal they had ever eaten, describing vividly every dish—the savory broth, the juicy steak, the fruit and pastry and cream. Then they amused themselves picturing the meals they would have when we got back, with the same mouth-watering emphasis on every detail, until I could have screamed with irritation.

I determined to obtain food from the village that night. Hunger and thirst warp your judgment and drive you to take chances which, reviewed afterwards on a full stomach from the security of an armchair by the fire, appear unjustifiable.

We approached the southern outskirts of the village after dark and found our road. Near it I saw a farmhouse, conveniently isolated. We walked up to the door of the kitchen which was open. Inside in the light sat two old ladies. I knocked and entered and asked to buy food. They were quite friendly and unsuspicious and seemed to accept the story that we were Germans whose truck had broken down on the road farther back and that we were now walking to Orani for help. They produced six eggs, a cheese, and large flat biscuits in lieu of bread. We drank a lot of water, filled our bottles, and loaded the food carefully in the packs. The question of payment raised a serious problem as I had only a 500-lire note, which of course they couldn't change. I gave it to them and said I would call back the next day in my truck with smaller money. We exchanged polite *"Buonanotte's"* and left. Not to have had some five and ten-lire notes was a bad oversight in the planning—it is just these little points which matter most and which get forgotten in the preliminary enthusiasm for the big Aim.

We filled ourselves up quickly on biscuits and cheese and then set off down the road. We met one or two peasants who answered our *"Buona sera"* without question, though generally if we saw them first and had time, we dodged off the road till they had passed. The road climbed steadily, winding round the contours and over bridges.

As we walked through another village, about a hundred dogs began to bark in houses off the main street, but no one came out. We reached the outskirts of Gavoi at 2 A.M.

There beside the road stood a water-trough fed from a tap, and beside the trough two youths. They watched us in silence as we drank the water greedily and then they asked for cigarettes. Our cigarettes had English markings and we checked ourselves in time. No, we none of us smoked. And then, anticipating their questions, I asked how far it was to the nearest "other" Germans. I thought I was being rather subtle, appearing to assume that they knew we were Germans. "Do you speak German?" became my invariable technique on similar future occasions. The youths seemed friendly and gullible and told me of a German camp at Fonni. I was confident that they suspected nothing. They pressed us to come and drink a glass of wine before continuing our walk. Their house, they said, was only just round the corner. Brown and Fry urged me to leave at once, but I was seduced by the idea of wine . . . "I've got them taped," I assured them. "I'm sure they're genuine—there's no danger."

We followed the youths up a dark side street, and they stopped at a house. They knocked on the door. And then I realized just how badly I had miscalculated the simplicity of Sardinian peasants. Over the door hung a huge heraldic sign—the sort of sign which you see over the doors of police stations anywhere on the continent.

"It's late and I think we ought to be getting on, after all," I said hurriedly. I did not wish to behave too suspiciously, in case my worst fears were unfounded. We turned to go back but one of the youths clung to me, insisting that a glass of wine would take no time. The door was opened by a man in shirt-sleeves and the other youth spoke to him in a low voice. I continued to regret politely that we must really be going and we walked away. I heard voices, excited voices, inside the police station behind me and then people running after us. Two *carabinieri* in uniform with rifles caught up with me. I changed my tactics. I became the haughty German officer. Did they speak German? No. Did I speak French? one of them asked. I did, and was able to tell him forcibly that I was in a hurry and what the devil was the fuss all about, anyway?

He seemed servile and apologetic. Would I wait just a minute longer till the "Brigadier" came? He was just coming now.

No, of course I wouldn't wait! . . .

But then the "Brigadier" arrived, a fat elderly little man out of breath, accompanied by two or three of his soldiers.

Could he understand German?

He regretted he could not. Obviously he was confused and lacking in confidence. I spoke to him through the interpreter in French. My sudden command of that language surprised me. I had never spoken it so fluently before—perhaps I never will again.

I have forgotten what I said, except that my tone was very indignant and haughty, as was appropriate from a German officer affronted in such a manner by *carabinieri*. The "Brigadier" was pacificatory, apologetic, scared. He was sorry I had been delayed but how did a German officer happen to be walking over this mountain road at this hour?

I explained impatiently that I was walking for a bet. We Germans were great walkers. I had wagered my Colonel that I could walk in the night from Orani to Fonni. Now, unless I was quick, thanks to this interference, I should lose the bet. My Colonel was waiting for me at Fonni to attend an important conference. If I was late he would be angry . . .

The "Brigadier" wavered. I could see exactly the doubts and the fears revolving in his mind. He was, like all Italian soldiers, terrified of offending Germans, even such preposterously unlikely Germans. I felt I must clinch the matter quickly before I lost the advantage of surprise.

"Satisfied now?" I sneered. "Good night," I added fiercely, and walked off with Brown and Fry behind. A chorus of faint "good nights" followed us. We dared not obey the temptation to look behind us and we tried not to walk through that village faster than a mere bet should warrant. In such circumstances the mind shifts into the back, somewhere between the shoulder-blades—and wishes it had eyes to see with. An unpleasant anticipatory sensation of vulnerability you have in your back, in such circumstances . . . But the shots we expected never came. Outside the village we left the road immediately, as a precaution. On the wild hillside we began to lose that constricted feeling in the wind-pipe and to breathe freely; our knees recovered their strength.

And I hope I had the good grace to say I was sorry.

I wished I knew just what those *carabinieri* had said to each other after we left. I believed they would telephone to the Germans at Fonni, discover the mistake, and send after us. We kept across country for a time and then, striking the road, walked along it again listening carefully. About 4 A.M. we heard a horse coming towards us and hid in a convenient culvert. The horse clop-clopped by and we never saw the horseman, but I am sure now it was only a peasant riding off to his fields. Dawn was near and we climbed uphill to find a good bush. It was a bad area for bushes—more like English parkland with oak trees and bracken and we settled finally among some large rocks, with no prospects of shade except from their shadow.

A tense, tiring day, though we boiled one egg each for breakfast and another for dinner and fed well off biscuit and cheese. There were flocks on the hillside round us all the time, scaring us with their bells, and we had to keep watch in turns for fear of being caught asleep. The sun rose in the sky and the shadows of the rocks dwindled to nothing and we none of us obtained more than an aggregate of four hours' sleep during the day. My nervous system resisted the impulse to sleep. If I dozed from sheer tiredness, it was never for more than half an hour, when some subconscious alarm bell would ring—an echo of sheep bells inside my head and I would wake guiltily as might a sentry who nods at his post. I found it less wearing on the nerves to keep awake.

In the coolness of evening we read our maps and planned the night's march ahead. We had covered a gratifying distance on the map the previous night and we agreed to continue to walk on roads, in principle, except through villages which we would skirt, however tedious and slow the detour might be. Now, owing to the news of Germans in Fonni, it seemed better to cut straight across the hills to join the road again south-east of it, after which there were no villages marked on the map till after Gennargentu.

The valleys on that night all ran across the line of our march. Consequently, to avoid climbing up mountains and down again, I tried to work round their flank, without changing height more than necessary. In my anxiety to spare us the fatigue of climbing up and downhill too often, I strayed farther and farther off our course till we hit the road from Nuoro to Fonni. We followed it and arrived by dawn in a place like Windsor Great Park, within sight of Fonni.

During the night we had found a potato field and from this day onwards we always boiled potatoes with the mutton—they gave us the much-needed bulk.

There was no ideal cover in the Great Park. We lay under a small oak tree and kept a careful watch. Shepherds and goatherds with their flocks and peasants on horseback passed nearby, but no one noticed us. We had brewed some tea at dawn on a discreet fire. The ashes smouldered on unseen by us, the dried leaves and grass caught alight and burst into a sizeable bush fire, which we heard before we saw it. We beat out the flames just in time, but the embers, in the tinder-dry undergrowth, were a menace for the rest of the day. We urinated on them in turns, to help keep them under control—it was impossible to extinguish them totally.

We hoped, when we set off, to reach the road south of Fonni within an hour or two, and to cover many miles along it that night. We should be crossing the Gennargentu range, and we could expect to find the road comparatively safe.

First we walked into a flock resting for the night, and the dogs went for us, with their infernal snarling barking. The shepherd called them off and he answered our grateful greeting, but it was the sort of thing which in our frayed nervous condition frightened us still, hours later. Next we met an old man who asked our business and who, when I told him we were Germans climbing Mt. Gennargentu for the exercise, strode away without a word. Then a small boy cutting a field of wheat with a sickle by moonlight. He stared hostilely and wouldn't speak. Another flock of shepherds with guns caused us to hide by a stream while they crossed it, and when we dared to start again, we met another peasant. He seemed friendly and insisted on showing us the best track on to the road which I told him we wanted to reach. On the way he led us to his family spending the night out in their fields, who begged us to stop with them. But we pressed on, keeping to the track he indicated till out of sight and then branching off it. Another flock suddenly, and dogs, and a shepherd who kindly put us back on the track to join the road. He also showed us a spring. We talked with him some time. He had fought with the English against "us" in the last war, he said. Now we were fighting together against the English. War was silly, wasn't it, and was hard on the poor soldiers who had to obey orders and didn't want to fight anyway? Like him in 1915, like ourselves now, out so late at night, carrying such heavy packs. A nice man.

He asked us how the battle was going in Sicily. This was our first definite news that it had begun and I questioned him about place names, but he knew very little. I assured him dramatically that we would kick the filthy English right off the island very soon. To my secret amusement he did not appear very convinced, though he made some polite and noncommittal reply. He was obviously pro-English and the temptation to confide in him was very great. But even if he was friendly, he would certainly talk about us to others. Mussolini had offered a reward for British parachutists, and I kept the impulse back.

It was 1 A.M. (15th July) when we finally struck the road. We were all of us footsore and stiff, and though we had been marching only three and a half hours, more tired than we usually felt after a full night's march.

By 2 A.M. we reached the summit of the pass over Gennargentu and the road began its winding descent. In total distance and time we were well up to schedule, with every prospect of reaching the R.V. two or three days before the 24th July. So I decided to halt and give ourselves the chance of a thorough rest till the following night. We climbed off the road into adequate scrub, pulling our sleeping-bags over our heads and slept—the first real sleep since the night 6th/7th July on board the depot ship.

I was woken at 11 A.M. by the noise of goats grazing all round me—bells everywhere. The goatherd, wrapped in a black cloak, stood motionless against the sky-line, staring apparently at us. An ominous sinister figure he made. Then the goats drifted on and their attendant spirit disappeared too, leaving me wondering whether he had really seen us—or if I had really seen him.

He and his goats passed by again in the evening. That sleep made a great difference to us all. Brown and Fry were both so tough and so cheery, they never looked as tired and stiff as I usually felt, and I had stopped early for my own sake rather than for theirs. However, they now confided that they, too, had been almost "done for" when I decided to halt and sleep. I knew they would have died rather than ask me to stop, such was our pride and our fear of letting each other down. Though I loved them for their trust and their loyal acceptance of my least reasonable prosposals (such as following the young men for a glass of wine), I found this sense of responsibility towards them a trying additional strain. At least it was pleasant now to feel that for once I had made a right decision.

We set off down the mountain again at a tremendous pace, bursting with energy and optimism and a determination to eat up the kilometer stones along that road. We counted ten of them in the first two hours. After that I plodded along in a sort of trance— the dumb misery of marching on a hard road; humming to the beat of my feet an inaudible chant indiscriminately composed from snatches of Beethoven, dance tunes, or musical gibberish of my own improvisation. The sheer boredom of marching always weighs on me more heavily than any pack.

We arrived outside Villanova about 3 A.M. and spent a laborious weary hour climbing round it. We branched off the road again as the first light of day appeared in the sky and found cover in a thick wood. We crawled into a large bush and fell asleep on ground comparatively soft with leaf-mould—not that the softness mattered much to us.

The shade was wonderful in that bush, owing to the trees around it. The sound of peasants with carts in the vicinity disturbed us all day, but we were well concealed—so well, that I watched a wild boar unaware of our presence pass the bush several times not six feet from my head.

I wondered, as we slipped back to the road after dark, what might be ahead of us in the night. I had grown to hate more than anything, more than the hunger or tiredness or boredom of long marching, the suspense which increased with every day of continued success and as the distance to the R.V. lessened. I hated more deeply with every day the sense of insecurity, the feeling that however safe we seemed to be one minute, some ghastly crisis might be impending in a space of seconds, that the bogey of sudden disaster lurked for us round the corner. At the start of each march I struggled to reconcile myself to bearing this cross and the cross each time seemed more and more unbearable. Now my spirit was, so to speak, still in the process of groaning, the nightly business of philosophic resignation was still in progress, when the bogey of sudden disaster stepped out.

The moon had only just risen and the light was obscure, when we saw a group of soldiers seated by the roadside ten yards ahead. Too late to avoid them, we walked boldly up to and past them. More and more Italian soldiers—for I saw to my relief they were Italian—obviously resting on a march, appeared beside the road. A company in numbers, with baggage carts still lumbering on to catch up the rest. We called *"Buona sera"* cheerfully and one or two replied. They were dozing and slow to suspect us. We were fifty yards beyond them when a voice shouted after us to halt. We marched on without looking back. Footsteps running on the road behind. I hesitated whether to run on or to stop and bluff. The latter seemed the best chance. Two soldiers caught us up. Who were we and so on? Germans from Fonni. But why were we walking on foot on this road? A training march, I explained. We Germans believed in keeping fit—we made a practice of marching long distances at night over mountains with heavy packs. I demonstrated my biceps and made other gestures indicating how tough and strong we were. They seemed impressed but not convinced.

"Well, we must get on . . . far to go . . . a hard life . . . Good night . . ." And we sighed, as one soldier to another, as we turned away. A stream of straggling foot-soldiers and a lorry containing more troops appeared coming towards us. I led off the road down a grassy hillside, dropping completely all pretense of self-assurance by running as fast as I could. At the best I hoped no one was watching us; at the worst, if they gave chase, the ground was in our favor. But I was afraid that if we kept on the road we should be stopped again—perhaps by an officer, whom I could not expect to bluff so easily.

No one came after us or fired. A bad beginning to the night and one which made us keep off roads and move cautiously along the shady side of river-beds. But we ran into nothing more alarming than a litter of wild boar in some reeds. It was nice to frighten somebody else for a change.

The railway line, two white ribbons threading through the valley, accompanied us much of the way. We crept past a small station, a pale ghostly building standing in its plot of vegetables, where not even a dog barked. The station marked the turning to Jerzu and as the time was by now 2 A.M., 17th July, we decided to use the road again.

We overtook an ox-drawn cart, a peasant lying asleep in the back, while the ox pulled slowly uphill. The wheels creaked noisily and we walked by without disturbing the peasant and were soon out of sight ahead. The incident was repeated, with very different consequences, two days later.

The road climbed a mountain and descended again till it crossed a gorge and then zig-zagged up the other side to Gairo Nuoro. We left the road and climbed down a precipitous goat-track to the gorge, which I planned to follow the next night past Jerzu, until eventually it joined the main coast road. The gorge was a "deep romantic chasm" if ever there was one, complete with "Alph," a sacred torrent rushing down the bed between mighty rocks and boulders. The moon was low to the west, casting one half of the gorge into deep and chilly shadow. Here surely we could spend a day unmolested and secure, and we began to search for a suitable hide-up. First light was about to appear at any minute.

We found an artificial channel, constructed of earth and carrying water from the torrent along the hillside, presumably for irrigation purposes. My heart misgave me. We followed it and came to two small terraces of beans. We squatted despondently under the dividing bank among the beanstalks. It was poor cover but dawn was breaking and there appeared to be nowhere better. Those thrifty Sardinian peasants . . . I cursed their ingenuity and persistence which could level up and cultivate even in such a place a small plot of earth.

"Mark my words," I said gloomily, "there is somewhere in these parts an aged crone whose only purpose in life is to totter out every day to this wretched crop of beans and to prune and count them with loving care."

I had hardly spoken when, glancing at the terrace above, I saw by the dim grey light of dawn an aged crone standing among the stalks. She had not seen us. She was dressed in black, a black shawl over her head and shoulders. With immensely loving care her bony fingers pruned the plants. Her lips moved inaudibly as though counting the pods. I watched her with horror.

I whispered to Brown and Fry to lie back and pretend to sleep. And I waited, holding my breath, while the crone moved slowly from stalk to stalk, working her way round every single one until she reached the end of that terrace. Then she staggered shakily down the bank on to our level. She began to work from stalk to stalk not ten yards away from us, and still she had not seen us.

I was lying back, too, with half-closed eyes, watching her. She was standing right over Brown and Fry when she caught sight of them and she stopped as if suddenly petrified. She stared and stared and her hand very slowly relaxed its clutch on the beans and traveled across to her mouth. I studied her old wrinkled face as I have never studied a face before. What was going on behind it? What would she do next? But the expression in those dark lackluster eyes was insoluble.

Brown and Fry gave a wonderful performance. Lying there still harnessed in their packs and accoutrements, with their blond hair and pale, clear skins and charming youthfulness, they made a picture of tired, sleeping warriors, a picture which told its own story. Burne Jones would have reveled in the sight of them. I thought I could detect a trace of tenderness in the old witch's face, so far as mahogany is capable of becoming plastic to that extent.

Then out of the corner of her eye she saw me, but her scrutiny was abrupt. She turned and tiptoed away, like a mother leaving the room where her child is lying asleep. I could not see where she was and had to assume she had gone to betray us. I "woke" Brown and Fry and decided to make at once back up the gorge, so that if we were pursued we should at least have the advantage of a start uphill.

But as we left the terrace, there was the crone again working quietly on the terrace above. She stared at us as we passed and did not answer our greeting. Her expression was still inscrutable, but now I could interpret it. The blond sleeping-warrior act had got her maternal instinct. She had tiptoed away rather than disturb them. No doubt she had sons or grandsons of their age serving in the army overseas. The whole episode was very touching. All the same, we hastened back up the gorge, keeping among the boulders by the torrent.

We caught sight of a man walking along the irrigation channel in the same direction as ourselves. He was repairing the earth walls where our feet had crumpled them and there was no avoiding him. We looked round us for a place to hide—a desperate hunted feeling. Then we noticed a sort of crevice under the rock, behind which we

had halted to be out of sight of the man. I stooped and looked in and
saw that the crevice was the mouth of a narrow tunnel leading to a
small cave. The tunnel was just wide enough for us to crawl through
one at a time. The cave was ideal for our purpose, adequately lit by
a window-like crack in the ceiling. A branch of the main stream, a
trickle of clear water, flowed through it and there was just room on
the pebbles either side of it for three men to lie down.

We felt almost perfectly safe; we had beautiful running water
and the shade we lay in was unalterably cool all day. The pebbles
made our sleep intermittent, but they were a price worth paying for
the other joys. We washed and shaved before the light failed and our
spirits were high when the time came to start.

We calculated to reach the main coast road that night and from
then the R.V. would be in sight. The date was 17th July. We could
hope to reach the R.V. by the 19th or 20th, which would leave four
days in hand to rest or if necessary to search for the others or to
descend to the pre-arranged point on the coast. Brown and Fry
began to take our successful return for granted and to visualize in
graphic terms the foodstuffs they hoped to find waiting at the base
and all that they intended to eat thereafter in the submarine and on
the Depot Ship and in the fleshpots of Algiers. I was pleased with
their morale, though their optimism, which I knew was wildly pre-
mature, grated on my nerves. So many things could still go wrong
between our present cave and the submarine. And my short experience of submarines had not filled me with confidence.

The gorge fell away more and more steeply and progress was
painfully slow, scrambling down over rocks at the risk of damaging
a limb. The packs had never seemed so uncomfortable and the belts
bruised our hip-bones raw with their weight of water-bottle, pistol,
grenades, etc. I had slightly sprained both knees many nights before
and had to bandage them for each night's march with the elastic
bandages we wore on our ankles for the jump. The bandages now
impeded me in the climbing and cut into the flesh behind the knees.
It was a warm night and we sweated hard but were able to relieve
our thirst from the stream as we went along.

After four hours' painful descent the gorge opened out into a
wide fertile valley and the torrent lost itself over a broad sandy river-
bed. The valley, in the full moon, was a wonderful inspiring place;

the mountains towered many thousand feet on either side, well wooded and terraced with vine and vegetables at their foot, gleaming with black rock towards their peak. We passed small white solitary cottages, and a tile-roofed chapel, but there was no sign of human life. For all its cultivation that valley was the stillest, most deserted spot I was ever in. Not even a dog's bark or a goat-bell.

The sandy surface of the river-bed gave a welcome relief to our limbs, jarred and stiff from the climbing. We covered the ground faster and at last, about 3.30 A.M., we saw the road ahead, where the valley finished.

We followed the road for a while, looking for signs of suitable cover, but the countryside was intensely cultivated with olives and vine. We were in a broad apparently fertile valley, and at length there was nothing to do but branch off to the eastern range of mountains. The mountainside was also well cultivated. The chances of being detected there were too great and we eventually climbed the mountain to its summit, an exhausting business in our weak state. I loathe climbing mountains.

On top we found a few leafless bushes, but the surroundings were wild and the dawn had started. We flopped down and slept for an hour. Thereafter the noise of peasants on the move in our immediate neighborhood prevented sleep. But in any case, we had reached that state of nervous exhaustion when the mind seems incapable of settling into unconsciousness.

The day was windless and the sun beat on us through the bushes until we almost cried. The hours dragged and time became an evil force smothering us. To help us defeat it we "brewed up" three times, using old tea-leaves we had kept. The brew was black and stinking but the business of lighting a fire smokelessly and cooking tea and drinking it, sipping it slowly to spin out the minutes, took our minds off our misery.

I was worried by the question of water. Below in the valley I could see the river Pardu, but it was dry. We had seen no springs on the mountain and though the valley was green, I was afraid that all the surface water supplies might be dried up. This boded ill for the next five or six days. I had identified the peak of Mt. Alberu about twelve miles away and we could reach it possibly in the next night's march, certainly the night after. But our bottles held only enough

water for three days on the scale of two pints per day. In this heat we
sweated so much we could not manage on less if we were to remain
strong enough to paddle or even swim out to the submarine. The
idea of water and the possible shortage of it obsessed me more and
more as the hours passed and I scanned the valley below in vain for
signs of it.

Evening brought its delicious relief of coolness, but our thirsts
remained and the strain of resisting the temptation to drink our
bottles recklessly was agonizing.

We studied the ground and decided to descend to the valley and
follow the river-bed parallel to the road until we had passed Tertenia, the last village on our journey. "Silly to take any risks now,
having come so far and with so many days in hand," we argued.
Once past Tertenia we might rejoin the road for the last five miles
until we reached the junction with the track which led off to Mt.
Alberu. Once past Tertenia we would have some reason to consider
our troubles over, except for the always doubtful question of finding the submarine. Brown and Fry were already disposed to consider
themselves safe. What sort of rations would Bryan have for us at the
base? Would there be lemon squash and tinned fruit? And so on,
bless them. I cursed them at the time, silently.

Supposing we couldn't find Bryan or anyone else there . . . supposing we couldn't find the boats he had brought ashore . . . supposing . . . The alternatives of disaster were endless. And, anyway, we
still had to march to the base successfully. So many things might
happen.

I did not wish to dispirit the others. When I suggested that we
should not congratulate ourselves too soon Brown exclaimed: "If I
got caught now, I think I'd shoot myself." The juvenile Fry made a
speculation about life as a prisoner-of-war and Brown, whose temper
was usually placid, for once shut him up angrily.

The descent to the valley took an hour. I tried a short cut which
failed and we had to force our way through clinging undergrowth
over loose rocks in the dark, for the moon had not risen. We crossed
the dry river-bed and our thirst had become so intolerable I broke
the resolution to avoid the road. I believed there might be water near
it. We met a peasant and I asked him where I could find the nearest
spring. He said there was *molto acqua* a mile farther along the road.

We came to a house and asked again from a man and his wife, and they sent their children to guide us to the spring close by. We should never have found it otherwise, for the water was collected and carried in irrigation canals out to the fields where it disappeared.

We drank and drank, while the children stared in wonder. Then we soaked our heads and splashed the cold water down our backs and on our faces. And then we drank as much again. After filling the bottles we filled our cork helmets and carried them like basins in our hands when we continued the march. We returned to the river-bed and the helmets slopped the water out as we stumbled along. When our thirst had fully returned we drank what water remained. It tasted of resin, which had been used in the manufacture of the helmets, and smelt of our own hair and was altogether most unpleasant.

The moon had risen and the houses of Tertenia were easily distinguished. We skirted the village by a few hundred yards but, even so, a dog began to bark. We walked on to a field of tomatoes and ate some, unripe and sour. Then we joined the road again and with Tertenia behind us strode along it. The hour was about 2 A.M., 19th July. We had five miles to cover for the turning off to Mt. Alberu on our left.

There was still no sign of plentiful running water in the neighborhood, which continued to worry me. I felt sure there was water, in springs and wells, but the difficulty was to find it without visiting houses. The take-off not being planned till 24th July, our water-bottles would not suffice, unless we found water on Alberu; otherwise we might have to walk back to the spring.

Ahead of us on the road we heard and then saw, as we caught up with it, an ox-cart, like the one we had passed a few nights earlier. We could wait for it to draw ahead, but that would prevent us reaching the turn-off to Alberu before dawn. And I did not care to spend a day in the valley where the cover was insufficient, nor did I want to climb a mountain, unless it was Alberu. Alternatively we could leave the road and try to by-pass the cart. But the ground was rough and we might not be able to walk fast enough. Or we could simply walk on and overtake the cart. This was the lazy solution which appealed to me most and which I adopted. That is my only justification for what followed.

A man was sitting up, half-awake, on the tail-board. And then I noticed several more men lying asleep behind him. I greeted the sitting man and asked if there was much water along the road. He said there was, in about a mile. We called "*Buona notte*," and in my confidence I slapped the bullock on the flank as I passed, causing him to swerve and no doubt stirring up the sleepers. However, we strode on and soon left the cart out of sight behind.

We always walked in single file. After ten minutes Brown said from the rear: "We are being followed."

"Are you quite sure?" I whispered, and kept walking.

"Three men, about a hundred yards behind."

"We'll walk faster. Don't look round yet, but when I say, glance back casually and see if they've dropped behind."

We lengthened and quickened our stride, but after some minutes Brown said the men were gaining on us.

"All right, we'll pretend to rest by the road. Make a business of off-loading the packs, as though it was a natural halt. We'll soon see what they want."

The three men came up to us and appeared friendly. Three ordinary peasants. Were they from the cart? In which case, where had it gone, because we could not hear its wheels, nor did it come in sight after five minutes.

I told the men we were Germans from Tertenia marching to Villapatzu; the old story. It came out quite slickly now. And the men seemed to accept it. But I wasn't happy about them, or about the story. I didn't know that there were any Germans in Tertenia. And it was suspicious that the men should have followed. And where was their, cart? I tried hard to convince myself—and the others—that all was well. I refused to believe that anything could be wrong just when everything ought to have been nearly right. But I blamed my folly for having stuck to the road with more bitterness than I can describe.

I tried to chat naturally to the men about water. Could we get a drink anywhere? They led us to a spring, hidden in the bushes near the road, which we would certainly have missed. They seemed overfond of us, unanxious to get on their way home and to leave us. I said we were tired and would sleep a while by the spring before continuing, and begged them, with how much politeness, not to bother to wait . . .

The mosquitoes round the spring were bad and the three men warned us not to stay or we might catch malaria. I countered that we had anti-mosquito cream. At last, to my relief, they showed signs of moving.

Then we heard the cart approaching. The men promptly pressed us to come back to the road and drink some wine. No, we didn't care for wine; we just wanted to stay and sleep. "Thanks very much all the same, please, please don't wait for us," and so on.

The men returned to the road to the cart. We looked about desperately for a good line of retreat, but the ground near the spring was boggy; we sank in to our knees and obviously we couldn't escape far without being heard or seen. But was this, after all, a trap? I could not, dared not, believe it was. There was still no apparent danger, nothing tangible to fear. Which was what made the incident so nightmarish.

The cart stopped and we could hear low voices of men talking. Unable to bear the suspense, I left the bushes and joined them. I said I had changed my mind and would like to buy their wine. They produced a small Italian army bottle of it, for which I gave them a 500-lire note. They laughed delightedly, all piled on the cart and drove on. I listened to their laughter growing fainter and fainter and felt better. I rejoined Brown and Fry and told them that they had only been simple peasants after all, who had just sold a pennyworth of wine for a pound and were chortling with joy at my expense. I believed the explanation because I wanted, desperately, to believe it. Then, allowing time for the cart to get well ahead, we started off down the road again.

I intended to leave the road and find cover as soon as I could, but the landscape on all sides was barren and open. There was no hope of reaching Alberu—all that mattered now was safety for the next day, if there was a next day. The premonition of calamity stifled me, try how I would to be optimistic. And when Brown whispered that we were still being followed I was not really surprised. I just felt rather sicker at heart than before.

There was only one man who might of course be a different one; it *might* be only a coincidence . . . We tried to out-walk him again and failed and stopped again by the roadside, this time pretending to urinate. The man caught up. I thought I recognized him, but I could not be sure. He did not speak but walked over to a shepherd who appeared with his flock suddenly nearby. They had been resting for the night by the road. I walked over, too, and asked him if we had already met at the spring. He denied it. The shepherd looked at me strangely, I thought. He was carrying a gun. Neither paid me any attention and went on talking together.

We waited and the man walked off, up the road ahead of us. The shepherd sat down with his flock. We followed the man until a bend placed him out of sight of us. Then we turned up the hill into some scrub, hoping that if he was hostile we might give him the slip. And at the same moment we heard the horses' hooves—how many horses we couldn't tell, but they were galloping down the hard road. And they grew louder and louder very quickly.

I saw now, only too clearly, what had happened. The peasants on the cart had sent back to Tertenia for help while they stuck to us.

We dropped our packs and crawled up the hill among the bushes. We might yet get away. I hoped the horsemen would ride on till they caught up the man. But the latter was running back down the road. As the *carabinieri* came round the bend we heard him shouting to them to stop—no doubt pointing in the direction we had taken. The shepherd appeared on the skyline above us, so it was useless to try and climb the hill undetected. We dived on top of each other into the thickest bush. There was still a chance the search would carry on up the hill, if they didn't find us at once.

We lay there while the *carabinieri* and peasants searched all round. They passed and repassed our bush without spotting us. I began to have hopes, however faint. I wondered whether we should have thrown grenades when the *carabinieri* were on the road instead of bolting and hiding. Now we were so cramped we could not even reach our revolvers without stirring the branches. A man was standing five yards away. We lay and prayed the search would move a little farther on, to give us time to relax our aching muscles. A twig moved, a leaf rustled; the man noticed. Before we knew it, we were the center of an excited mob, shouting, firing their rifles in the air, pulling us by the limbs, seizing our arms and possessions, screaming orders at each other and at us—an experience which might have seemed almost amusing if we had not felt so bitterly humiliated.

CHAPTER SIXTEEN

The Enemy

BITTER HUMILIATION SOUNDS a forced and rather improbable emotion, but it was real at the time. Though I have forgotten much else, the memory of my first hours of captivity is still exactly clear. Thankfulness to be alive, fear of what might await us, disappointment, despair; those were all there too, but humiliation at first predominated. And I can still picture, as if it happened yesterday, the moonlit scene on the mountainside with ourselves the center of the dangerously excited group. The shouts and firing stopped at length and we descended to the road. The order of march was discussed. A peasant produced a rope and tried to shackle us, but we protested angrily we were soldiers, not convicts, and to my surprise, the *carabinieri* pushed the peasant roughly aside. Though allowed to walk unfettered we had the feeling of a wounded bird watched by a cat. The smallest unwarranted move might be the excuse for an ugly pounce with gun or sickle. The peasants, I feared, were a bloodthirsty crowd. The *carabinieri*, more anxious to return triumphantly with their prisoners intact, probably saved us.

As darkness slowly lightened, the motley procession filed down the road back to Tertenia. A posse of mounted *carabinieri* rode in front; others, leading their horses, marched beside us. A rabble of shepherds and peasants, each continuously boasting (I imagined) of his own part in the night's drama, pressed on us from behind. The bullock cart brought up the rear. An occasional *contadino*, startled to meet such a crowd on his way to the fields before dawn, would stop to hear the sensational news, to shake hands with our escort and jabber his congratulations. There were grounds for congratulation. Three potentially dangerous parachutists, ruthless men who gave no quarter, had been caught without firing a shot. I blamed myself for that.

"You had guns. Why didn't you use them?"

I sensed reproach, contempt, in the *carabiniere*'s question, and it stabbed my conscience on a sensitive part. Why hadn't we shot? Or thrown grenades? Everything had been so sudden, so confusing. Amos, Kempster even, would surely have done otherwise; and then, since escape was out of the question, would have died, butchered most likely with knives. Yes, our capture had been disgraceful though it might still prove to have been the wisest course.

He who fights and runs away
lives to fight another day.

The foolish jingle ran through my head in time with my tired feet. I glanced over my shoulder. The silhouette of Mt. Alberu could be seen quite clearly now. And I glanced at Brown and Fry trudging along so silently, so grimly. Were they blaming me in their hearts for landing them in this mess?

The *carabinieri* whistled and sang. Relief accounted for much of their elation. Searching for one armed man in darkness can be a more intimidating experience than facing a whole squadron of enemy tanks by daylight. I thought of nocturnal expeditions with the Palestine Police after some Arab bandit, of the chilly menace in every shadowy cactus or olive. Perched on Caesar, I had felt vulnerable beside the police on their ponies. Caesar . . . where was he now?

Stretching out a hand, I patted the nose of the nearest horse. His master, fearing a sudden ruse by so desperate a character, reached quickly for the rifle slung on his shoulder. I laughed reassuringly. "I used to have a horse too," I mumbled in pidgin-Italian. He half-scowled, half-smiled at me, not sure which was the proper course. Fraternization with the enemy . . . How strong is the impulse; and how human! I longed to say, "You know we probably have so much in common." If Brown and Fry hadn't been there . . . Their mute presence reminded me of the part I must, supposedly, play.

We reached the water point where I had bought the wine. And, farther on, the bend where I had slapped the bullock in passing. What on earth had prompted that crazily impulsive gesture? But for it, we might by now be on Mt. Alberu, perhaps sampling Bryan's stock of base rations. Had our present capture compromised the R.V. for the rest? Or had the base party already been rounded up and our whole march thus been futile from the start? What would the future be? Incarceration as prisoners-of-war? A firing squad as saboteurs?

The procession entered Tertenia at dawn. The horses clattered on to the cobbles from the dusty road, dogs barked, a cat streaked up a dark alley. I imagined drowsy eyes peeping at us from behind the shuttered windows and reflected that half a world away Lucinda would be going to bed. Our reunion was further off than ever. I wondered what account of my doings or my fate would ultimately reach her.

The *carabinieri* led us into a bare room in the police station. The peasantry slipped off to spread their news or hung around outside to see what would happen next. While Mussolini frowned on us from a picture frame, the *carabinieri* stripped us, of our few possessions, watches, identity cards, cigarettes, money; and in my case a photograph of Lucinda, which they thought would be returned to me after interrogation. Stained and crumpled, it lies before me now. They were almost friendly and gave us a bowl of *pasta*. We had done much to raise their prestige that night and *carabinieri*, of all men, are sensitive to their prestige. Conspicuous by their slightly absurd uniform, they are changed by it to something more and something less than men. They are inordinately vain. Flatter their self-esteem and they will give you macaroni. Threaten it and they will give you something less pleasant, as I learnt to my cost on a later occasion. For, like most policemen, they are bullies at heart.

The much-needed food raised our spirits. "What will happen to us now, do you think?" Brown asked cheerfully and a less phlegmatic look from Fry echoed the question. "Oh, a prison camp, I suppose. Don't worry. With luck the Allies will be here before they can send us to Italy."

Youthfully zealous for our honor, we discussed the circumstances of our capture, reassuring one another that resistance would have been futile, even had it been possible in the cramped position of our bush. "I just couldn't get my revolver out in time," Brown said. We all lied in more or less the same way.

Tertenia was transformed when, towards midday, we were led out into the sunlight. A dozen soldiers, steel-helmeted and heavily armed, awaited us in a lorry. The streets were lined, the windows and balconies crowded with spectators, mostly women. The ex-assistant-director in me noted the admirable grouping. We held ourselves proudly, for it was undeniably pleasant to be the focus of so much curiosity. Give me an adequate female audience and, I think, I might manage to die bravely on the scaffold.

In a film-conditioned age stock situations prompt stock attitudes. I had seen many actors play just this part in my time. Now, though I had lost everything, though I was exhausted in body and depressed in spirit beyond words, though the future was at best indefinite, at worst lethal, I could not help recalling how Ronald Colman behaved once in a similar predicament. I imitated his wry smile and his gay, ironic wave of farewell, as I climbed after Brown and Fry into the lorry. There was no applause.

We drove northwards along the coast, then north-westwards across the Gennargentu range. I thought I recognized parts of the twisting mountainous road and wondered whether Amos, Cope, and Morris, hidden in the scrub, might perhaps be watching us. The midday sun beat down on the open truck, as it swayed recklessly round the corners. The driver seemed bent on hurling us into the ravine. One of the soldiers was sick into his helmet and we viewed his distress maliciously. "Why not stop the truck?" I asked the sergeant. He looked pretty sick himself. If he did stop was there any point in jumping out? But three of us couldn't make a dash for it and I welcomed the excuse not to try and escape. Prisoners-of-war, I was to discover, are always glad of an excuse not to try and escape.

After three hours we arrived in a small town not far, I reckoned, from Ottana airfield. The lorry drove up a narrow street and stopped at some sort of military H.Q. I was ordered to get out, Brown and Fry to stay.

We had been together in the Barsetshire Yeomanry. That in itself was a considerable bond. Then we had trained for months with Bomfrey's Boys. The past two weeks had drawn us as close to one another, almost, as men can be. And we said goodbye now as though we would meet again on Monday morning, after week-end leave.

The soldiers led me up a dark staircase to a door flanked by sentries. Now for my first interrogation, I thought. Remembering the gloomy American Major in Algiers I could not but feel apprehensive. The sentries threw open the door. With a soldier on either side of me I marched forward.

I had half-expected to find harsh lights, tiled walls, a resounding floor, a table and two chairs, something between a prison cell and a public lavatory. Instead, the room used by the local Military Intelligence as an office was apparently the drawing-room of a private house, and I had a quick impression of carpets, curtains, and ornate furniture. As I entered someone I could not see left by another door at the farther end.

If the room's appearance was an agreeable surprise, so was my interrogator's. Middle-aged, benevolent, and rotund, a Latin edition of Pickwick, he sat at a small writing-table behind a vase of carnations. The latter had been put there, no doubt, by whomever had just left—his wife or more probably his mistress. A map of Sardinia—the only sign of the room's present use—was stuck to the glass of a large gilt mirror on the wall behind him. He reminded me of a pre-war friend, a jolly family man and the proprietor of a Soho restaurant, dressed up now, it might be fancied, for the part of an Italian Captain in some amateur operetta. His badly-cut tunic and breeches were made of grey silk, his cardboard riding-boots were too wide at the top. The Captain rose politely to greet me; then, mindful of our respective roles, sat down quickly again, pointing me to a chair in front of him. On five separate occasions since the war I have seen the identical gesture, half-courteous, half-fussy, made by our local Registrar of Births.

To a prisoner-of-war any Interrogation Officer must appear potentially brutal, but hardly this one. Still, you could never be sure. There were no thumbscrews lying around on the table, though I noticed with disquiet a heavy metal ruler. The ubiquitous Mussolini scowled from a picture frame suspended between wall and ceiling above the mirror.

I was face to face with the Enemy at last.

The Captain offered me a cigarette. "You must be tired. You have been so very—energetic." Apart from a slight accent, he spoke perfect English.

Evidently he was using the soft-soap interrogation technique first. The American major had specifically warned us against it. I was relieved. I felt I could withstand soft soap rather better than metal rulers. Enjoying my cigarette, I prepared myself against what might come. Name, rank, number . . . That, we had so often been told, was all we should give. And that was all this musical-comedy Captain would get from me.

However, he had them already, with those of Brown and Fry, from the identity cards taken by the *carabinieri*. The snapshot of Lucinda was folded into the flap of my card and the Captain spread out the two so-different photographs side by side.

"Your wife?" I nodded.

"And you?"

"I'm afraid so."

Some time or other in the desert I had amused myself by adding an ink moustache and side-whiskers to the terribly simpering face. The result was not flattering. The Captain said nothing, but he clearly thought Lucinda had made a disastrous choice. However, he gave the pictures back to me. Then, like the Registrar of Births, he began to copy the three names with meticulous neatness on to a form, ruling a line underneath each. Was it my fancy or did they come at the bottom of a list already long? The carnations blocked my view. Doubtless some of the other parties had been caught. But which? And how many were still at large? Did their fate depend on my silence now or, perhaps, on how skilfully I bluffed?

I stared through the window at the house across the narrow street. A patch of stucco on its outer wall made a funny face. Inside, a peasant woman kneaded *pasta* on her kitchen table. I could see right through the house, past the vegetable garden and across cornfields, to where vineyards patterned the lower slopes of wild hills. The hills must be somewhere near Ottana, perhaps those we had hidden in.

The Captain finished writing. "And now," he said, pleasantly, fingering the ruler, "please tell me what you are doing here in Sardinia."

I folded my arms. "I can tell you nothing."

It sounded absurdly pompous and rude, an outrage against all the canons of conversation. But the Captain only smiled and put more questions. I stuck to my formula. I still couldn't see him as the Enemy. Yet he was. And, to him, I was. Three weary years of war and the destruction of the Italian Empire by the British lay between us.

He seemed particularly interested to know *how* we had come.

"Not, surely, by rubber dinghy? That would have been too far even for you to walk. Besides, we should certainly have caught you. But if you came by plane where are your parachutes? You see, I admit we haven't found them yet."

"I can tell you nothing," I repeated woodenly.

Of a sudden the Captain's face darkened. He scowled. He was no longer my jolly Soho *restaurateur*, but cold, prefectorial, simian, like the portrait above his head. Pickwick had become Mussolini.

"Are there any other British *saboteurs* on this island?"

My heart stopped a beat. The question's implications were quite clear.

"We're not saboteurs. We're soldiers."

"Then, why aren't you in uniform?"

"But this *is* uniform!" I tapped the pips on my shoulder strap. I felt hot in the face, chilly in the stomach.

"Not one that can be identified. Those cork hats, for example?"

"They're standard equipment. The lining of an American steel helmet."

"I dare say. But you are *British*. It would have been wiser to wear something more orthodox. To avoid unpleasant . . . misunderstandings . . ."

The soldiers beside my chair shifted their feet, their rifles clinked. In the house opposite the woman prodded the *pasta* viciously into a pot. My heart pounded and my stomach felt very chilly indeed.

"The Germans at Ottana say you told their sentry you were Italians. That was before the planes exploded—about six, I believe. We saw the fires from here. A good night's work, I congratulate you. But the sentry was a mistake. You should have . . ." And the Captain drew a podgy hand across his throat.

"Ottana . . . ? Sentry . . . ?" The innocent blankness sounded quite unconvincing.

"In the dark, with those helmets, he believed you. Otherwise, he would have raised the alarm. Oh, yes, the Germans are *very* angry." The Captain gave a silly little giggle.

I glared at him, trying to guess what he was driving at. But who can ever tell what a Latin is really thinking? I had a bright idea.

"Well, it couldn't have been us with the sentry. None of us speak a word of German."

"No? You spoke it all right at Gavoi. You told the *carabinieri* there you were Germans on a night march! And on several other occasions. I have the details here." The Captain paused. "Our relations with the Germans just now are . . . not good. I do not wish to make them worse. They want us to hand you over—as *saboteurs* . . ."

So that was it. He was threatening to hand me over to the Germans unless I talked. Jolly *restaurateur*, my foot! Just a cowardly, spiteful little wop. Fear is at the roots of anger as damp generates heat in a haystack. I began to feel angry. And supposing I did talk? I reflected. Of course he would hand me over just the same. He was too scared of the Germans not to.

"Now, will you tell me where you hid your parachutes?" The Captain spoke quietly, earnestly. I had the curious impression that he was asking me a favor.

"We didn't come by parachute."

The door opened at the farther end of the room. It was exactly behind where I sat and I could see part of it in a section of the mirror not covered by the map. A shadow of annoyance, I thought, crossed the Captain's face. I was watching his face by this time as if my life depended on it. Someone walked towards us over the carpet. Perhaps his mistress had come to interrupt us? I hoped so. But whoever it was the Captain took no notice and asked some more questions. The newcomer sat down close to me. He was a man. I could hear his breathing and see part of a trouser leg in the mirror. Who was he? A thug with a truncheon?

"You still say there are no other British sab—I should say soldiers, at large on the island?" The Captain looked over my shoulder with a faint smile on his lips. I didn't like it at all.

"None."

"Not even that one?" And he pointed behind me.

I turned, to see Amos. A beard, darker than I would have expected, fringed his thin face, accentuating its pallor. I waited for him to speak but he stared non-committally at the ceiling, like an El Greco saint. What on earth was all this? I supposed I had better keep on with the pretense, so I turned round again to the Captain. He was smiling in triumph.

"I never saw him before in my life," I said emphatically.

The Captain stopped smiling. He looked quite astounded. Aha, I had shaken him . . .

Fortunately my powers of resistance to interrogation, whether by soft soap or by ruler, were tested no further.

Amos spoke behind me. "You're being perfectly splendid, old boy, but I'm afraid it's a waste of time—we're all in the bag."

The Captain laughed. Amos laughed. I laughed too, in a mystified sort of way. Beside me the two soldiers grinned; dressed-up oafs whose faces, like two ponds, merely reflected the weather.

"Ah, well," the Captain said, "poker's a dull game when you know your opponent's hand." And he passed me the paper off his table. It was a complete list of all the parties on Operation Swann. Dazed, I read it through. No one was missing. Our three names were bracketed under those of Amos, Cope, and Morris. Against each of the other parties was written their landing-point on the coast. Against ours was a question mark.

"Didtheothershaveanyluck?" I asked Amos quickly, to fox the Captain.

"None. You needn't be careful. We have no secrets from the *Capitano*. Except one." Amos seemed quite at home. I found his self-confidence reassuring, though I knew it was put on.

"Except one," the Captain laughed. "Well, I shall try and keep my side of the bargain. Now, I'll go and fetch some wine. I expect you'd like a talk." And he left the room. Our two soldiers sat down promptly on a sofa and smoked.

Forgetting our present situation for a moment, I asked Amos the question I longed to know above all others.

"Was it you in that bush?"

"Yes, of course. Why did you go rushing off? We searched for you for hours."

"And we searched for *you*!"

We exchanged notes. Like us, they had soon abandoned cross-country marching in favor of roads and had been caught two days ago on the coast north of Tertenia. Then Amos had been brought here. He had spent the first night with Kempster, Jim, and Bryan

in the local jail. Bryan's base party had been rounded up almost on
arrival, the others before reaching their objectives. Possibly there had
been some leakage of information from Algiers, but, in any case,
malaria accounted for much. Two or three men died in the open
before capture, others, luckier, were now in prison hospitals. The
three officers were all well and had been sent on to a prison camp in
the north.

"Why weren't you sent too?"

"I'm coming to that. Things are pretty tricky for you and me."
My stomach went chilly again. I had known there must be a snag
somewhere.

Amos spoke quickly before the Captain returned. "As far as I
can make out all P.O.W.s are brought through this town and it's
just our bad luck Ottana is so close. The Germans knew nothing
about us until the day before yesterday. They thought the *Italians*
had blown up the planes. A sentry saw an Italian officer coming off
the airfield—there is some business about that I can't follow. Anyway, there was a hell of a row and the Captain tells me that as they
couldn't find anyone else to shoot the Germans shot the sentry." I
am afraid I was glad to hear that. "Typical of the sods," Amos went
on. "But now they *have* heard about us being here, they are hopping
mad. To give him his due the *Capitano* was keeping quiet about
us. He is on our side, but, of course, shit-scared of the Germans.
Anyway, he sent the others off yesterday because they had nothing
to do with Ottana and, as he knew I had, he hung on to me. The
Commandant of the airfield came here to see me yesterday afternoon. Awful brute, like some outrageous caricature of a typical German, which is to say like a typical German. Really, it was quite an
unpleasant scene."

That, I felt sure, was an understatement. "What happened?"

"Oh, a lot of shouting and threats. Anyway, I persuaded him I
don't speak the language, so it couldn't have been me who fooled
his sentry. He went away, but I'm afraid he'll come back if he knows
you're here. The *Capitano* wanted to send me off in a truck last night
to join the others. Instead, I made him give me dinner—very good
too. I slept it off on his sofa. We're very good friends, the *Capitano*
and I."

"Why didn't you go?"

Amos grinned. "I knew you'd turn up before long. I thought it would be nice to see you."

"What was all that about a secret and a bargain?"

"I was working it out with him after lunch. Then you came along and he shoved me out. In civilian life he's a silk merchant. He lived for years in England, selling shirts. We found several mutual friends."

"I didn't know you were in silk. Or is it a by-product of tar?"

"Oh, I was in lots of things I haven't told you about. But to come to the point. The way the war's going in Sicily and with, who knows, Sardinia next on the list, the Captain hopes to be out of the army in a month or two. That's why he is so interested in finding our parachutes. That quantity of pure silk will be worth having. You didn't tell him, did you? I couldn't hear every word behind the door, and though you sounded wonderfully bored, I thought I'd better come back. For the second time in a fortnight our lives might be said to hang from those chutes."

"I see. Then the bargain—?"

"Quite so. As I told him at dinner last night and again at lunch today, every fortune that was ever made depended, in the first place, on taking one bold chance. This is his chance. If he sends us *both* safely away from here, we will give him the map reference . . . Oh, I've been praying that you would be caught quickly. The sooner we get out of this place the better. I wouldn't put it past the Germans to come and grab us."

"Amos, you're wonderful. But surely the parachutes aren't worth the Captain risking his neck for—a few hundred pounds?"

"Well, there's more to the bargain than just that. The Captain really wants to set up business in England. I have led him to suppose that I have a good deal of influence in silk circles. Perhaps, even, I have misled him a little . . . I am, in case you didn't know, a director of Harrods, Selfridges, Harvey Nicholls, Marshall & Snelgrove, and Peter Jones . . ." He paused. "Ah, young fellow, you may be able to rush about more energetically than I can. But this situation calls for something you can't supply. Age, wisdom . . ." Amos tapped his forehead. "That stuff."

I had never seen him facetious like this before and I realized that he had been—still was—more frightened than his manner betrayed.

But at that point the Captain returned with a bottle and three glasses. He poured the wine and said how nice it was to be talking to Englishmen after so long. It was almost a party atmosphere. But not quite. Amos had begun to say something about a truck to take us away at once, when a rumpus broke out on the landing.

Several voices spoke at once in Italian and one, loudly and unmistakably, in German. The Captain turned white. As a rule, people only turn white in books, but now, in spite of a brown skin, the Captain definitely turned white. The door banged open and a German officer, brushing past the Italian soldiers, strode in. He was obviously in a highly emotional state and he flourished a revolver.

"That's the bastard," Amos muttered. "At least he's alone. Or has he left the others downstairs? One would like to know."

The Commandant of the airfield sized up the situation at a glance—futile treacherous Italian I.O. drinking wine, actually *drinking wine*, with the very *saboteurs* who had destroyed his planes, caused him to shoot a sentry, and brought down on his own head an almighty rocket from Luftwaffe H.Q., Sardinia. Recognizing Amos, who stood out by his height, he walked straight up to him and knocked the glass of wine from his hand.

Hastily I put my glass on the table. I always hate to see wine wasted.

Amos, with studied insolence, took out a handkerchief and wiped himself. The Commandant shouted something about "*verdammte Frechheit . . .*" but the words he used in the following minutes hardly matter. An Oxford don of my acquaintance maintains that all German conversation sounds like "*Heilige Himmelfahrt mit Schweinsbraten und Kartoffelsalat nocheinmal,*" and that that, in fact, is all it is. Metaphysics . . . and Food . . . And again. There may be something in the theory.

But as the Commandant spoke no English, hardly any Italian, conversational interrogation of the polite variety I had experienced with the Captain was impossible. There was nothing left for him but a tantrum and he gave the sort of grossly exaggerated performance one hears occasionally in a provincial repertory company. And not only there. I listened recently to a Third Programme play in which a Nazi was presented as raving and raging in much the same manner. Afterwards the critics crabbed the part as "unrealistic." I, too, disliked the performance and found it embarrassing, but it was certainly not unrealistic. Critics seldom have much acquaintance with life.

Amos, whose supercilious face and bearing drew on himself most of the tirade, understood not a word. The Captain and I followed pretty well, though, of course, I was at pains to hide my moderate knowledge of German. There was a lot of stuff about the rules of war and dirty *saboteurs*. The trivial sentry incident apparently mattered more than the aeroplanes. And as it concerned myself alone I felt like a schoolboy for whom, unless he owns up, the whole school will be punished.

The Commandant, I learnt afterwards, had been lunching in the town when he heard of the arrival of another British officer. An impulsive man, his plan was probably to brow-beat the Captain into handing us over on the spot, but his impetuous arrogance had placed him at a disadvantage. He was alone, as it turned out, except for a driver in the car; he had stormed into this H.Q. with an insulting lack of ceremony; and he was now in the midst of Italian soldiers who, if militarily contemptible, were nevertheless armed and who showed every sign of their hostility to himself. Anger, I repeat, springs from fear. In no time the Commandant's anger was out of control. And a German out of control is a ghastly sight, like a bus-load of screaming children heading downhill towards a precipice; with this important difference, that the German is not, in fact, being run away with. His rage is calculated. Hitler always knew what he was doing when he gnawed the carpet. The only safe reaction—hazardous though it must seem—to a German in this state is firmness. To cower is folly. It has been proved over and over again.

Jabbing the pistol into Amos's stomach, the Commandant shrieked at him to turn round and march out of the room. Amos stood quite still. Then, with the expression of a fastidious duchess lifting a Pekinese's turd off her sofa, he took the barrel between finger and thumb and moved it away.

"When I hear the word gun I reach for my culture," he said coolly. He turned to the Captain. "Are you going to allow this lout to humiliate you in front of your own soldiers?"

It was a cunning jibe. And it worked. The Captain, all honor to him, for he was visibly shaking, summoned his courage.

182 GOING TO THE WARS

"These men are our prisoners. You have no right to be here. Please get out!"

He spoke in Italian and the soldiers, of whom half a dozen had crowded into the room, edged menacingly towards the Commandant. The latter's face was contorted, livid. If he shot Amos—as, too evidently, he would have liked—the soldiers would leap on him. You could see his mind working it out. His rage, as I say, was deliberate, insincere. Theater stuff. He switched it off, like a spotlight.

"You will hear more of this," he said to the Captain.

And he strode out of the room.

We listened to his footsteps on the stairs; then to the car driving off. Amos spoke first.

"If the entire German nation, like the sorcerer's apprentice, was sucked by mistake into one of its own gas chambers, I should bear the news without flinching. How about some more *vino*?"

Half an hour later, Amos and I, with an escort, climbed into a truck. The Captain saw us off.

"A prison has been improvised for you on a farm near Sassari. You will be reasonably comfortable. I know the Lieutenant in charge. As it happens he was my schoolmaster; a nervous fussy little man and a Fascist. He's been told to treat you well—after all, we may be *your* prisoners soon!—and I think he will, if you behave. He's anxious not to lose his temporary commission."

"Are we likely to be moved across to Italy?"

The Captain smiled and shrugged his shoulders. "That depends on your army. You know more about their plans than I do. But don't try and escape. We'll easily catch you. And you'll catch malaria. That's a joke, isn't it?"

"Just about. Do you think you will have trouble over this with the Germans?"

"I don't think so. I've been on the telephone to our H.Q. and reported the incident. They say I did right. They are going to protest, but, in any case, the Germans will be leaving Sardinia soon. Then I expect we shall be allies, not enemies. Let us hope we meet again some day in a happier spirit when this strange phenomenon called war is over." He paused and gave us a look of infinite pathos.

The look said, "I belong to an ancient and civilized race which has been defeated and humiliated and which will soon be bankrupt.

I am a proud man, in my way. But *please* tell me where you hid those parachutes?"

We told him, as near as we could on the map. I have never been able to discover, though I have tried, whether he turned the information to good account.

Bumping along in our truck to join the others in prison, Amos said: "Well, here we are, far from anywhere that really matters, as Oliver would put it. So long as the Germans don't grab us I can't say I mind being in the bag much, do you?"

"Not if we don't stay too long. I told Lucinda I'd be home before Christmas. I hoped she might be able to park Comus somehow and join me there."

"Don't worry, you'll make it easily. Even if they want to, the I-ties are much too short of transport to move us to the mainland."

But they were not.

CHAPTER SEVENTEEN

Intermezzo

SENTENTIOUSLY PERHAPS, I wrote in an earlier chapter that I was concerned with people rather than with military history. But in war, obviously, the two are inseparably related, as the tiny individual thread is related to the pattern on the carpet. If I tend to see patterns where none exist, that, after all, is my trade in life as a painter.

The day of my capture was 19th July 1943. Curious to know what else happened on that date, I have turned to volume 5 of Sir Winston Churchill's book.

"On 19th July a strong force of American bombers attacked the railway yards and airport at Rome. Havoc was wrought and the shock was severe. In Sicily itself the Americans were advancing steadily under the spirited leadership of General Patton." In Italy—I paraphrase for brevity—Badoglio prepared to arrest Mussolini; and in London and Washington the Combined Staffs debated whether the next landing should be made in Sardinia or at Naples.

Within a month all four of those events shaped, or at least touched, the unimportant thread of our lives. Or did the thread, in spite of them, follow a pattern we spun for ourselves? The truth lies somewhere between.

Five men in a room.

There was nothing to do except to kill flies and mosquitoes, nothing to read except Amos's by now tattered copy of *Through the Looking Glass*. In short, as in a play by Jean-Paul Sartre, there was nothing—beyond ourselves, our primitive bedding, and the four whitewashed walls, on one of which hung the usual picture of Il

Duce. We called it Humpty Dumpty. For we were, as Amos had said on the submarine, in the Sixth Square.

"The Seventh Square is all forest," he read aloud. "However, one of the Knights will show you the way out—and in the Eighth Square we shall be Queens together . . ."

"We shall meet Fizzy there," Kempster said.

My thirtieth birthday was a month nearer than on the submarine and I worked, furtively, on my poem about Life. The poem struck me then—but, alas, not now—as rather beautiful and sad. It began:

> *Outside the prison gate*
> *Italian guards expectorate.*

and ended

> *Nothing left that's lasted*
> *Except the memories remain*
> *Of youth's slow-dying torment*
> *At thirty*
> *the loss exceeds the gain.*

"The first month was the worst," Hilary once told me, describing his own prison experiences. "Since then we've got used to it and life is really quite fun. I have voluntary church parades every day!"

But in our prison, outside Sassari, we had none of the facilities of an organized *campo concentramento*, which, with Hilary, we enjoyed later for a while; no mail, no Red Cross parcels, no amateur theatricals, no cigarettes, no variety. Above all, no variety. The atmosphere was not unlike that of a prep school in which the usual proportion of masters to pupils had been reversed. True, we didn't play games; but we were led out for a walk every morning in the yard.

Escape was pointless, unless we were moved towards Italy. We lived in dread of that, and of some sudden reprisal by the Germans for the Ottana incident. As the Captain had hinted, our best hope for freedom was to cause no trouble and to wait philosophically for deliverance.

But male human nature is ill-designed to support boredom. The danger was in ourselves.

Jim and Bryan, like so many healthy and unimaginative young men in captivity, suffered the most. They grumbled continually about the food, the hardness of the beds, the absence of cigarettes. Then, sinking into despair, they rotted before our eyes.

An American pilot called Hank gave us news of the raid on Rome and of progress in Sicily. Returning from the raid, he had landed in the ocean, had drifted for two days in a rubber dinghy on to the Sardinian coast, and thence had been sent to join us. We welcomed, at first, this infusion of new life into our stale company, but after the tenth hearing of his sufferings to exposure Amos and I silently wished him back in the Tyrrhenian Sea. A naïve character whose crew-cut extended within as well as over his head, he clearly thought us a bunch of decadent Limeys, though Kempster's tough good looks and much vociferated intention to escape impressed him.

While Jim and Bryan rotted, Kempster went mad.

He could not forgive himself, or the planners in Algiers, that his own part in Operation Swann had been unsuccessful. Reaching the airfield only to find it disused, he had marched across half Sardinia in search of another, literally dragging his patrol with him. No one could reasonably be blamed, least of all himself, for this gallant failure. But then none of us, least of all Kempster, were reasonable.

We all talked much of escape, to pass the time, but only Kempster, keen soldier that he was, had landed in Sardinia scientifically equipped. Steel files, handkerchief maps, silk cords, and gold coins were sticking-plastered all over his body. Like a schoolboy showing off his treasures, he revealed this collection to us one day and we laughed so hilariously that the *carabinieri* came in before he could get dressed. They spotted the corner of a map hanging out of his shirt. We were searched from head to foot, the guards were doubled, our walks stopped. The withered elderly Lieutenant, who had treated us well hitherto, was much shaken. He kept the *carabinieri* patrolling the wire fence round the yard, or sent them on surprise visits to our cell. And thereafter, like schoolboys, we teased them by picking noisily at the walls and floor.

Kempster, as I think I have said, was partially German and obsessed with war. Having lost his escaping tools, for which he blamed us all, he sat morosely on his bed dreaming of military exploits that might have been and might yet be. Or he concentrated on keeping fit. He walked naked five miles every day round the room. It made us giddy.

"What will you do after the war?" we interrupted him at his exercise, preferring talk to giddiness. He sat down and said defensively: "I shall go on fighting."

"Who against?"

"What does it matter? War is eternal. Look round you everywhere. Look at Nature red in tooth and claw, look at business, look at marriage. It's all war. Why not accept it? I do." He rose again suddenly and stood declaiming, as if in a pulpit. He was half-terrifying, half-comic.

"I acknowledge in myself the impulses towards Death and Power which, multiplied a millionfold, seem to me to have more basic connection with the final disaster of war than all the history-book stuff about ideologies, land hunger, scraps of paper, broken pledges, and the rest. To fight is the proper state of man. In every child flourishing a wooden tomahawk, in every old man bent over his chessboard, I see the symbol of all wars that have been, the seed of all wars that are to come."

"Why, that really sounds fine, what you said," Hank exclaimed. "It had something. It was . . . It was sorta poetry."

"It was sorta his German grandmother coming out," Amos said.

Kempster looked at him contemptuously, then began walking again to keep fit. He was mad, quite mad.

Amos and I kept fit by bickering.

Amos's Englishness had always irritated Kempster. Now, under the stress of prison life, it often irritated me. A differing attitude to "foreigners" can sharply divide two Englishmen on the Continent, however close their friendship. And this was the first time that Amos and I had, so to speak, come abroad together. I was disposed to like our Italian guards and their Lieutenant. I thought they treated us as well as could be expected. Both Amos and Kempster (their only bond) combined against me over this. It was our duty, Kempster maintained, to make ourselves a nuisance. And Amos, maliciously amused by my dilemma, supported him.

"A disgraceful way to treat British officers," they both said at every opportunity.

But it would be unfair to name one more than another. We were all to blame. For the sake of peace we suppressed our private tensions, but we expressed them, in an exaggerated form, against the Lieutenant and his *carabinieri*. As the officer commanding Operation Swann, I was continually being driven to voice some general and, to my mind, unjustified grievance. But, morally a coward, I have never found it easy to resist the demands of my friends. In this case it would have been better for us all if I had. Every morning, as our official spokesman, I marched into the *Tenente* to complain that we were being eaten by bedbugs, that the cheese was too hard, that the wine was undrinkable, or whatever else our perhaps mistaken sense of duty had invented for the day's grievance. In the end we really came to believe we were ill-treated.

In retrospect our behaviour was childish and self-destructive. Perhaps we suffered a nervous recoil from the strain of the past month. Perhaps, too, we showed off a little to one another and to Hank, the stranger. However it was, our six interacting personalities produced a disastrous compound. At the end of three weeks we were no longer six grown-ups, we were a committee. Our joint attitude became, to say the least, arrogant. But we pushed our arrogance too far.

We heard of Mussolini's downfall a fortnight after it occurred. He, too, though we did not know it, was a prisoner in Sardinia, on the island-port of La Maddalena. It may have been this irony which prompted the Lieutenant to come in and remove the picture from our wall. As a Fascist his emotions at this time must have been greatly strained. Already fed up with us, he was in no mood for being chaffed.

"Ho, ho," we all cried; "so Humpty Dumpty *has* had a fall."

And we danced round the room triumphantly.

The Lieutenant walked out, beside himself with anger.

When, the next morning, I marched into his office as usual, I decided to begin, diplomatically, by thanking him for favors received.

"I want none of your thanks," he snarled venomously. "You're ungrateful *priggionieri*, and I'm sick of you. I've arranged for you to be sent at once to Italy. And good riddance!"

So after that we hated him openly and he hated us.

La Maddalena, the largest of a cluster of islands off the northeast corner of Sardinia, was at that time an Italian naval base, in use by the German Navy as well. To us, this north-east corner of Sardinia had an additional significance and interest. Long before, in Africa, we had planned that if things went wrong, this was the part of the island to try and reach. It was wild, it was the closest point to Corsica, there would certainly be fishing boats which might be bought or stolen. In prison, when we had considered the possibilities of escape, we always planned to aim for just this area. There was a feeling of destiny and good omen that we had now been brought here en route for Italy, instead of being flown direct by aeroplane from Sassari. We congratulated ourselves on having waited.

A launch took us from the railway station to the island and we had a good chance of observing the town and harbor. We passed several seaplanes at anchor and numerous small fishing boats against the wharves. We sailed to the far end of the port, on the south side of the island, where the town dwindled to a few barrack-like buildings. Opposite one of these we disembarked.

We found ourselves in a naval barracks. The buildings, surrounded by a high wall, were grouped round a courtyard with one building planted in the center. We were ushered through a barrack-room, into a smaller room opening off it, full of wooden double-decker beds of the kind proverbial for their bugs.

But prison life in the naval barracks took on a congenial shape. Lunch and dinner we ate in a mess prepared in the building in the center of the yard. At least three naval waiters attended on the six of us, while others crowded in the doorway until chivvied off by the *carabinieri*. Even the latter, taking their cue from the sailors, became increasingly friendly and fore-bearing. And, as we had hoped and were now quick to notice, they became increasingly slack guarding us.

We considered many plans for escape during the first three days. The boldest was to capture a seaplane in the night and fly it back to Africa. Hank thought he could work the seaplane once we got on board. But the first insoluble snag was how to get out of the prison. The windows were heavily barred, the door was padlocked at night. Kempster did not allow us to forget the loss of his files which would now have been so useful. The *carabinieri* slept outside in the large barrack-room. We tested their precautions by knocking on the door in turns during the night and asking to go to the lavatory, which we were allowed to do under escort. The trick helped to tire the *cara-binieri*, particularly as one of them was sick with malaria, so that the others had to do extra duty. By the third day they were notice-ably worn.

Amos and I preferred the idea of stealing a small boat and try-ing to sail either to Corsica or Sicily. We were convinced that, in any case, not more than two of us could escape and stay undetected for the necessary length of time—at least half an hour—to get suffi-cient start.

On the fourth afternoon a *carabiniere* mentioned that a destroyer had arrived from the mainland and would take us across to Naples the next day, 20th August. Amos and I decided to try and escape the same night and the others generously agreed to help.

Our plan was to escape after dinner, always a sociable meal, when the friendly sailors showed photographs of their families and when, afterwards, we gossiped in the doorway before walking back across the yard to our room. The *carabinieri* took no trouble to keep us in sight, since there was no way out of the yard except by the guarded main gate. At the time dinner ended about 9.30 P.M., the night would be dark until moonrise an hour later. We would slip away from the others between the mess and the barrack-room. If the *carabinieri* didn't come in immediately to count us we might have perhaps half an hour in which to find some hitherto undiscov-ered way out of the barracks. Once outside, we would try to steal a boat or, if that failed, to hide on the island. It would be something to miss sailing with the destroyer. For then, even if we were caught there was a chance the Allies would arrive before another boat could take us.

We had saved up bread and went into dinner with our pock-ets bulging and with two full water-bottles. But the *carabinieri* sus-pected nothing and the meal passed without incident. We spun it out till the darkness was complete, then made to leave. One of the sailors produced the photo of his girl and told us she had been killed in the raid on Rome the previous month. He bore us personally no ill-will.

"You English only bomb military targets. The Americans bomb civilians."

"Here you can't say that! I was on that goddam raid," we heard Hank protest, foolhardily, as we walked quickly towards the barrack. We passed our door and made a tour of the yard. Sailors stood chatting in groups, but paid no attention to us. We could find no way out, so doubled back to the mess building, on its far side.

From its shadow, we watched the others still standing in the light of the door twenty yards away. Hank was arguing with his sailor, Jim and Bryan were laughing with the rest, while Kempster expounded in English his theory of war to the *carabinieri* who, understanding not a word, listened somewhat restlessly.

The main gateway loomed out of the darkness another fifty yards beyond the mess. The gate was open—we could see the harbor outside. There was no silhouette of a sentry visible against it. Casually we walked across. We kept outside the circle of light from the mess door and prayed that Kempster could hold the *carabinieri* from glancing our way. By good luck the sentry at the main gate was talking to his girl. We slipped through and turned quickly to the left, along the road that led away from the port towards the east end of the island. We walked on, restraining ourselves with difficulty from running. No one shouted. Soon we were several hundred yards clear of the barracks.

Finding no boat on the water's edge, we turned inland towards the north-east coast and reached the sea again after a mile, where it cut across the island in a long narrow gulf. And there, hidden under the rocks, was a boat with two oars and a sail, as if placed for us at that exact spot by Providence. The moon rose, an hour too soon for our purposes. Keeping in the shadow of the bank and wading up to our necks, we pushed the boat towards the open sea, half a mile away. Beyond that, somewhere, lay Corsica. Progress was too slow, so we climbed into the boat and rowed quietly.

The mouth of the inlet, overlooked by two headlands, was four hundred yards wide and we had almost reached it when, on the rocks above, we saw a sentry. His back was turned. We could not tell what guards might be with him or on the other side. The only chance was to try and slip between the two headlands though, as the sea was calm and brightly moonlit, we were well aware how easily we could be seen. Stealthily we rowed towards the center.

A voice shouted after us from the bank. We shouted back cheerily and rowed faster. Then a shot rang out, the bullet passing between us. We shouted again, this time indignantly, a quasi-Italian gibberish, hoping that the guards would believe they had made a mistake. It was a vain hope. The two headlands had by now come alive, dozens of figures moving over them in the moonlight.

We rowed on as fast as we could towards the center of the all-too-narrow opening.

They started firing from both sides; rifles and then a machine-gun. The impulse to jump into the water was almost overwhelming. We stopped rowing. The firing ceased. Italian voices shouted to us to come into the bank. It was the only sensible thing to do.

We bluffed the soldiers for a while that we were German naval officers out for a night's fishing. They were friendly but insisted that, as we could not produce a pass, we must wait for their officer. He was away for the moment at R.H.Q. and had been sent for. We passed the time pretending to accept the formality in good humor, while they congratulated us on our good luck in not having been hit. There was still a faint chance.

The officer arrived, out of breath and excited. He rushed up to a hatless soldier and, prodding him with a revolver, ordered him to surrender. Then, the ludicrous mistake having been pointed out, he rushed at us. We held up our arms while he searched us for weapons.

The hatless soldier tried to calm him, explaining that we were German naval officers, but he cursed the soldier for a fool and said that we were escaped British prisoners. He had just heard all about us from R.H.Q.

So that, we realized sadly, was that.

As we marched wearily back towards Maddalena, we passed innumerable soldiers hunting for us in the countryside and our Italian officer shouted to them that we had been found. He was a delightful man and, chatting with him in French, we heard that the battle in Sicily was over. Before the war, he published school books in Milan. Owing to Mussolini's fall, all the books would now have to be re-written, and he looked forward to a brisk trade, if only he could get started again.

He was amazed that we had tried to escape. Wasn't it better to remain safely as prisoners till the war was over? We explained, without truth, that much as we enjoyed being prisoners with the Italians, we had an even stronger desire to fight Germans again.

"Yes," he sighed, "the Germans are the true enemy. We ought to be fighting them together."

Handing our escort over to a sergeant, he said goodbye to us outside the town, making a really charming speech about the fortunes of war.

Our escape had caused some commotion. The streets were thronged with troops and civilians who joined in the procession. Amos and I felt rather pleased with life in spite of the disappointment. It had been an exciting escapade and we could not blame ourselves that it had failed.

"I'm afraid the *Capitano* was right about catching us easily," Amos said. "It remains to be seen whether we catch malaria."

As we approached the naval barracks we recognized the Lieutenant waiting outside. He walked up and spat with great gusto and accuracy into our faces. Then he followed us into the barrack-room where the *carabinieri* stood glowering. One of them hissed furiously, "So this is how you return the kindness we've shown you." His face was quite hideous with malignity.

So was the Lieutenant's. Our own faces must have expressed a supercilious contempt we certainly did not feel, for he muttered that we would soon take that smile off. Then he cleared the barrack-room of the crowd and left us with the *carabinieri*. The time was about 3 A.M.

The next dozen hours are not pleasant to recollect even at this distance. The door was locked on the others, though we suspected, rightly, they would be peeping through the keyhole. The *carabinieri* ordered us to lie on the floor. Then covering us with pistols and rifles they set about getting their own back. They concentrated first on Amos, smacking his face, kicking him, spitting and throwing water, and one brought a rifle butt down, though Amos warded the blow off with his arm and suffered only a broken wrist-watch. They repeated the performance on me. Then they withdrew to their corner of the room to sleep, after assuring us that we would be shot in the morning.

We were unhurt, but thoroughly scared. We did not take the threat of being shot too seriously, but we dreaded a further onslaught. Amos had dysentery and my bladder, weakened by the sea water, was bursting. We were wondering if we dared draw their attention to us again by asking to go to the lavatory, when one of the *carabinieri* walked over to me. He asked me the question I so badly wanted to ask him. Gratefully I said "Yes," and half-raised myself to get up, whereupon he struck me very hard in the face and pointing his pistol at me, ordered me to stay where I was. We glared silently at each other for what seemed minutes. There was murder in his eyes and in my heart.

So we stayed on the floor in a state of physical mess and mental anguish. In the morning the Lieutenant visited us, apparently to gloat, for he paid no attention to our request to be allowed to go and clean ourselves.

About 3 P.M. we were summoned before two Naval Intelligence Officers. We showed them our condition and they were deeply shocked. They told the *carabinieri* to take us at once to a water trough where we washed. Then they interrogated us about the escape. They thought we must have been helped by sailors in the barracks. In the end they believed us, that we had escaped unaided, and found a boat by accident.

Later in the day we were taken by launch to the waiting destroyer. We heard from a friendly sailor that the Lieutenant had been sacked as a result of our escape, and would accompany us no farther. We last saw him staring in our direction from the quayside, a frail exhausted figure. Relief at being rid of his prisoners may have compensated him for disgrace, and I do hope so. Three years afterwards he and the four *carabinieri* were sentenced by a War Crimes Tribunal to varying terms of imprisonment.

I would, I think, have shot all of them on that day, if I had been in a position to do so. But cold-blooded revenge is a sterile satisfaction, like writing a book. As to how far their treatment of us was a war crime, the reader will have formed his own opinion, and I doubt whether it will differ greatly from my own. I protested in vain against the futile retaliation, but I suppose it gave employment to the uniformed lawyers at the War Office.

"Can't have British officers beaten up by Wops, you know," one of them said to me. He was laying the foundations to a successful post-war legal career, like a vulture building its nest on bones.

Passing through Rome two days afterwards, we saw ample evidence of the "havoc and severe shock" wrought upon the railway station by Hank and his companions. Posters of Uncle Sam wielding a tommy-gun and labeled GANGSTER stared at us on the platform. An evilly-disposed crowd gathered, eager to know if we were Americans. But our *carabinieri*, equally scared as ourselves, said we were English and hastened us on to the train. It was probably the only occasion in Hank's life when he was glad to be mistaken for an Englishman.

"Sardinia" (I quote Sir Winston Churchill for the last time) "so long thrust forward in Staff argument as the alternative to the assault on Italy, fell into our hands for nothing, as a mere bonus, on 19th September . . ."

By then our *campo concentramento* in the Abruzzi had been taken over by the Germans and we waited, with some thousands of others, for the train to carry us off to the *Vaterland*.

So ended Operation Swann. Whether it achieved anything that a flight of Spitfires could not have done better, whether it caused even mild alarm in German and Italian circles on the island, scarcely matters now. We had had no illusion about our chances of success and we accepted our fate without bitterness. Nor, for the majority, was that fate a particularly hard one. Most of the officers and men returned safely in due course, either via Germany or, having escaped, through Italy. Some, like Kempster, died escaping.

He was a strange complicated person whom I regret not knowing in the post-war era. I think he would have remained a soldier, fighting voluntarily in Korea, Malaya, Indo-China, or wherever. There is usually a war somewhere and he claimed to be in love with war. Perhaps his end was the one he sought. As the Germans loaded us on to the train at night he dashed suddenly across the line for the cover of the hillside. It was a wildly gallant and suicidal bid for freedom.

In the next hours, lying packed with thirty others in a cattle truck, Amos and I thought much of that crumpled body, left under sacking beside the line. It was a deterring thought. The train moved slowly out of the mountain station, then halted in a cutting. We heard the sentry pass and repass. There was a small ventilator on the roof of our truck, just wide enough for a man to crawl through. He would have a drop. And then what? . . . But would there ever be another chance?

"God knows why I followed you," Amos whispered to me half an hour later, as we lay under a bush watching the train gather speed. "You've got Lucinda to return to and all that. If *I* get home I shall only be popped in the bag again—by my creditors!"

PART FIVE

Finale

CHAPTER EIGHTEEN

The Seventh Square

AT THIS POINT I pause.

Twelve months of empty wine bottles clutter my table, a tilth of cigarette ash and used match-sticks lies ankle-deep round my feet. And I sit wondering where I shall ever find the stimulus to carry me through to the end.

There is no lack of raw material. A ten-year-old account, written at the time, intimidates me with its detail of life in the Abruzzi. The story goes on and on, adventurous incident piled on incident, till interest fails. Besides, what do they amount to, these hair-breadth escapes, narrow shaves, and the rest? Buchan invented better ones. Mine actually happened—but then what recommendation is that? Truth is less readable than fiction, and our story is already stale as yesterday's newspaper. Hundreds of escaped P.O.W. had the same experiences as Amos and myself; dozens have already published them. Why, even as I write this, my eye falls by chance on a review of some of these books in a week-end paper. The reviewer, born, I believe, about the time I sat with Lucinda and the Prendergasts on the Piazza, plunges straight to the heart of the matter.

"One is becoming as bored of these escape stories as of their tellers, beamish boys galumphing their way home through a tangle of generous peasants, Fascist spies, and boastful partisans. They march great distances, but Einstein, one imagines, goes farther every day without stirring a foot. Cave life in the mountains, *chianti* and *pasta sciuta* in lofts by candlelight, tappings on the shutter, sudden arrivals and hasty departures, even the final dash through the lines, all are by now situational clichés, unredeemed, as a rule, by literary skill . . ."

Thanks to that young man I see my way suddenly clear. I shall, quite simply, skirt my own tangle of spies and peasants; and, since I cannot hope to redeem my situational clichés, I shall omit them. As for stimulus—well, there's still a drop of South African hock in one of the bottles and a few cigarettes left in the last packet. Here we go, then, for our final dash . . .

We spent the day, 15th December, making puttees from an old coat and rubbing pork fat on our feet and boots against the snow. The boots, provided with so much else, by Sam, were too small, but at least watertight and hobnailed. Our intended march could hardly be attempted without them. We studied a small guide-book map stolen from the prison library and waited impatiently for darkness when Sam had promised to return with a rucksack full of food for the journey.

The Eighth Army, so far as we knew, was held up on the river Sangro, thirty miles and two mountains south of our cave. The mountains, Genzano and Greco, were both about 7,000 feet. The re-entrant between them was said to be full of Germans. We planned to reach it the first night, to lie up there the next day and then the next night to cross the Monte Greco. Below the latter, on the far side, the village of Barrea on the Sangro was rumored to be within the British front. If, in the past eleven weeks, all the rumors retailed to us as facts had come true, the Allied advance would by now have swept over us, but Sam had heard about Barrea on the B.B.C., and the news had been confirmed by others.

In any case, now that we had the boots, we knew we must take the future into our own hands and face the long-deferred ordeal. Amos's malaria seemed momentarily dormant. And our existence in the snowbound cave had become an intolerable strain. I dare say suffering ennobles, but it also demeans. Amos and I had reached a state of starving misery when the unequal division of one single walnut could leave a sense of grievance for days.

Still more was our existence in the cave a strain on Sam, though he never complained. German troops were billeted on most of his neighbors and continually raided the others for food. No one knew any longer whom to trust. Though Sam kept our presence secret, his furtive excursions up the mountain, particularly now that the snow had fallen, must inevitably be noticed and bring him sooner or later into disaster. Only the week before a German patrol, rounding up cattle hidden in the beech-forest, had strolled past our cave-mouth, missing him by minutes. The falling snow had covered his footprints or the Germans would have searched inside, where we lay huddled, pretending to be rocks.

With darkness, we wondered nervously whether he would come now. A dozen things might have happened to hold him up. But there he was suddenly against the sky in the cave-mouth. He was greatly excited.

"My God, lucky I killed them pig and we eaten him. Them Germany peoples come this morning but they not find much."

He had lived in America, hence his nickname, and spoke a delightful brand of English.

"Sam, how awful for you. What did the bastards take?"

"Oh, nothing. Some chickens, some corn. The cow, she in the cave O.K."

We were especially glad the cow was safe. In palmier October days we had often drunk her milk and, later, when the German raids had forced us up the mountain, she had accompanied us some of the way to a lower cave.

But Sam made light of his losses. He had brought, as well as the rucksack, a dish of macaroni, still hot in spite of his three-hour climb through the snow, and he pressed us to eat it quickly. Then he tried, for the last time, to dissuade us from setting off. The saintly man was in tears, on our account.

"No good in the mountains. Too cold, too far. Amos, him bloody sick. Them Germany sons of bitches catch you."

"Don't you worry, Sam. If we get stuck up there we'll come running back to you."

He brightened, I can't think why.

"You promise? That's good. Come back and stay in my loft for the winter till your peoples come."

We, too, were near tears. We loved him and we wanted to say much that could hardly be said. But there were no minutes to waste, and we bade him farewell, promising again to return if we met difficulties. Climbing upwards, we looked down and waved several times in the next quarter of an hour at the small figure standing on the snow by the cave. But for that providential young reviewer, I would write at much greater length all we felt about Sam.

The pack he had given us was so heavy with food we had to jettison some of it. We walked slowly, for the boots soon blistered our feet, and we gained the mountain's ridge about 2 A.M. The last hour had been over hard snow and near the top Amos had slipped, skidding two hundred feet down on his back. His language, when he regained my level, was unprintable.

There was cloud on the ridge and it began to snow. Guessing the direction, we descended towards the dangerous valley, but at our slow pace we despaired of reaching it that night. Yet how else could we lie up the following day? And if we reached the valley, where absolute concealment would be essential, should we be able, in the cold, to lie still for more than an hour or two?

Amos struggled along, stumbling at every step and breathing with difficulty. I begged him to hurry. Ten years younger and in good health, I felt shamefully fresh, though I had carried the rucksack all the way. I was becoming desperately worried when, as so often before, Providence saved us. We walked on to a shepherd's hut half-buried under snow and, entering it, found two Italians asleep by a blazing fire.

Giovanotti escaping the German call-up, they had come to the hut that evening and were leaving at dawn to try and reach the Eighth Army. They had no idea where the line was—perhaps in the valley ahead—but they, too, were quite sure that Barrea was in our hands.

We spent the day beside the fire, tending our tattered feet and eating Sam's provisions. In daylight the snow cleared enough for us to see the valley three miles away across our route. The fir trees were black and menacing as if bristling with Germans, though it should be possible to keep above them along the ridge which joined Genzana to Greco. By evening we felt restored, though neither of us had slept. At the back of our minds had been the fear of Germans coming to the hut.

The second night's march was a long-drawn-out agony. The boots pinched our swollen feet, though the pain perhaps focused our thoughts away from more substantial dangers. We by-passed the valley successfully without dropping more than a thousand feet, and came up again on to an interminable undulating snow-field, like a vast deserted room under dust-sheets, copper-colored by the full moon. At the end of it, a small conical peak guarded the pass over Monte Greco. It looked an hour away. But size and distance are hopelessly deceptive in snowy mountains at night. When, after hours, the peak had come no nearer we wondered if it was really there at all.

It was too cold to halt and each lifted his feet mechanically through the snow, to a private rhythm.

Freude, schöner Götterfunken
Tochter aus Elysium.

I hummed a travesty of the famous bars over and over again for six solid hours without stopping.

We passed many single wolf tracks; and, once, human tracks, those evidently of a patrol. They were quite recent and came up from the valley, crossing our route over Monte Greco in a wide circle. The patrol had turned aside to visit a shepherd's hut and then had descended again towards the valley.

"Don't let's jump to hasty conclusions," Amos muttered; "but it looks very much as if we're in no-man's-land. In which case we've only to keep going . . ."

To encourage us, a short artillery barrage rumbled behind the hills to our east, and the flashes lit up the sky. Distant gunfire had often echoed over the mountains in the last month, but this seemed very close indeed. We kept going . . .

At last the conical peak was definitely there, towering above the pass. We reached the latter at 4 A.M. The gradient leveled off and for an endless mile we waded through deep snow. I don't think I have ever felt more utterly tired and miserable. Then the descent began, until the pass narrowed to a steep valley. We climbed down rapidly, passed the snow line, and just before dawn sat under a rock to check our position. Keeping back two tins of Italian bully for emergencies, we ate the rest of Sam's food.

The early sun promised a wonderful day. As the mist cleared, we identified the village of Barrea on the River Sangro a mile below us. The river disappeared into a gorge, then ran out on to a plain by Castel di Sangro, five miles to the east. We checked and rechecked the roads we could see with those on the map, until we were certain that the village below us was Barrea. If it really was, we had but to walk downhill for half an hour to meet the Eighth Army. Only one thing puzzled us—the complete absence of military activity. No troops were visible in the village, no lorries on the road running from it towards Castel. It must mean that the line, so far as one existed above the snow, stretched across the mountains *behind* us, as Amos had guessed, and that we had been on the safe side of it for hours already.

We warned one another not to be overconfident. Yet, what other explanation could there be?

The damp glistened on Amos's beard and pale emaciated face. He rubbed his hands for warmth, or perhaps for joy.

"When we're *quite* sure, let's walk *very* slowly down the hill," he said. And my own thoughts sped to the anticipated scene of rejoicing and reunion. Home before Christmas after all . . .

Some shooting began on the other side of the Sangro, and we became attentive at once. The guns were firing from the direction of Castel and we watched the shells bursting two miles away on the road between it and Barrea. The shelling did not last long but it threw a very different light on our position. There could be only one explanation—the German line was still in front of us. We saw a party of men with a laden donkey leave Barrea, cross the bridge, and move over the hillside below us. The sound of their voices drifted up to us quite distinctly. They were Germans.

We lay up till nightfall, then Amos set off first, as arranged. There was little enough hope of being able to creep past sentries alone; together, there was none. His tall silhouette vanished into the night, but for ten minutes afterwards I heard his nailed boots scraping over the rocks. Then I followed him.

Like him, I moved slowly and painfully, my own boots making an appalling noise, or so it seemed. We had agreed that the best chance was to keep high up on the mountain, where the line of outposts would be thinner, and in two hours I arrived where I expected them to be. A steady procession of men and mules passed backwards and forwards a hundred yards farther down. Then I heard German voices immediately ahead. At that moment the full moon rose. I had been in pitch darkness hitherto, but was now exposed on the barest of hillsides. I could not crawl farther unseen, and decided to make for the Sangro below on my right. Hidden in the shadow of a spur, I crossed the mule track between trains of pack animals. I was so tired and thirsty I was quite reckless, feeling that only colossal luck could help me and that only the highest stakes were worth playing for. After a long and difficult climb I reached the bottom of the gorge.

The gorge, a mixture of rock and forest, rose up precipitously about two thousand feet on both sides and the river, thirty yards wide, roared deafeningly between them. I had no strength left to climb back the way I had come. My only hope was to try and follow the river down, till it debouched near Castel di Sangro, though I might run into a patrol using the narrow track between river and rock. There were many footprints where the track was muddy.

I drank a stomach-full of Sangro, then sat down to think for a bit. Sooner or later I would have to cross a German line in or just outside the gorge. The best chance might be to get into the water and creep along submerged. I can remember thinking how silly it would be to drown, but not caring much either way. Then I fell asleep.

When I woke the moon had passed some distance over the sky and was, most fortunately, diffused by mist. It was about 3 A.M. I started to walk. After an hour the track ended and a sort of bridge of San Luis Rey spanned the river. On the right bank another path continued and I followed it until I could see where the gorge opened out and the river flowed on to the plain. The path was a yard wide, between sheer rocks on one side and the bank, covered with sparse bushes, on the other.

I came round a bend to find myself within five yards of a German soldier. He stood in shadow and I first saw the glint of his rifle. I pressed myself flat against the rock, out of sight from him unless I moved. Very slowly I peered round to see what he was doing. There were two sudden flashes, almost in my face, and it was a few seconds before my tired mind grasped the fact that he had fired at me. I crawled backwards on my stomach and was crossing the path into the river when he fired a third time. And missed again.

I was into the river faster than a snake, and worked my way along with only my eyes and nose above water. I expected to see him at any

moment on the bank above me, but I progressed safely in this way
for a hundred yards, then crawled into the bushes to try and restore
some warmth. I continued to crawl alternately in and out of the river
for the next hour. A minefield, conveniently wired off on the south
bank, suggested that I was in no-man's-land, so I crossed it with
infinite caution and came to a deserted and ruined village, where a
black cat gave me a fright by running suddenly over the street. In
early daylight I crossed the Barrea-Castel road and climbed a hill.
There were shell holes everywhere in the muddy ground, but no sign
of life. I opened the tin of Italian bully and scooped the meat out
with my fingers. I reached the hill-top as dawn broke, but the morning mist was too thick to see anything. I longed to be challenged by
a British sentry, but there were none about.

Descending the hill on the far side, I met three Italians on don-
keys.

"Are there any Germans round here?" I asked them in Italian.

Suspiciously, they asked if I was German. Hearing I was English,
their manner changed immediately. They embraced me and told me
to keep going for half a mile when I would reach their village, Mon-
tenero, and find English soldiers everywhere.

"*Niente tedeschi, niente tedeschi!*" they laughed.

The sun broke through the morning mist as I came in sight of
the village. Approaching it, I deliberately dawdled and finished the
last mouthful of Italian bully.

"Well, here you are," I said aloud. "I suppose you'll remember
the next minutes all your life."

And I was quite right.

From a hundred yards away the much-battered buildings appeared deserted. Then I noticed a Bren-carrier behind a wall, a few
trucks under camouflage netting in a yard. As I limped slowly into
the main street, a solitary shell whistled overhead, exploding somewhere at the farther end. A group of British soldiers, the first I had
seen, in long leather waistcoats and khaki cap-comforters, chatted
unconcernedly in a doorway across the cobbles from me. I glanced
shyly at them, but they took no notice. Just another bedraggled
peasant haunting the ruins of his home . . .

The conventional inhibited Englishman is ill-equipped by temperament for such occasions. I would have liked to dance, to shout,

to make some kind of demonstration. A Frenchman, an Australian, would have done it naturally, but somehow I could not. So I walked slowly on, holding off the pleasure of the long-awaited moment, the exclamation of surprise, the greeting from a compatriot.

English voices and laughter came from a house. I crossed the threshold and found, in what had been the peasants' kitchen but was now the usual military desolation of a billet, two half-dressed Privates cooking breakfast. One of them saw me, standing there grinning at them.

"Christ, Nobby, look what the cat's brought in," he said.

I tried to be hearty but failed. "I've just come through. I'm soaked. Can I warm up by your fire?" I heard my bored voice say politely.

Neither of the soldiers was much surprised by this sudden entry of what was, to all appearances, a dank and bearded Italian, who spoke fluent English with a B.B.C. accent. Sensibly enough, they were more interested in breakfast.

"What are you? Escaped P.O.W. or something?"

"Yes."

It didn't cause much of a sensation and they asked no more questions. They treated me, as they might have a stray dog, with a sort of cheery kindness and without fuss. In a few minutes I was sitting naked before their fire, drinking a cup of char and feeling the warmth return to my numbed body.

A Corporal and others of the section came in for their breakfast. My back view may have mildly surprised them.

"Bloke's an escaped P.O.W.," Nobby explained.

"Lucky sod. They'll send you home," the Corporal said, offering me a Players.

Savoring every puff of the tobacco, every sip of the tea, I wondered whether Amos was doing the same somewhere nearby. We had so often pictured just this situation in the past three months. Superstitiously, I put off asking them if they had heard of him. If they had, they would surely say so. And I didn't want to hear them say they hadn't.

Long-anticipated pleasures seldom come up to expectation. Neither the tea, the tobacco, nor even the warmth were now quite as delicious as I had imagined they would be. The scene was un-

real, unbelievable. Though the soldiers' gossip around me was vivid
enough.

"Ginger, go and swipe some clothes for him off the C.Q.M.S.'s
truck," the Corporal said to one of the men.

"Do you think the C.Q.M.S. can spare me something?"

"The C.Q.M.S. won't know," Ginger winked as he left the room.

Certainly I was back with the British Army all right.

Later, in the miscellaneous garments swiped by Ginger (the
C.Q.M.S. would, I am sure, have supplied them voluntarily—but
that, of course, would have been more trouble) I visited R.H.Q. in
another part of the village. Nothing had been heard there of Amos
and the C.O. refused at first to credit my story that I had walked
through his outposts unobserved, until I traced my route for him on
the map. Evidently I had indeed walked slap through C Company's
position.

"Can't think why they didn't shoot you," the Colonel said irritably. "Remind me to have a word with the Company Commander
about that," he added to his Adjutant.

He seemed to treat my personal survival as a discredit to his
blasted Battalion. He was about my age, had a pink face and a
toothbrush moustache and the manners of a bilious Scoutmaster.
We disliked one another on sight.

I ventured a facetious joke. I hadn't made one for years.

"It was only eight o'clock. Perhaps they were all still asleep."

"That is not very probable."

We had little in common and I was glad when he told the Adjutant to take me over. The latter rang through to Brigade and then to
Division, but they, too, had heard nothing of Amos. The Divisional
I.O. wanted to see me as soon as possible, so the Adjutant arranged
for me to travel back there on a truck.

"Be a good chap," he whispered as we parted, "and don't mention that you walked through our lines unopposed."

"Of course I won't," I smiled. Nor have I, till this day. I should
say he was a very good Adjutant.

From the truck I looked back across the plain at the way I had
come. The sun shone fully now, defining clearly the dark cleft of the
Sangro Gorge and behind it the snowy mountains Amos and I had
traversed so painfully.

The driver drove the truck at a desperate pace over the potholes in the steep winding road. I had not come thus far to break my neck in an accident and I said so.

"The f——— shell this stretch of road when they see anything to shoot at."

After that I agreed he should drive as fast as he liked.

There was no news of Amos at Divisional H.Q., where I lunched. Nor at Corps H.Q., where I arrived for tea. When, in turn, my various interviewers found that I had no information of any military importance to give them they quickly handed me and the problem of my disposal on to someone else. During the day I came to feel, quite unreasonably, that no one I met on the Staffs was sufficiently stirred by my dramatic return to the bosom of the Eighth Army.

"Lucky sod, they'll send you home," nicely expressed the general sentiment.

The Eighth Army had changed a great deal in the year since I had known it in the desert. Keen, efficient, and all that, doubtless it still was, but I felt it had lost something of its old spirit. What was lacking? Style, perhaps? A sort of debonair flourish to its way of life? The cap badges, the vehicle signs, the hundred details of uniform and equipment which make up the external personality of an Army, and which from long training my eye critically noted as a matter of course, were all unfamiliar and contributed to my sense of having arrived among strangers. They were friendly strangers and I was pleased enough to be alive and among them. But still they were strangers. Nor, during the day, did I meet a soul who knew Amos even by name and who might thus take a personal interest in his fate. A year before in the Desert that could hardly have happened.

Presuming that he had met with the same difficulties in crossing the line that I had, there were three possibilities. Either he was already dead, shot by an outpost or blown up on a mine; or he had been retaken; or he was still lying up and would try again this night. In the latter case, in his already weak condition and without food, he would need fantastic luck to succeed. There was nothing I or anyone else could possibly do for him, and try how I would I did not feel hopeful.

"Don't worry. I expect your pal, what's-his-name, will turn up all right in the morning," said the G.S.O. 2 at Corps. He was friendly, he was helpful. But my disorderly appearance in his tidy office was obviously a great bore.

Some months later I myself became a G.S.O. 2 on a Corps H.Q. As such it fell to me occasionally to entertain, in my own tidy office, other young men who had just "come through"; disheveled, impatiently-arrogant young men, their egos inflated by successful adventure, claiming, as by right, my undivided attention for their selfish worries. I much resented being trampled on by them, yet had to admit the justice of it. I knew how they felt. Moreover, by that time Lucinda had rejoined me. I was content to be trampled on.

The present G.S.O. 2 was far from home, far from his own Lucinda, if he had one. Harassed by more pressing military affairs, he wished to relegate me to some organization that had been set up for the disposal of escaped P.O.W. Whence, traveling through the usual channels, I might hope, he said, to be back in the U.K. within a month. Certainly within two. That was not nearly fast enough for me.

Adept by this stage of the war in short-circuiting the military bureaucracy, I played my last card.

"Does Army H.Q. know that I've come through? For reasons I can't go into it's terribly important that they should. Can we ring them at once?"

The G.S.O. 2 looked skeptical.

"Who might be interested there?"

Who indeed? A happy inspiration guided me. It was the last link in the long chain of good luck that lay behind. Guessing wildly, I gave Alan's name.

The G.S.O. 2 reacted at once. "Oh, does he know you?"

"Try him and see."

Alan, I shortly gathered, waiting while the G.S.O. 2 put through the call, was now a Brigadier. And in two minutes I heard his unmistakable voice, muffled against the G.S.O. 2's ear.

"*What!* He's with you there now? Why the hell didn't you ring me before? Let me speak to him at once!"

Sheepishly, I was glad to see, the G.S.O. 2 handed me the apparatus.

"Good evening, Brigadier . . ."

The ensuing conversation, memorable though it was and moving to me though it still is, more by its tone than its actual content, is hardly worth recording. Alan promised he would have me flown back to the U.K. within a week; by Christmas, in fact. And, as always, he was as good as his word. For the present the G.S.O. 2 was to arrange for me to spend the night in the Casualty Clearing Station at Campobasso, where Alan would send a car to collect me the next day.

Apart from fatigue and two blistered feet there was apparently nothing wrong with me that a good night's sleep could not put right. In the morning I knew I should be ready to move on. Meanwhile, there were certain immediate comforts to be relished.

I fell in love with the Sister on sight. She was struggling, I discovered, with the prospect of Christmas decorations for the ward, and I offered to do some drawings—hypocritically, since I knew I would not be there to carry them out. Together we planned a frieze to be hung round the walls. She wanted Father Christmas and reindeer. I preferred my own idea of turkeys dressed as Generals.

Tucking me up, she slipped a hot-water bottle under the sheets.

"Don't tell the others, but I've put some medicinal brandy in your Bournvita," she whispered, handing me a mug.

As I lay back on the pillow and smiled gratefully at her, so starched and white, I thought she was probably the most beautiful woman in the world.

Except one.

CHAPTER NINETEEN

The Pattern Completed

NATURE IS NEVER STATIC. Tides mysteriously turn, the moon having waxed begins imperceptibly to wane, and death itself, I have read somewhere, is only the last phase in a long process of dying which supersedes, at some indeterminable moment around the age of thirty, the long process of growing up. In the case of my own life, looking back ten years or so, I like to place this moment of transition from incline to decline, from immaturity to maturity, in the Casualty Clearing Station at Campobasso. I had jumped out of the train carrying me to Germany on my thirtieth birthday. I see the final effort of crossing the Allied line as my youth's last fling. The same night, shaving off my beard in the Casualty Clearing Station, I noticed my first grey hairs. At that point I started to die—quite an agreeable process so far.

Those were hardly my thoughts as, too tired and too excited to sleep, I lay cozily in the dimly-lit ward taking stock of my situation. Still, I was aware, I think, that a change had come about, that "Youth's slow dying torment," as I had fancifully called it, was over and that the individual in the hospital bed was no longer the same who had ridden over the Quantocks in 1937, who had married Lucinda, who had gone to the wars and who had thereafter, according to Amos, gone steadily to the dogs. Would Lucinda find him sufficiently the same? Or rather, since she must have changed no less, would she find him sufficiently different? To Comus, who had not known his father, the fact that he was missing, perhaps lost, could hardly matter. But what had Lucinda been suffering in the past six months?

If the young man in me was dead, so was the keen soldier. Whatever charitable interpretation others may have put on my actions, if they troubled to put any at all, I had no illusions about them myself. I had joined Bomfrey's Boys, had jumped into Sardinia even, on the hunch, tenuous but positive, that that was my quickest road for home. Though the road had wandered farther and farther afield, I had followed it with some strength of purpose. Now, mostly through luck, I was in sight of home, and I suffered the acute depression, the especial sense of failure, which only the successful accomplishment of a long task can bring. The war of a sudden was no longer my war.

It is a P.O.W.'s duty, we had so often been told, to escape in order that he may continue to fight for his country. My own reasons for escaping had been entirely different. I had escaped to rejoin Lucinda and Comus, and for nothing else. So far as I was concerned, the country could look after itself. But the war would go on. I would remain a soldier. It was rather annoying, I reflected, that I had no obvious disability like a wound.

I knew nothing in those days of the possible psychological causes of illness and perhaps it was as well. Today it strikes me as no accident that within a week of my reunion with Lucinda in England and with the Normandy invasion impending, I was stricken with the first of many acute malarial attacks. I remained, appropriately, the color of a daffodil till the day in November 1945, when the Demobilization Center at Guildford issued me with a bright-blue pin-stripe suit and a green pork-pie hat. Neither of which Lucinda has ever allowed me to wear. But enough of myself.

In the Yeomanry concerts which R.S.M. Burge organized, primarily for the display of his own vocal and histrionic talents, one ballad always particularly delighted Amos and me. Most of the R.S.M.'s other songs were monotonously obscene or, far worse, agonizingly sentimental. The theme of this one, as I recall it, was an old sailor yarning about the past to an audience of skeptical younger men. The ironic refrain in which we all joined with mounting enthusiasm after each verse went

Hardships?
Hardships, you bastards?
You don't know what hardships are!

Amos and I turned the refrain into one of those small, but so important, private jokes, by which soldiers make their unnaturally tedious life supportable. Whenever one of us showed an inclination to grumble, to exaggerate the importance of some temporary inconvenience, the other had only to murmur "Hardships, you bastards? . . ." for the inclination to be overcome.

Many times in the writing of this book, particularly towards the end, I have thought I heard Amos's quiet mocking voice behind me whisper "Hardships . . ." I trust the effect of the hallucination has been salutary.

In a way it was appropriate that he, the older friend in any young man's life, should have passed out of mine for ever on the day that, according to my perhaps too conveniently tidy theory, I finally grew up. Passed out of it, that is, in the physical sense. The memory remains. Summoned up by a chance taste, sight, or smell, by some association of ideas or for no apparent reason at all, friends from the past reappear in my thoughts arbitrarily, disconcertingly; the dead more vividly, I find, than the living. Muggs, the Colonel, Fergie Deakin, Voles, Burge, Kempster, and nameless others . . . they haunt my dreams, sleeping or waking. That is their revenge.

Invited to lunch recently in a famous London club, I thought of Amos and of his debts, long since written off, as I parked my car on the open space where his gallery had once stood, in that area behind St. James's Street primarily dedicated to the display of scarlet cardinals sipping port. A few minutes later, as so often happens, I came on his name again.

"Are you *sure* Brigadier Bone is expecting you?" asked the plum-colored janitor, quizzing my battered hat, my stained overcoat, my bulging portfolio. And I noted that whereas he led other guests unquestioningly into some inner smoking-room or library, myself he held, pending further investigations, in the limbo of the hall.

So, to pass the time, I glanced at the list of fallen members on the club war memorial. I was startled to see Amos's distinguished name among them.

"Killed in Italy, 1943?" was printed beside it.

The uncertainty of his exact fate, which has caused me personally so much anxiety and trouble, would have amused him who loved to weave mysteries. I had forgotten he used to belong to this club. Then, among many other memories, I recalled an occasion during the Battle of Alamein when he and I, smoking furiously, had sat under the lee of Victor Bone's tank, discussing the seeming uncertainty of our prolonged existence on this planet. Amos had pulled a letter from his pocket and shown it to me. The letter, highly acrimonious, was from the secretary of his club threatening to suspend his membership unless he paid a debt of £350. Gleefully Amos had torn the letter up.

"The one good thing about all this," he had said, waving at the smoke and hubbub around us, "is that none of my creditors—or my wife's creditors either for that matter—can reach me here!"

Perhaps he is still saying it.

CPSIA information can be obtained
at www.ICGtesting.com
Printed in the USA
LVHW010811301118
598733LV00002B/2/P